SEE YOU AFTER THE DURATION

*The Story of British Evacuees
to North America in World War II*

Michael Henderson

Foreword by Sir Martin Gilbert

PublishBritannica
London   Baltimore

First printing

ISBN: 1-4137-3868-0
PUBLISHED BY PUBLISHBRITANNICA
www.publishbritannica.com
London   Baltimore

Books by the Same Author

From India with Hope
Experiment with Untruth
A Different Accent
On History's Coattails
Hope for a Change
All Her Paths Are Peace
The Forgiveness Factor
Forgiveness: Breaking the Chain of Hate

To our granddaughter Lola, a US citizen

Contents

Illustrations

Acknowledgements

I would first of all thank my brother, Gerald, and various generations of the Hinchman family, as well as Ginny (Rorstrom) and Ted Boyd for their help and my wife, Erica, for reading and rereading many drafts.

I am grateful to the many evacuees, listed by their evacuee names, who were willing to share their reminiscences, orally or in writing, briefly or at length, and I wish there had been space to include all their experiences: Alys Acworth (Rickett), Pat Ayckroyd, Patricia Backlar, Anthony Bailey, Janet Baker (Baroness Young), Granville Bantock, Jim Baynard-Smith, John Bland, Vivien Brawn (Srivastava), J.M.Brice (Gasper), Shirley Catlin (Baroness Williams), Ellie Bourdillon (Vickers), Yvonne Bowerman (Evans), John Patrick Bradley, Barbara Chance (Mellor), Faith Coghill (Garson),Toby Coghill (Sir), Jennifer Clarke (Richards), Harry Collins, Diana Cran (Lamming), John Crawshaw, Keith Douglas-Mann, John Eden (Lord), Elizabeth and Margaret Ewert, Charles Fay, Joan Flewers, Jane Fry (Redway), Martin Gilbert (Sir), Valerie Green, Brian Hall-Tomkin, Eric Hammond, Margaret Hanton, Muriel Harrington (Russ), Jane Harris, Ron Hart, Denis Henry (Sir), Richard Himsworth, Robin Hitchcock, Robin Holland-Martin, Alistair Horne (Sir), Dorothea Hudson (Desforges), Ken Humphrey, Janet Hutchison (Paine), Ruth Hutchison (Mackenzie), Anne Hutchison (Mackay), Ruth Inglis, Henry Jacobs, Anne James (McCready), Daphne James (Dunkin), Derek Johnson, Barbara Jones (Shawcroft), Brian Joseph, Mary Justham (Jolliffe), Blanche Lawson (Sayers), Isabel Lawson (Raphael), Louise Lawson (Milbourn), Susan Lawson (Berl), Grace Leader (Baldock), Martin Lobkowicz, Mark Lucas, Alastair Macbeth (Dr), Neil Maidment, Jessica Mann, Clifford Mathews, Sheila McDougall (Lamont), Meggie Milne (Weston Smith), Lord Montagu of Beaulieu, Penny Moon (Jaques) and her mother, Ruth Moon, Bridget Moore (Whyte), Jean Moore (Phillips), Tony Moore, Gwen Newstead (Saull), Maggie Northcott, Ann

Norton (Brunsdon), Caroline Norton (Lucas), Fabian Pease, Richenda Pease (Lady Huxley), Veronica Pease, (Farrington), Richard Price, Brian Proctor, Jean Proctor, Dorothy Pye (Jones), Martin Revis, Tony Robinson, Juliet Rodd (Boobbyer), June Roper, Fred Rosenbaum, Hazel Sands (Wilson), Carmen Silvera, Ian Skinner, Brian Snelling, John Spooner, Anne Spokes (Symonds), Clare Stephen, David Stronach, Gillian Stronach (Ferguson), Tim Sturgis, Anne Tatham, Jeremy Thorpe, Rosalind Tolson, Geoff Towers, Jennifer Trusted, Anthony Thwaite, Heather Turvey (Hodge), Ralph Wedgwood, Bridget Whyte (Moore) John Wilkinson, Douglas Wilde, Margaret Wood, Margaret Wyatt (Fitter).

My thanks, too, to those Americans and Canadians who provided information, pointed me in helpful directions or helped in other ways: J. Sinclair Armstrong, Mal Barter, Marita Barter, Betty Buck, Bernard Cavalcante of the US Naval Historical Center, George Chase, Joe Cronin, Russell Ellis of Rockywold-Deephaven, Larry Gilmore of the Columbia River Maritime Museum, Louise Higgs of the *Halifax Herald*, Alice Forbes Howland, Hunter Ingalls, Robert Kuehn, Joan Kunhardt, Stephen Lyons of Canadian Pacific Archives, Mary Putnam Mitchell and Penny Nichols from South Pond Cabins, Bob Morrison, Paul Nanton, Hugh Putnam, Albert-Lauritz Rasmussen, Jack and June Robinson, Timothy Riddle then with the Home for Little Wanderers, Peter and Suzanne Runton, Cliff Scott of The History Associates, Commander Ted Watt, Peggy Wood, staff at the Todd Pacific Shipyards, Barclay Feather, Frank Millet, Anna Longstaff and others at Milton Academy, headmasters John Bigelow, John Green and Tom Army, and also Kate MacKenzie, from the Rectory School, Gayle Lynch, archives assistant at Brown University, Nancy Williatte-Battet, archives assistant at CP Rail, Dan Haacker and the staff at the Milton Public Library, and John Hamlin who did research in the Boston Public Library.

Among those to whom I am indebted in Britain are John Cranwell, Gowen Bewsher, Dr Peter Collinson, Audrey Fay, Jill Henderson, Lt Cdr A Hague, Lt Cdr Peter Hinton, Ruth Inglis, Bob O'Hara, Cherry Martin, Dr Martin Parsons, Kenneth Poolman, James Roffey, as well as the staffs at the libraries of Chatham House, the English-Speaking Union, the *Illustrated London News* and the Fleet Air Arm Museum as well as Rose Wiseman and others at my local public library in Bideford. Also to Margaret Warren in Ireland. A special thanks to Sir Martin Gilbert for his foreword.

For publishing advice I thank David Godine, Noel Hodson, Annabet Suter, Meriel Talbot, Gordon Scott Wise and in particular Hugh Nowell. I am grateful for the computer skills of a neighbour, Roger Tisdale, and for Blair Cummock for processing the photographs.

I would like to acknowledge with gratitude the willingness of Jocelyn Statler and her family to let me quote from many of the letters exchanged during the war and contained in her book *Special Relations.* I am grateful for permission to draw on material from other works: to Anthony Thwaite for his poem 'Evacuation 1940,' to Judge Edgar Fay for his wartime letters, to the Home for Little Wanderers for the extract from *Advocate,* to Tom Curren for his reflections in the newsletter of the Lakes Region Conservation Trust; to Blake Simms for the lines from the poem by his father about the *City of Benares* and to Athalie Warren for her poem on the same subject, to Ann Spokes Symonds for allowing me to draw on her excellent compilation of the Oxford experience *Havens Across the Sea,* to Sir Alistair Horne for material from *A Bundle from Britain,* Anthony Bailey for material from *America Lost and Found,* Kevin Barrett for material from *The Young Ambassadors* and Granville Bantock for material from *Lucky Orphan.* The extracts from Vera Brittain's *Testament of Experience (1957)* are included by permission of Mark Bostridge and Rebecca Williams, her literary executors, and the British Children's Prayer by G. Schirmer Inc. Strenuous but not always successful efforts have been made to discover all rights holders but if any emerge after publication acknowledgment will be added in later printings.

On photos, my thanks go to Alastair Macbeth for returning evacuees, to Granville Bantock for children from the Actors' Orphanage, to Milton Academy for the school chapel, and to the *Christian Science Monitor* for our arrival in Boston.

Foreword

I am honoured to be asked to write this foreword to Michael Henderson's book. He and I are among several thousand British children and youngsters who were evacuated to Canada and the United States in 1940.

Millions of children suffered cruelly during the Second World War. More than a million Jewish children were murdered during the Holocaust. A total of 7,736 British children—whom we had left behind, as it were, to face the music—were killed during the relentless German aerial blitz over the British Isles.

Our tribulations in crossing the Atlantic and being taken in by other children's parents were very low down indeed on the scale of suffering. Of the twenty-eight ships in my convoy, eleven were sunk, but all four ships with children on board got through. Seventy-seven children were drowned when one of the evacuee ships, the *City of Benares*, was sunk: the only child victims of the 1940 sea evacuation, but their deaths brought an end to the evacuation scheme.

The British evacuees were especially fortunate. Many of us, Michael and I included, found the people of the United States (in his case) and Canada (in mine) both welcoming and supportive. We were far from home, and yet, in the main, made to feel at home. We were educated in a far-off land, acquired a strange accent (rapidly lost on return), and learned a great deal about a world that would never otherwise have crossed our ken. Links of Anglo-American and Anglo-Canadian friendship were formed in those days that have lasted to this day, more than sixty years later.

I was one of 727 children who were brought back to Britain in April 1944, in time for D-day and the flying bombs. Michael was sent back, more sensibly, a year later, in time to witness the surrender of a German submarine. On my return I was introduced to my mother with the words, 'This is your mother', and I replied (I was just seven years old), 'How do I know she is my mother?' She was a stranger in my eyes. Similar in intensity are the many vignettes that Michael Henderson presents, not only from his story but from many others that he has assembled.

My passport for the return, which I still have as a precious possession, states that it is 'valid duration war'. No one knew in 1940 how long that duration would be, or indeed if the British would survive the bombing blitz and expected German invasion. This book is the story of that duration. It will bring back vivid images to the minds of all those who were part of the evacuation, memories that hark back now to an age that is long gone, to manners and morals that seem antique today, to simplicities and certainties that no longer exist.

For those who were not part of the saga Michael Henderson so brilliantly recounts, there will be myriad surprises, affectionate vignettes, and warm tributes amid the difficulties and uncertainties of exile.

The memories of individuals can have an unreal, egocentric aspect that does no service to history, only to individual vanity. Michael Henderson avoids this pitfall, producing instead a vivid portrait of the events, moods and atmosphere of a fast-moving, fearful and inspiring era.

One warning to readers of this book. It is a true history of a traumatic period, and there were several occasion when in spite of myself—I found tears in my eyes. As a little boy, not then four years old, I sang bravely and strongly the song 'There'll always be an England...', and forty years later chose it as my first record on *Roy Plomley's Desert Island Discs* radio programme, and now, sixty-four years later, cried involuntarily as I read its words in this magnificent volume.

Sir Martin Gilbert

Introduction

In 1939 King George VI visited the United States, the first British reigning monarch to do so. At that time Harry Hopkins was a confidant of President Roosevelt. His wife had died and he was living in the White House with his young daughter. He was anti-British and unmoved by the hoopla surrounding the royal visit.

On the night of the State banquet for King George VI and Queen Elizabeth, however, his daughter had a fever and to her dismay the doctor would not let her out of bed, even to take a peek over the staircase at the royal couple. Word of Hopkins' daughter's disappointment reached the Queen. And so, when she was dressed up in her crinoline, decked out with the Order of the Garter and her jewels, and wearing her tiara, she went to the daughter's bedside. Later Hopkins told an English friend, 'That is how I first came to think you people must have some good in you after all.'

I discovered the same and more, about Americans, at roughly the same impressionable age as Hopkins' daughter. For when I was 8 and my brother, Gerald, 6, we were evacuated to the US from wartime Britain and stayed with an American family for five years.

In 1978 I returned to the United States, living in Portland, Oregon for 21 years. Many Americans hearing about our wartime experiences have urged me to write about them. Many Britishers, even with the exposure to all the nostalgia for World War II at the time of its sixtieth anniversary, have little idea of the overseas evacuation. Other books exist by evacuees to America including excellent accounts written some years ago by Anthony Bailey and Alistair Horne[1]. But every account is different and personal, shaped by the age and experience of the author and sometimes the length of time each stayed in an American home and attended American schools. None attempts to give— as far as I have discovered—an overall or thorough picture, particularly of the private evacuations.

For young Americans and Canadians the passage through grade school and junior high school is a time of change and discovery but few of them can have that period so clearly framed as my brother and I did. It began with an ocean voyage in a liner escorted by a battleship and five destroyers across the submarine-infested waters of the Atlantic and ended with our return trip in an escort aircraft carrier across those same waters believing, but not taking it for granted, that all enemy submarine commanders knew the war was over. It was a dramatic change of mood, of culture, of language, of accent, of perspective, even of humour. It was a switch from shorts and gartered long stockings and school cap to dungarees or corduroy knickerbockers and ski cap and an introduction to the decimal system. And then five years later it was back to school blazers and school scarf again, and to the archaic calculations of pounds, shillings and pence.

Some of the book is based on a child's memories and reflects an innocence that had not yet grasped the horror of war. The fallibility of that memory was underlined for me some years ago when I wrote in an article for one of my American schools that I had played the part of Nathan Hale, spy or patriot depending on your country, in a school play. It was a surprise to get a letter from the widow of one of my teachers pointing out that the part was played by another boy and sending a photograph to prove it! I had genuinely come to believe this fiction. There is the danger, as Eric Hoffer writes, that 'we can remember minutely and precisely only the things which never really happened to us'. So, I am quite prepared to have a few readers who were present at events I describe getting in touch with me to set the record straight. Gerald and I wrote a letter home every week for five years. I assume that they would have been a wonderful if juvenile source of information. Unfortunately, they were all thrown away before I ever thought I would write a book. As I read through the material I have gathered over the years I am persuaded that the sense of duty and of love of country, in fact of two countries, that I think comes through in books I have written, played a significant part in my decision to devote the last fifty years of my life to addressing the causes of conflict and division.

The arrival on American shores of Gerald and me in August 1940 was recorded by a front-page photo in the *Christian Science Monitor*, taken as we waited for the immigration inspection in Boston. My brother has his tongue out at the photographer. The caption states, 'Gerald's impression of the proceedings seems a bit questionable.' Our impressions of the United States, however, have never been questionable. They have always been marked by gratitude.

The close relationship our two countries, Great Britain and the United States, enjoyed in those war years and afterwards cannot today be taken for granted. Despite the great opportunities for travel and communications, many in Britain do not know the generous side of America that was our good fortune to discover early on. This book is first of all an expression of gratitude to the Hinchman family who took us in for five years, to Ginny Rorstrom, now Ginny Boyd, who looked after us for two of those years, and to women like Sylvia Warren whose tireless energy and devotion, without remuneration, found hundreds of us a home away from home which, if things had gone terribly wrong, would have then become permanent.

I hope with this book to recall for the older generation some of the spirit and attitudes of those war years and help the modern generation know what life was like then, even if some attitudes may seem quaint by today's standards. That we were patriotic is indisputable, and with what historian John Keegan has called 'the fierce patriotism of a war child'. Tremayne Rodd[2], an English evacuee in kindergarten on Long Island, learned that America had beaten Britain in the War of Independence. His stout response, 'It's not true. I won't have it.' And another evacuee, 10-year-old Douglas Wilde, was quoted in the *Winnipeg Free Press*, 'Hitler is trying to scare the people of England, but he isn't doing much of a job of it.'

My first chapters spell out the context of the time because I have discovered from many conversations how hard it is for parents today to understand that parents of yesteryear could have been willing to send away their young children on such a hazardous voyage. When our daughter, Juliet, was eight I realized more than I ever had before how dire the circumstances and prospects must have been for our parents to part with us. Many motives played a part. Fear for the safety of their children was probably the overriding consideration of parents. 'Children shouldn't be on the front line,' was one father's remark. In an article in *Christian Century* in 1941 Dr. Maude Roydon wrote, 'To many British people the fear that their children could be brought up Nazis was worse, even, than the fear of death.' Some saw evacuation as the means to streamline the country for the battle against the invader. The broadcaster, J.B. Priestley, describing his first night as a Local Defense Volunteer, wrote[3], 'I remember wishing that we could send all our children out of this island, every boy and girl of them across the sea to the wide Dominions, and turn Britain into the greatest fortress the world has known; so that then, with an easy mind, we could fight and fight these Nazis until we broke their black hearts.'

Some saw evacuation in an even more positive light. Reporter Jean Lorimer, who had travelled out to the United States on the same ship we did, wrote in 1941, 'We sent our children to build stronger, finer foundations of love and mutual trust overseas at a time when…all the powers of evil seemed to prosper.'

Alistair Horne records how his father told him as he set off for the United States, 'We're going to lose everything, old boy. But you're my only son, and my most precious possession, and I just want you to come through it, even if I don't.' Sadly, his father died after an accident in the blackout in 1944. Happily, our parents survived. But they, I am sure, had no idea in 1940 that our separation was going to last five years. Just as American and Canadian hosts could not have imagined that the generosity of their offer of homes at a time of crisis would be so stretched out. Not many people were as prescient as Harold Macmillan, later to be prime minister, who, when asked in 1940 how long the war would last, replied, 'Twelve months if they win; five years if we do.'

I know that our separation does not compare with the suffering of many children, whether those killed or imprisoned or tortured. It was not a good war for the younger generation. 'Children,' the *Oxford Companion to World War II* points out, 'were the victims of the Second World War to an extent quite unknown in previous conflicts.' It is estimated that thirteen million children died as a direct result of the war. More than a million Jewish children perished in the Holocaust; only 11% of Jewish children in Europe in 1939 survived the war. The deaths were on all sides, with 5,586 German children killed, for instance, in the Allied bombing of Hamburg in July 1943, and uncounted thousands of Japanese children victims of the A bombs on Hiroshima and Nagasaki in 1945. Seven thousand seven hundred and thirty-six British children under sixteen were killed by enemy action during the war. At the end of the war it was estimated that there were also millions of abandoned children in Europe.

Evacuations of children were, therefore, not the worst things that could happen to them. Evacuations to escape the bombings also took place in Germany and Japan but the largest number of evacuees was in Britain with the first ones leaving the big cities two days before war was declared, followed in the next days by 827,000 unaccompanied children and 524,000 mothers with preschool children.

According to Foreign Office records[4] 13,973 children were sent overseas for safety from June 1940 to the end of 1942, travelling to Australia, Canada, New Zealand, South Africa and the United States. Of these 2,664 were evacuated under CORB[5], the government scheme. To the overall total must be added an unknown number of children who were sent in 1939 and in the first five months of 1940. The evacuation figures for Canada are 7,030 (1,532 CORB) and for the United States 3,103. The United States and Canada were certainly safe havens. The only mainland American children who died as a result of enemy action were not killed in an air raid but lost their lives in an explosion of a Japanese balloon bomb in Oregon—five children and one adult.

Of course, not every evacuee looks back on those war years with pleasure. There were many mismatches and some were abused. Some mothers who accompanied their children found difficulty getting work and some children were shunted from home to home. A few had no home to return to. Some social scientists and others regard the whole overseas evacuation as a terrible mistake. But for many of us who spent the war years in North America new horizons were opened. Gerald and I and many of our friends who were evacuated rate those years as a gift for which we have always been grateful. I would say the same as another evacuee, Felicity Hugh-Jones, 'I don't think I would have missed it for anything.'

My one regret is that the generosity so freely displayed to British children did not extend to all those children on the continent whose need was greater than ours. It is gratifying to learn of the *Kindertransporte*, trains which brought ten thousand German and Austrian children to safety in Britain in 1938 and 1939. Nine thousand of them were Jews. One of the children, a friend in Portland, Oregon, Fred Rosenbaum, enjoyed British hospitality for two years. 'It was a wonderful experience,' he wrote to me, but adding 'one that no one should ever experience.' In 1999 he presented a plaque to the British Parliament as thanks for rescuing the 10,000 children. Some of those children went on to America. From the outset the US Committee for the Care of European Children had been concerned over the dire straits of thousands of children on the European continent, particularly those whose Jewish background put them constantly in danger of their lives. They tried desperately to cut the red tape that would release them for migration. But as the Committee stated in its final report, "The entanglements proved too thick and only a few continental children could be extricated during the war years and brought to the hospitality of American homes.'

In 1940, as we waved goodbye to our parents in London, I apparently used the latest grown-up word I had acquired. 'See you after the *duration*,' I shouted. This book is about that duration.

Michael Henderson
Westward Ho!

21

1
1939

As for the time in which we live. Is not England at last taking its proper place, sacrificing all, standing alone against evil? Alone in arms, but backed by prayers and carrying the hopes of all peoples of the world. Few would not find it exhilarating thus to stand armed in the last ditch with good comrades in so righteous a cause.
—Col. Josiah Wedgwood, Memoirs of a Fighting Life

The 3rd of September 1939, the start of World War II, is for English men and women of my age as indelibly marked on our memories as the 7th of December 1941, the Japanese attack on Pearl Harbor, is for Americans sixty-five and older. Prime Minister Chamberlain's dramatic announcement that we were at war with Germany was particularly shocking for those of our parents' generation as it was only 21 years after the end of World War I, which was supposed to have been the 'war to end all wars'.

Our father had been a private in the trenches in France in the Great War, as it was then called. One thousand one hundred old boys (alumni) from Mill Hill, his school—whose enrolment at that time varied between 150 and 265— were in military service. All 15 members of the school's 1913 rugby team were in the forces overseas and eight of the team were killed. Such statistics could be repeated at many schools. On the first day alone of the 1916 Battle of the Somme about as many British soldiers were killed as were Americans in the whole Vietnam War. It was 15 times British losses on D-Day, seven times the losses at the Battle of Waterloo. And that was but one battle. Our father, fortunately, survived, as did our Irish grandfather who was also in the army in France and was wounded.

So it is perhaps not surprising that in the 1930s many British leaders and most of the British public allowed their horror of war to blind them to Hitler's intentions. Those in public life whose desire to prevent another war let their judgement be coloured have been pilloried and yet their motive was honourable. 'The British tendency to appease Germany had many sources,' writes John Lukacs[6]. 'They included the gradual recognition of the British people that Germany had been treated unfairly by the Treaty of Versailles and thereafter. There was the almost universal wish of government and people to avoid a British involvement in another war in Europe, at almost any cost.' Indeed, Andrew Roberts in his biography of Lord Halifax,[7] British Foreign Secretary in the late 1930s, says that the policy of appeasement 'once occupied almost the whole moral high ground' and the word was 'originally synonymous with idealism, magnanimity of the victor and a willingness to right wrongs'.

The threat of another war and particularly its potential danger to children was a concern of people and of governments all through the thirties. The most frightening aspect was the unknown effect that airpower was going to have. During World War I Britain suffered 103 air raids, from zeppelins and bombers, that killed 1,413 people and left another 3,400 injured, more than half the casualties in the greater London area. And the advances in aerial warfare in the twenty years that followed, whether in Manchuria, Abyssinia or Spain, raised horrifying spectres. Stanley Baldwin, a former and future prime minister, told Parliament in 1932, 'I think it is well for the man in the street to realize that there is no power on earth that can protect him from being bombed. Whatever people may tell him, the bomber will always get through...the only defence is an offense, which means that you will have to kill more women and children more quickly than the enemy if you want to save yourselves.'

In 1934 Winston Churchill, who was to become prime minister in 1940, warned in Parliament that under the pressure of continued air attack on London 'at least three or four million people would be driven out into the open country'. In 1936, in the light of events in Spain, the figure for possible deaths from bombing in England was raised to 600,000. And the great increase in the size of the Luftwaffe in 1936 and 1937 heightened the sense of alarm. Before the Second World War, as Harold Macmillan pointed out many years later, the British people feared aerial bombardment 'in much the same way as the Cold War generation feared nuclear attack' and historian Andrew Roberts wrote in 1991, 'The sense of dread about another war then was analogous with the way we feel about a nuclear war today.'

Successive governments may not have believed that war would come but were in no doubt what they felt the effect would be if it did. As early as 1925 a government committee met and discussed the threat the country would face if it came under air attack. In 1931 the Imperial Defence Committee set up an Evacuation Sub Committee. The Committee concluded that the 'morale effect of air attack in a future war would be out of all proportion'. All agreed that whatever happened, in the event of war London must be able to continue its job of supplying the needs of the nation. Anyone whose presence in the city threatened to hinder this objective had to be removed beforehand since they would 'merely add to the risk of casualty and to the possibility of confusion'. Committee member Maurice Hankey expressed the opinion of all when he declared that, just in case it came to civilian evacuation, it might be good to 'have a scheme in place'. By 1933 evacuation plans had been made public. In 1937 the Home Secretary said, 'We regard the question of evacuation as being very urgent.'

Some people, fortunately, were not convinced that Britain would be indefensible against bombing. Particularly those experimenting with a new discovery, radar. In fact, as Prime Minister Neville Chamberlain flew back from his Munich meeting with Adolf Hitler in September 1938, and claimed that there would be no war, his plane was tracked by five radar stations and plotted on the first ever radar Filter Table, a table that would play a significant part in the Battle of Britain. In the late 1920s work had begun in some countries on the basic ideas for radar. The Royal Navy had developed a proposal for a patent in 1928 but by 1934 nothing had been done about it. A few influential individuals saw the futility of Britain's defence and sought an effective early warning system. Churchill led the general cry for rearmament, decrying the 'cursed, hellish invention and development of war from air'. Frederick Lindemann, an Oxford professor, later Churchill's scientific adviser (Lord Cherwell), in a letter to *The Times* said that although it was true that there was at present no means of preventing hostile bombers from depositing their loads of explosives, incendiary materials, gases or bacteria upon their objectives, that no method could be devised to safeguard great centres of population from such a fate appears to him 'profoundly improbable'. He wrote, 'To adopt a defeatist attitude in the face of such a threat is inexcusable until it has definitely been shown that all resources of science and invention have been exhausted.'

However, the development of radar was necessarily secret and the public mood was one of fear mixed with a certain unreality. On 25 March 1939, for instance, the 'menace' was illustrated by a dramatic drawing in the *Illustrated London News*: 'an artist's vision of the nightmare now haunting the imagination of Europe under arms—surprise air raid on a great city'. In May anti-aircraft weapons and air raid precautions (ARP) were demonstrated in Hyde Park but that same month holidays on the continent were still being advertised as 'so easy to arrange nowadays'.

A year earlier, on 27 May 1938, the House of Commons held its first Committee on Evacuation meeting. It was decided by July that it would be possible, with Government help, to clear three to four million people out of the city in 72 hours. On 29 September the Home Office issued details of its plans. The government laid out four principles: 1) there should be no compulsory evacuation 2) billeting in the reception areas should be compulsory 3) the government would meet the initial costs of the evacuation 4) school children could be evacuated with their schools.

The country was divided into three zones—evacuation, reception and neutral. Local authorities in the reception areas were ordered to carry out a housing survey to determine how many evacuees could be accommodated. In the evacuation area key local authorities, such as the London County Council, were made responsible for planning the actual evacuation. Detailed transport arrangements were made involving the use of trains, buses, the Underground and even passenger boats. It was ordered that every child evacuee was to wear a tied-on luggage label bearing its name, that of its school and of the evacuation authority[8].

On 30 August 1939 the government issued its Get Ready for Evacuation signal. It was expected that the Germans would attack as soon as the war began. At 11.07 am on the 31st the evacuating authorities received the awaited Evacuate Forthwith signal. The greatest family and social upheaval Britain had ever known, Operation Pied Piper, was about to begin. The government's priority was to get children away as swiftly as possible from danger areas.

Parents were alerted on the radio and in the newspapers to send their children to the schools ready to be evacuated. All normal train and bus services were cancelled and hundreds of special trains were assembled. Some 200,000 children were evacuated from London on that day alone. And the operation continued for two more days. By the evening of September 3rd, 1,473,391 people, most of them children, had been placed in reception areas. Richard M. Titmuss writes in the official *History of the Second World War*, 'From the first day of September 1939 evacuation ceased to be a problem of administrative planning. It became instead a multitude of problems in human relationships.' Operation Pied Piper, this greatest ever evacuation of children from the city to the country, was an amazing feat but it has been well documented in a number of books[9] and is beyond the scope of this one.

However, another potentially enormous evacuation was shaping up. It had begun even before the outbreak of war with a trickle of children who were sent privately for safety overseas. But with the disastrous war situation, with the overrunning of European nations by the Germans and the evacuation of British troops from Dunkirk, with the offers of help from Commonwealth countries and from the United States—and the desire to make it available to all and not just to those who could afford it—this option of overseas evacuation came increasingly into official focus.

It was on the evening of the first day of the war, 3 September, that the liner *Athenia*, on its way from Liverpool to Montreal, was sunk by a German U-boat. Out of the 1,418 passengers and crew 112 people died, most of them American students returning home and refugees. It was a portent of worse to come.

In 1939 the United States meanwhile was coming out of a depression. President Roosevelt's New Deal legislation had included massive Federal programmes for public works and industrial expansion and a Fair Labor Standards Act that legislated minimum wages and maximum hours. But there were still more than eight million unemployed and twenty-three million more were receiving some form of public assistance. Militarily the United States stood at 18th in the world and the country had almost no munitions factories.

The New York World's Fair that year had as its theme 'The World of Tomorrow'. Germany did not participate. King George VI and Queen Elizabeth were two of the 25 million visitors.[10] The fact that President Roosevelt served them hot dogs at his Hyde Park residence made headlines. The *Illustrated London News* commented, 'If Americans still cherished any doubts about the democratic simplicity of the British royal family these were finally dispelled by the visit this month to Washington and New York of the King and Queen whose frank and unaffected enjoyment of the tumultuous welcome accorded them won the public affection wherever they moved.' An important transatlantic link of friendship had been established. Eleanor Roosevelt noted, 'We all knew the King and Queen were returning home to face a war', and the King asked, 'Why don't my ministers talk to me as the President did tonight? I feel exactly as though a father were giving me his most careful and wise advice.'

Despite economic difficulties at home, foreign policy was beginning to overshadow the domestic scene. President Roosevelt told Congress at the beginning of the year, 'We have learned that the God-fearing democracies of the world, which observe the sanctity of treaties and good faith in their dealings with other nations, cannot safely be indifferent to international lawlessness anywhere.' Acts of aggression, he said, 'automatically undermine all of us'.

Immigrants to America from Europe were making their mark, whether in arts or science, and having an influence. Albert Einstein, who was to become an American citizen the following year, wrote to President Roosevelt, 'It may be possible to set up a nuclear reaction in uranium by which vast amounts of power could be released.' This would also lead to the construction of 'extremely powerful bombs of a new type'.

Hitler's *Mein Kampf* was on the American non-fiction best-seller list. British Prime Minister Chamberlain's umbrella and hat became motifs in fashion accessories and prints while 'blackout fashions' included white hats, flashlights and containers for torches. Dictaphone was advertising its product as 'How to please a dictator'. In November 1939 Britain's finest copy of the Magna Carta was deposited in the Library of Congress for safekeeping. In December the *Boston Post* made King George VI its 'man of the year'.

The outbreak of the war in Europe underlined the divisions in American attitudes. A Gallup poll indicated that 58% of the people believed that the United States would be drawn into the war in Europe while 65% favoured boycotting Germany. National hero Charles Lindbergh led demonstrations against US intervention, while his mother-in-law, Betty Morrow, worked in London to help Britain. President Roosevelt in one of his radio 'fireside chats' assured the country, and those soon to be voting in the election the following year, 'This nation will remain a neutral nation but I cannot ask that every American remain neutral in thought as well. Even a neutral cannot be asked to close his mind or close his conscience.' It was clear, however, that there was no guarantee that the US would come to the aid of Britain if the situation became perilous. Britain's ambassador to the United States, Lord Lothian, in one of his periodic surveys (April 1940) of American attitudes was of the view that 'the United States is 95% anti-Hitler, is 95% determined to keep out of the war if it can, and will only enter the war when its own vital interests are challenged, though these vital interests include its ideals.'

It is hard now to live into the mind of people at that time. News of Hitler's excesses was no secret. But rather like events in more recent times in the Balkans or in central Africa they had not reached that mass awareness that provokes swift or immediate response. The rights and wrongs were not seen in the sharp relief of later years.

There has always been a strong isolationist streak in the American attitude to the world. And the world then as today did not always welcome American intervention. Harold Evans has written in *The American Century*, 'Isolationism was no more an American monopoly than appeasement was a British one. Before Winston Churchill took power, the rulers of the Western countries did not seek or welcome American involvement in Europe.' He points out that at the beginning of the war American industry made no distinction between trade with Germany and trade with the democracies: 'As the dictatorship grew ever more menacing, American industry blithely supplied them all with materials essential for their war machine.' In fact, between 1936 and 1940 American investment in Germany increased by 40 percent.

No document better makes the ambivalence of attitudes clear, that reveals that issues were not as black and white as they became with hindsight, than the issue of *Life* magazine that was published eight weeks[11] *after* the war had begun. In 1939 it was not at all clear who was going to win and it is almost as if bets were hedged on the outcome, with the United States a spectator.

There is, for instance, a whole page with photo and drawing with the headline: 'A German hero phones his mother: "I just sank a battleship"'. The accompanying article starts: 'To the select fellowship of naval immortals who, in small boats, stealthily, perilously, have ambushed and conquered mighty ships of war, there was added last week the name of Guenther Prien. Blond, boyish, diminutive (5 ft 5 in), he was hailed not only in Germany but by the British Admiralty and the seadogs of the world for his professional skill and daring in guiding his submarine into the dangerous waters of Scapa Flow on the night of October 14 and there torpedoing the 29,000 ton British battleship *Royal Oak*.' The article describes how afterwards Prien and his crew were entertained by the *Fuehrer* in his apartment, decorated and taken to a vaudeville show in the *Wintergarten*.

There are two pages on the 'great debate' on American neutrality: 'The edge had been taken off the debate by the debaters' lack of candor—the pro-repeal senators concealing the fact that their real motive was a desire to help Britain and France beat Hitler, the anti-repealists hiding the fact that their major aim was to stop the President from implementing his pro-Ally sympathies.'

Two pages feature the achievements of German pilots in shooting down British planes. In one photo a pilot gets an ovation from squadron mates, in another a pilot is congratulated by his superior officer. On the opposite page there is a picture of a German bomber shot down and also two RAF prisoners 'proudly photographed by the Germans Propaganda Ministry in friendly conversation with a German infantryman'. 'One sour note,' the paper says, 'was a report that a French pilot escaping from his plane was machine-gunned in the air by German planes.' There are six pages of photographs headed 'England mobilizes 1,500,000 of her women for the war.'

Life follows this with seven pages headed 'Paintings by Adolf Hitler—the artist who turned statesman wants to pick up his brush again'[12]. The spread begins: 'The last important conqueror in Europe to be greatly interested in art was Napoleon. His interest was largely acquisitive. It consisted in swiping Italy's art treasures and putting them in the Louvre. Adolf Hitler has a deeper personal interest in art. He himself was a painter whose struggles with art brought him no success and little satisfaction. But Hitler has never stopped wanting to be a painter. In his famous pre-war conversations with Sir Neville Henderson, published in the Blue Book, he told the British ambassador: "I am an artist and not a politician. Once the Polish question is settled, I want to end my life as an artist."' There is also a focus on architecture with the dramatic quality Hitler liked. His mansion near Berchtesgaten and its furnishings 'suggest that in a more settled Germany, Adolf Hitler might have done quite well as an interior decorator'.

The same ambivalence was evident in newspapers on the West coast. The writer, Vera Brittain, who was in Los Angeles three months later, at the beginning of 1940, found it an educative experience for a British traveller 'to read publications which presented England's naval misfortunes with the same laconic detachment as Germany's aerial defeats, and treated Winston Churchill's dramatic speeches with hardly more respect than the picturesque pronouncements of Dr. Goebbels'. In the Los Angeles window of the Hamburg-Amerika Line she noticed a large placard inviting Americans to help in breaking the British blockade: YOU CAN NOW SEND FOOD PARCELS TO GERMANY.

Over the next months the worsening scene in Europe, and particularly the dire straits in which Britain found herself, were increasingly brought home to the American public, not least by the nightly radio broadcasts from London by CBS correspondent Edward R. Murrow. American poet Archibald MacLeish was to write of those broadcasts the following year, 'You burnt the city of London in our homes, and we felt the flames.'

2
A Special Relationship

Hitler may hurl hell towards England at any moment and certainly he will strike soon. America must act instantly. America must say to England, 'Our bars are down to your children. Send them by the thousands, it is our duty and privilege to give them a home.' There is no conceivable reason for not taking 60,000 children if England wants to send them, and more too. And let us stand side by side with Canada to relieve her of any part of the burden of providing for children which her war effort might make difficult.
—New York Daily Mirror, 24 June 1940

I send you this line to say how warmly we have appreciated the many generous offers which have been received from private sources in the United States to look after children from this country during the war.
—Letter on 25 June from British Foreign Secretary, Lord Halifax, to the US Ambassador to London, Joseph Kennedy

By the spring of 1940 an invasion of Britain by German forces was widely expected. The strategic situation was so bad that twelve Regional Commissioners were appointed by the King to provide for the continuation of civil government in the event of an invasion. If that were to happen each Commissioner would become in effect the civil governor of the region, with full powers and in liaison with the local army commander. 'Twelve dictators in waiting' was how lawyer Hartley Shawcross described them. On 17 May

Canadian Prime Minister Mackenzie King wrote in his diary: 'The Blitzkrieg might lead to destruction of Britain and France within the next few weeks.' On 21 May a senior US diplomat, James Pierrepoint, wrote in his diary: 'We have to face the possibility that there may be complete German victory.' Indeed, the US Ambassador Joseph Kennedy warned Washington that backing Britain meant backing the losing side.

In Britain, 26 May was proclaimed a National Day of Prayer. The King[13] and Queen carried gas masks at the service in Westminster Abbey. The Archbishop of Canterbury, Cosmo Gordon Lang, told those who attended that they were living in an hour darkened by greater dangers than had ever threatened the nation and that the mere act of prayer would bring calmness, courage, and self-control. 'It will yet be proved,' he said, 'that the spirit of free men is stronger than the subservience of men who are the cogs of the machine.'

On that same day Mackenzie King received a report that facing an air superiority of about 5 to 1 'it is unlikely that the UK can withstand such an assault for many weeks'. And, the next day, according to the authors of the *Finest Hour*[14], you did not have to be a defeatist or even an appeaser to feel that the war had been all but lost: 'This was, after all, what just about every well-informed person was saying in every capital city in the world.' On 28 May a Foreign Office paper suggested that secret plans should be considered for the evacuation of the royal family and government and the immediate removal of the Crown jewels and other precious stones and securities to another part of the empire. Churchill rejected this firmly, 'No such discussion can be permitted.' One cabinet minister obtained suicide pills. A Foreign Office memo stated: 'We are afraid to our bones these days, of the words "Too Late". If things should go really badly with the French people next week (or with England) the escape of some really large number of children would become urgent beyond all urging.' It quoted Raymond Gram Swing, the American broadcaster who was the BBC's commentator on American affairs: 'I want so much to arouse people to the need of mercy on a scale never shown in history, which predicted scale alone would be of use.'

There was one bright spot that no one had dared to envisage. Between 26 May and 3 June 338,226 men of the BEF[15] along with some French troops were rescued from the northern French port of Dunkirk. They were carried by nearly 900 ships and small craft, the famous 'little ships'. 'Wars are not won by evacuations,' cautioned Churchill, who had expected to get 20,000 to 30,000 home. 'But there was a victory inside this deliverance.' The stories of valour surrounding Operation Dynamo as it was called led to the morale-building 'Dunkirk spirit'. On 4 June Churchill made the famous speech: 'We shall fight on the beaches, we shall fight on the landing grounds, we shall fight in the fields and in the streets, we shall fight in the hills; we shall never surrender.'

According to writer Richard Hough, 'The shock of Dunkirk, the nature and extent of this defeat, the fall of France a few days later, the realization that Britain had lost her only European ally and, with her Empire and Commonwealth overseas, stood alone against the might of the new German Empire; the knowledge that the nation was more vulnerable to invasion and conquest than for 900 years: all this led to a sharpening of determination and an inspiration of warlike spirit, as mighty and memorable as that aroused in the American people by Pearl Harbor eighteen months later.'

On 8 June historian Arthur Bryant (later Sir) with some foresight wrote in the *Illustrated London News*, 'It is the business of the Royal Air Force to do in a new age what the navy in its classic and youthful days did for England in the past. It has to encompass us with a living moat, behind which our traditional liberties can survive and flourish.' That week the widely read magazine had a page headed 'How to recognize Nazi parachutists: dress, arms equipment'. And the following week a double-page spread, 'Meeting the threat of air-borne invasion in Britain: suggested measures for foiling Nazi troop-carriers.' The magazine noted that as a provision against any possible invasion by German parachute troops, members of the Manchester Police were receiving instruction in the use of rifles and revolvers: 'Events in Holland abundantly prove such measures of precaution to be necessary anywhere within flying distance of Germany.' At the end of the month another double-page spread was 'a guide to the identification of enemy aircraft: German fighters, bombers and troop carriers'.

On 20 June Churchill, always mindful of how much Britain's future would be determined by the United States, told a secret session of the House of Commons that the heroic struggle of Britain was the best chance of bringing the Americans into the war. It would depend on Britain's resolute bearing and holding out until election issues were settled there. If Britain could get through the next three months she would get through the next three years. On 29 June the *Illustrated London News* used the phrase the 'Battle of Britain' to indicate the next phase of the war.

A senior British general and later Field Marshal, Alan Brooke (Viscount Alanbrooke), who was to become Chief of the Imperial General Staff a year later, wrote in his diary on 2 July 1940: 'The more I see the nakedness of our defences the more appalled I am! Untrained men, no arms, no transport, no equipment. There are masses of men in uniform in this country but they are mostly untrained, why I cannot think after 10 months of war. The ghastly part of it is I feel certain that we have only a few more weeks left before the Boche attacks!' Former US Secretary of State Henry Stimson said, 'France has been conquered and the sea power of Britain seems to be trembling in the balance. We may be next.'

By June only a third of the American people believed Britain would win the war. CBS was already considering how it would cover the invasion. A review of American papers and their letters columns showed a large majority in favour of keeping out of the European war. But in the United States as in all the Commonwealth countries the mounting threat to Britain was also provoking an outpouring of support.

Starting early in 1939 offers of refuge began to arrive in Britain from a number of countries and soon after war was declared overseas evacuation schemes were put forward for the Dominions. In 1939 100,000 Canadian women, for instance, offered their homes to British evacuees. But in view of the experience of British parents with the internal evacuation the idea of overseas evacuation was not universally popular. Many families who had the means or who had relatives overseas to whom they could send their children took advantage of the fact.

As the situation worsened in the first part of 1940, more and more offers of help poured in. Elspeth Huxley wrote[16]: 'All over Canada and the United States, from the bustling seaboard cities to the flat and sun-soaked prairie towns, from the mansions of the millionaires (patrolled, like barons' castles of old, by armed bodyguards) to the cramped frame houses of the poor, men and women offered the safety of their homes to children from the battle zone.'

The Foreign Office was watching developments closely, particularly as to how they affected relations with these countries. They were not keen to give any sense of a weakening of British determination to resist which they were worried evacuation might convey. A respected but maverick member of Parliament, Col. Josiah Wedgwood, had written Churchill on 10 May when he became prime minister with suggestions how he could show that his government was different from that of his predecessor. One point was to approach the United States and 'get them to take and keep our useless mouths. Their conscience would make them consent; at worst the race would survive; they would be by far the best propaganda for armed help.' He gave notice to the effect that he would raise the question in the House of Commons.

An internal Foreign Office memo of 15 May states that this question was 'tantamount to admitting that we think ourselves so little capable of defending these islands that we are already contemplating large scale evacuation of the civilian population. The part of the question which suggests that the US government should foot the bill could hardly avoid a most unfortunate reception in the United States particularly when it is remembered that there is widespread unemployment there, part of which is represented as being the consequence of our blockade policy.'

Another memo the same day states, 'It seems to me that the idea of a more or less large scale overseas evacuation ought to be explored, if this has not been done already, by those whose business it is to consider these things, so that if things do not go well we can reduce our commitments here to the minimum and put ourselves in a position if necessary to carry on the war from Canada or Newfoundland. It can hardly be doubted that in those circumstances the United States would have to come in on our side. In this case it would be more a question of evacuating the royal family, the government, parliament and the ministries and services rather than the "useless mouths" contemplated by Mr. Wedgwood's question.' The writer makes an additional point: 'I can think of few things more calculated to wreck our future relations with America for the better part of a generation than to pour a flood of refugees into America, however ready they might be at first to receive them.'

A further Foreign Office memo on 23 May comments: 'At the present moment American opinion is in a state of complete dither about their own defencelessness and they are trying to make up their mind whether their best line of defence is in France with the Allies or in America. It is a close thing in which direction their mind will be made up and any signs of panicking or despondency on our part would probably decide them in favour of disinteresting themselves in Europe and concentrating on the defence of their own shores. It therefore behoves us to continue to show the Americans that we are worth helping, that we are determined and resolute and that, with their help, there is a good chance of our winning.'

Wedgwood had told the Foreign Office that his primary object was not to make it easier for us to resist but to preserve the species. A Foreign Office official minuted 'If the idea is to preserve the species I do not think that, even at the worst, enough children would not be left in the British Isles for this purpose.' And Sir Alexander Cadogan noted, 'Cannot Col. Wedgwood be ignored or snubbed. Is it not commonly known that he is mad?' The Foreign Office fears were removed when the Colonel withdrew his question. Colonel

Wedgwood commented,[17] 'Churchill considered it likely to damage the morale of the country; and though America is ready enough to help now at once, the "sea-evacuation" has been postponed, till a more urgent occasion. My own opinion is that we should all fight much better with our sword arms free and no anxiety for our families. It is not panic but a precaution with a military value.'

The more urgent occasion was soon upon the country.

With the worsening military situation, companies in the US and Canada such as Hoover and Kodak and Warner Brothers offered to take in children of their employees in Britain and university faculties extended hospitality to children of their opposite numbers. Invitations came from churches, schools and school districts, from the Red Cross, the Salvation Army, the Legion of Mercy, the Society of Friends and from private individuals. From all across the United States came letters and telegrams offering hospitality. Some went to the State Department, more to the British Foreign Office, a few even to the King at Buckingham Palace. After Dunkirk, Canada House was besieged by applications for entry into Canada.

The American Secretary of the Rhodes Scholarships appealed to American Rhodes Scholars to help in plans to house British children in the United States for the duration of the war. He suggested that they should receive into their families one or more children of Oxford or Cambridge dons or children of other universities. Invitations came from McGill University in Montreal and Swarthmore College in Pennsylvania. The University of Toronto's Women's War Service Committee contacted friends at the universities of Birmingham, Manchester, Oxford and Cambridge. Two days after the French surrender a canvass of Toronto faculty produced 147 offers of homes and 51 offers of financial help.

Clubs and organizations in the US and Canada set out to find homes. Canadian Rotary Clubs offered to be a clearinghouse for children. Miss Helena Mills John, General Secretary of the English-Speaking Union (ESU) in a 13 June letter to Malcolm MacDonald at the Ministry of Health says she has received a cable from Frank S. Coon, the General Secretary of the English-Speaking Union of the United States: GUARANTEE CARE HUNDRED CHILDREN PRIVATE HOMES PLEASE CIRCULARISE MEMBERS. She adds, 'I am venturing to write on this occasion to you personally as I would like to say that if any plans are being considered for the evacuation of British children to the United States, the ESU would wish to take part in those activities particularly as it is the largest British-American organisation in peace times and also because I believe I am right in thinking that the original suggestion that the United States should offer refuge to British children came from the American English-Speaking Union and their offers of help in this connection have been repeated again and again since September. Through our British and American Schoolboy Scholarships Scheme we have had many years experience with regard to the sending of British boys to live in the United States for a year at American private schools and during the holidays, and should be very glad to cooperate with the Ministry with regard to this new proposal.' There was general agreement that the ESU in the UK and the USA would work with the central organisations in the respective countries and not set up separate schemes.

On 1 June *The Times* published the official offers from the dominions to take evacuees, urging the country to take up their 'generous offers of hospitality'. In that month alone, just to take *The Times* as an example, there were seventeen overseas evacuation stories printed in the paper. Immigration offices were flooded with inquiries about entry permits, particularly mid-month when papers outlined a scheme for sending 100,000 children to the US.

The mounting number of offers and the generosity behind them sparked the government to considering how to respond.[18] Elspeth Huxley makes it clear why the government was anxious to make the opportunity more equal: 'In England, as the papers filled with pictures of the children of the well-to-do posing happily on the country estates of Long Island and Quebec, feeling grew that the safety of the nation's children was too vital and too sacred a thing to be bought with gold. Why should the son of the rich man sleep in security in New York's gay lighted towers, the roar of traffic bound on peaceful errands in his ears, while the son of the poor man dozed in crowded shelters below our dangerous cities, menaced by the bomber's drone? It was unfair; and something ought to be done.'

Geoffrey Shakespeare, MP, Parliamentary Secretary in the Dominions Office, was asked to chair an interdepartmental committee to consider the offers of hospitality which had come in. They met for the first time on 7 June. He had initially been doubtful about overseas evacuation feeling that dangers could not be overcome by running away from them. But he felt increasingly that the war effort would not be helped by keeping the children and that the opportunity should not be let slip. It was essential, he believed, that the scheme should be open to all alike 'and no one must get the benefit of it solely by wealth'.

Within two weeks of the first meeting of the committee the report was finished. 'In peacetime three months would have been required for a review of this scope,' he wrote later. He presented his report to the war cabinet on 17 June but while doing so was interrupted by a messenger informing Churchill that France was surrendering. At that point, Shakespeare wrote later, 'All interest in the evacuation of children was eclipsed by the stark magnitude of this momentous event.' Shakespeare withdrew from the cabinet meeting not certain what had been decided. However, next day consulting the cabinet minutes, he found that the Children's Overseas Reception Board, or CORB as it became known, had been approved. It would seem that Prime Minister Churchill had been preoccupied with the situation in France and may not have even realised a decision had been taken. Had he done so, he would have most likely opposed it. A few days later he told the cabinet that 'a large movement of this kind encourages a defeatist spirit which is entirely contrary to the true facts of the position and should be sternly discouraged. It is one thing to allow a limited number of children to be sent to North America, but the idea of a large scale evacuation stands on a very different footing and was attended by grave difficulties.' He admitted later that the possible ramifications of overseas evacuation were not fully appreciated by the government when it was first raised: 'It was not foreseen that the mild countenance given to this plan would lead to a movement of such dimensions.'

A Foreign Office summary of what happened records that after the war cabinet meeting on 17 June it had been decided that the offers coming in from Canada and other Dominions to receive and look after children from this country for the period of war, 'offers which represented a natural movement of sympathy', could not be neglected. The question arose what attitude should be adopted to similar offers from the US. 'The Secretary of State was advised, and represented at the war cabinet, that from the point of view of relations with the United States it was essential that such offers should not be cold-shouldered: if a large quantity of children went, say, to Canada and one, or only a few, to the United States, we risk forfeiting in the latter country sympathy which we could not afford to lose, and might even expose ourselves to the criticism that we thought the United States were not good enough for us.'

For Secretary to the CORB Board Shakespeare took G. Kimber from the Dominions Office where he had been secretary to the Interdepartmental Committee. An interesting sidelight on this appointment: The weekend before that Committee had met Kimber asked for leave for urgent, private business. He gave no reason but leave was granted. He returned on Monday very brown. 'Have you been sunbathing at the Lido?' Shakespeare asked. 'No, sir,' he replied. 'I've been with my sailing boat to rescue survivors from the beach near Dunkirk.' Shakespeare, who tells the story, comments, 'I hope the story of the gallantry of our amateur yachtsmen will one day be told.'

The cabinet had approved telling the House of Commons about the scheme. 'The favourable response that greeted Mr. Attlee's announcement in the Commons,' writes Michael Fethney, author of a history of CORB[19], 'was nothing compared with the rapturous reception given it by the press and public at large.' Only three days after the cabinet decision, the CORB offices in Berkeley Street opened on Friday at 9 am with a clerical staff of thirty. The morning papers had carried an announcement and by 10 am an estimated three thousand people were waiting in a queue that stretched several hundred yards. Then, too, an avalanche of post began to arrive, an estimated 7,000 letters a day, 94% from working class families. The government was seriously alarmed by the scale of the response and Shakespeare was told by the cabinet to 'curb the enthusiasm'. He went on the radio on the Sunday to try and do so.

But the requests continued to flood in. And after ten days the application lists had to be closed. Within two weeks of being set up CORB had received applications on behalf of 211,448 children, which was about half those eligible. 'This suggests,' says Fethney, 'that, if the scheme had remained open much longer, it is probable that a majority of parents would have sought the CORB escape route for their children.' In fact, a statistical survey conducted by Home Intelligence in July showed that parents of approximately one million children were prepared for them to go. There were in addition 19,000 applications from those desiring to be escorts. The ratio of escorts to children had been fixed at 1 to 15, and in addition a doctor and two nurses to every 100 children. To cope with all the administration, within less than a month the staff had expanded to 620 men and women, and within six weeks from the day Dominion governments had invited Britain to send children overseas the first CORB children had sailed from Liverpool. At the same time the US embassy tried to cope with some 4,000 people in line, 2,000 phone calls, 1,000 letters and 500 telegrams every day for several weeks.

The Dominions would not take any payment. 'Hospitality was to be freely offered, and no finer proof could be found of the spirit that sustains the British Commonwealth of nations,' wrote Shakespeare. In Canada it was announced that the province of British Columbia was prepared to absorb 10,000 children immediately and through the Canadian Medical Association came offers from physicians of homes for children of 1,000 British doctors. The Canadian Parliament went so far as to pass a law giving income tax relief to those who received evacuee children in their homes. Many gifts were received towards expenses. The wife of the South African High Commissioner, for instance, provided enough funds collected from women in the Dominion to buy tropical kits for several hundred children destined for South Africa. Another gift was L25,000 from the Government of Fiji. In Britain Simon Marks provided L7000 of clothing.

A spokesman for CORB was quoted in the *New York Times*, 'The youngsters we are sending abroad are the cream of British childhood. It is a thoroughly democratic set-up and doesn't make any distinction between rich and poor.' In a debate in the House of Commons on 2 July Shakespeare said, 'These children will form friendships, contacts and associations in the Dominions, and the silken cord which binds the Empire together will be strengthened beyond all power to sever.' However, in the same debate Conservative MP Rear Admiral Sir Tufton Beamish said that overseas evacuation could produce 'despondency and alarum' at home. He claimed that in his part of Sussex 'panic and evacuation' had already begun among the 'wealthy and leisured classes' who were evacuating themselves and their children 'all over the country'. He warned that the Germans would without hesitation torpedo a children's ship.

Even the dangers of crossing the Atlantic did not deter parents. In early July the former Blue Star luxury liner *Arandora Star* was sunk off the coast of Ireland with the loss of 714 lives—ironically not children but for the most part Italian and German internees. After this sinking it was announced that the official overseas programmes were cancelled while private schemes were permitted to go ahead unhindered[21]. James Griffiths, Labour MP for Llanelli, told the House of the 'great resentment' in his constituency because children of 'responsible public men' had been sent overseas while 'poor children' were left behind. He declared that the common people did not ask for 'anything more than the ordinary protection which everyone else gets, but they resent it and feel indignant if rich people are looking after their own children and allowing the children of the poor to stand all risks.'

The next day the government reversed its position. The scheme had only been postponed, not abandoned and any future overseas evacuation would be regulated 'with a view to restoring the balance between classes'. So CORB's life was extended.

In the United States action to help the evacuation was accelerating. In fact, a Gallup poll that summer indicated that five million American families would be willing to take in British and French children. Since 1938 some Americans had been coming together as the National Non-Sectarian Committee in an effort to find ways of bringing child refugees from the continent. Now they felt impelled to widen their focus from German children to the children of all European countries. Members met in early June 1940 with Mrs. Roosevelt. She invited a large number of people from various relief and charitable groups to meet with her to consider organizing into a committee which would be concerned with all European children and would set up an immediate program to channel the growing pro-British sentiment into a supervised child care program with good placement practices. By the end of June, writes biographer Doris Kearns Goodwin, 'Eleanor had found her first wartime cause in the movement to open America's doors to the refugee children of Europe.' With the entire continent under Nazi control, and England living in fear of imminent invasion, the public cry for evacuating as many European children as possible reached a crescendo.

A Foreign Office report records that the British Ambassador to the United States, Lord Lothian, was instructed to form an influential committee in the United States for the purpose of taking care of children during the war. 'After we had given instructions to our ambassador, and when the latter had enlisted Mrs. Roosevelt and many influential personalities, and when these in turn had entered on the scheme with enthusiasm and with publicity extending all over the States, it did not seem that we were in a position to change our minds and leave all these people in the lurch. While the United States went to great lengths to remove all obstacles in the way of the Board's sending children there, an unfortunate impression arose that we were endeavouring to blame them for the slow progress of the Board. This situation was eased when the Lord Privy Seal[22], on the advice of the Foreign Office section concerned, and at the request of the Secretary of State, attributed the difficulties at this end to the loss of the services of the French fleet for convoy work.'

The role played by Lord Lothian as ambassador to the United States, appointed on the eve of the war, helped significantly to ensure an American public and leadership that was well informed about British circumstances and policy. He was already well known to many influential Americans. For more than twenty years he had been Secretary of the Rhodes Trust. He had first come to the US in 1909 and claimed, 'I always feel fifteen years younger when I land in New York.' In speech after speech he laid out the issues facing Britain and the world. He was a man of deep moral and religious beliefs. 'I am certain that in the end moral principle is more powerful than bayonets and guns,' he told a Pilgrims Society dinner, 'and that when, in addition, it is backed by guns and bayonets it will inexorable and speedily prevail.' At an annual Columbia

41

University lunch he said, 'Since I came to the United States as ambassador I have always endeavoured to speak perfectly frankly to the American people. I think it is the duty of the free peoples to put before one another exactly what they think, provided they leave one another perfectly free to draw their own conclusions for themselves.' It was not his business, he believed, to try to tell anyone what they should do but to see that they were 'informed of the essential facts'. Indeed, he did this so effectively that one midwestern paper warned that the 'subtlety of his propaganda will consist of the fact that there will be no propaganda' and that he was, in short, 'a very dangerous man'. In his last speech written before he died, and read for him by a counsellor of the British Embassy, he said, 'The Sermon on the Mount is in the long run much stronger than all Hitler's propaganda or Goering's guns and books.'

An article in *The Spectator*[23] said that to a quite abnormal degree Lord Lothian saw men as men and cared less than nothing for rank and place and 'that was part of the secret of his success in the United States. He loved America, and made himself at home, with zest, in the American way of life.'

Paying tribute to him in January 1941, Lord Halifax described his performance as ambassador—which lasted 16 months until his death in December 1940—as 'one of the outstanding achievements of British diplomatic history'. 'To bring Britain and America nearer to each other was for Lord Lothian a labour of love for which he was marked out by temperament, interest and experience.' He was buried in the National Cemetery in Arlington.

Whoever deserves the credit, Lord Lothian or Eleanor Roosevelt, a new organisation, the US Committee for the Care of European children, was set up with a national office in New York. It was chaired by business executive Marshall Field, with leaders from the three major religious faiths, and dedicated to a non-sectarian approach. Soon phone and personal inquiries mounted to some 2,000 a day and 170 affiliated local committees were started. Members met daily with officials of the US Children's Bureau, the State Department and the Attorney General's office to find a way for groups of children to meet immigration laws written to prevent the exploitation of foreign child labour. Finding homes was simple compared with the legal challenge of getting children admitted in the first place.

Initially, the US government refused to issue visitors' visas, subjecting the children to its British immigration quota of 6,000 a month, with every child needing an individual guarantor who had to submit an affidavit of financial competence. Ships with children bound for the US would have to dock in

Canada since US rules prohibited the entry of anyone whose passage had been paid by his or her government. The Neutrality Act prohibited American ships from entering British waters.

On CBS radio Mrs. Roosevelt called for an administrative ruling that would allow the children to enter as temporary visitors rather than immigrants. 'The parents of these children will recall them when the war is over...therefore (they) should be classed as temporary visitors and not as immigrants...Red tape must not be used to trip up little children on their way to safety.'

Some Americans suspected that the enthusiasm shown in some quarters in Britain for having children come to the United States was a ploy by the British to provoke an incident that would draw her into the war. Breckinridge Long, head of the State Department's visa section, felt that refugees would endanger US security as Germans were using any opportunity to send in spies as visitors. He opposed any special arrangements: 'The very surest way to get America into the war would be to send an American ship to England and put 2,000 babes on it and then have it sunk by a German torpedo.'

Thanks to an intervention by President Roosevelt in mid-July a new ruling was issued whereby visitor visas would be issued to British children 'upon a showing of intention they shall return home upon the termination of hostilities'. This was through a 'corporate affidavit' which allowed a non-profit organization to guarantee support of a specific number of children and to receive within 48 hours 'blank visas'. These could be sent abroad to be filled in with the names of children awaiting exit. Six days after the ruling the State Department issued 1,000 visas. The reception and care of children had to be in conformity with the standards of the US Children's Bureau.

A 2 August front-page headline in the *New York Times* read: '200,000 children seek haven; drive here to ask funds for them/leaders in every field are enlisted in $5,000,000 campaign to rescue them from war-threatened Britain.' It was accompanied by an editorial 'They must be saved'. It recorded that Representative Thomas C. Hennings of Missouri has made public three facts: that there are children available for ships to bring back; assurances that 98% of the children are not children of the rich ('It would be a hard-hearted person who would wish to see a child hit by a Nazi bomb because its parents were well-to-do, but it may relieve some minds to know that the poor have not been forgotten.'); and that the American seamen's union has volunteered to man the rescue ships without pay 'an act which ought to make every American proud of our merchant marine'. 'All that stands in the way of the rescue is first, enough money, and, second, an amendment to the Neutrality Act. The sooner

43

that amendment is passed and the money raised, the more lives we can save. It is time to up anchor and sail.' In mid-August Congress amended the Neutrality Act to allow American ships to transport children from Britain but it contained a provision requiring a safe passage by Germany.[24]

Only British children aroused the sympathy of Congress. When Congressman William Schulte of Indiana tried to broaden the use of the visitor visas to any European child under 16, his bill was killed even before it reached the floor. This partiality, according to one writer, 'reflected the widespread feeling that the United States and Britain were blood-relatives sharing a common heritage'.[25] Sadly the sentiment of support for British children did not extend to some of those who most needed help. 'The crucial difference, in terms of American public opinion, between the British and the German children, was that the British boys and girls were mostly Christian, the German children mostly Jewish,' writes Kearns. 'The widespread paranoia about foreigners combined with anti-Semitism to cast a net so wide that everyone except the British children were caught in it.'[26]

By the end of the summer, the US Committee's report states, 600 British children had found their way to the United States with its help and 200 more were on their way. This was regarded as only the beginning in spite of the fact that in mid-July the British government, apparently weighing the effect on morale of a general exodus of children, had announced postponement of its evacuation plans. A voluntary organization in London called the American Committee for the Evacuation of Children, composed of American businessmen in London and sponsored by the US Ambassador, had stepped into the shoes of CORB to work with the committee in selecting and processing children. The American Committee had 3,500 children on its registry and the US Committee had already engaged sea passage for 1,000 of them when tragedy struck with the sinking of the *City of Benares* (see Chapter 6).

Thanks to this 'semi-official scheme', as Shakespeare called it, 838 children between the ages of 5 and 16 went to the United States. As well as the 110 children of Oxford and Cambridge professors who came to New Haven, CT, to live with Yale faculty members, there were 84 children of employees of the Hoover Company in Perivale placed with Hoover employees in Canton, OH; 156 from the Kodak Company in Harrow in the homes of Eastman Kodak employees in Rochester, NY; and 47 offspring of Warner Brothers' employees in London who were divided between Warner Brothers' employees in New York and California. Fifty-four children from the Actor's Orphanage in Chertsey, Surrey, went together to the Edwin Gould Foundation in New York. Fewer than 200 continental children managed to get through to America in that grim half of 1940. And no CORB children went to the US even though 30,000 had opted for passage there,

There had been many difficulties like medical tests and coverage, financial guarantees, and rigid immigration laws, which had slowed down the process. Shakespeare noted another problem: 'Ships in wartime are as diffident and erratic as girls with whom we are in love. They are neither reliable nor punctual. Ships which were booked to carry our children were often sunk or damaged and alternative plans had accordingly to be made. Another factor which slowed down the rate of evacuation was the withdrawal by the United States government early in July of American ships from belligerent ports and seas.' President Roosevelt blamed the delay in evacuating the children on the British government's failure to provide enough ships. Many were filled with enemy prisoners sent to Canada.

'If comments may be ventured,' said the writer of the earlier Foreign Office report, T.M.Snow, 'they would be that it was, perhaps, unfortunate that the CORB found themselves unable to give any practical effect to the Foreign Office wish that they should send at any rate some children to the United States.' The last remaining difficulties had nearly been resolved when the whole scheme came to an end.

3

Boston Hospitality

Your Home May Save a Child's Life
—August 8 headline in the Boston Transcript

It was through friends of friends of friends that we found our way to our American host family. We were at first a completely unknown quantity to each other.

Our father, who was in the family shipping business and had served in the Army during World War I, had rejoined on 3 September when war was declared. He was in Movement Control and was sent down from the War Office to Fowey, the picturesque China clay port in Cornwall. Equipment was being loaded there for the BEF in France. He and our mother lived in the Fowey Hotel, which had been requisitioned by the services. My brother, Gerald, and I were at boarding school in Surrey and went down to Fowey for the 1939 Christmas holidays. As we passed through Plymouth in the train we could look over to the dockyard and HMS *Ajax* which had just returned from its epic battle with the German battleship *Graf Spee*. It had lost its topmast and two gun turrets had been hit and we could see the gaping holes.

In Fowey the harbour was a constant source of fascination with freighters coming in and out shepherded by three tugs known to us at least as Freeman, Hardy and Willis[27]. I had a ringside seat sitting up in my Fowey Hotel bed as I had developed a case of German measles. Fowey's greatest literary son, Sir Arthur Quiller-Couch, who had been the town's mayor in 1937 and whose house was just below the hotel, captured the spirit of the harbour well when he wrote that it 'combines perpetual change with perpetual repose'. A few other images are retained in the memory of this seven-year-old like the scavenger hunt where I came back triumphantly with one of the wanted items, an air raid warden's helmet. And the fact that in the hotel dining room one tray on the table had small pieces of cheese each with a little flagged stick in it so that it didn't get confused with somebody else's ration. Our father was once machine gunned in the docks by a German plane and dived under a train for safety. It was, he realized afterwards, an ammunition train.

Gerald has three distinct memories as a 5-year-old: 'The first was being allowed on a special occasion into the room of the hotel used as the officer's mess. I was impressed seeing one of the officers hurdle over the back of one of the sofas. I think he was wanting to impress the ladies. Secondly, I remember walks on the hills above Bodinnick Ferry through the lovely banks of yellow primroses, and thirdly, sitting on the bench beside the old Fowey Church, being read to from Edward Lear's book about the owl and the pussycat and other such characters. It was not long after that our parents told us that we were going to go and stay with a family 'for the duration'. I had no idea what it meant. It sounded like an extended holiday.'

The author (left), his brother, Gerald, and mother on the eve of the boys' departure for the United States. Father was already in the army.

Through the Fowey harbour master, I believe it was, we were put in touch with a woman in Boston who was working with Sylvia Warren, who was organizing the reception of English children in the area and so began our lifetime's friendship with a generous American family, the Hinchmans.

Forty-seven-year old Sylvia Warren ran stables at River Bend, Dover. At the beginning of the war she and her circle of friends got in touch with friends in England offering help for their children. Three of those she took in were Martin, Dominik, and Oliver Lobkowicz, 11, 9 and 6 respectively, who had escaped to England from Czechoslovakia. Martin says, 'The reason she took my brothers and me herself was that for many years she had bought her Irish hunters from my great aunt, Edith Somerville of *Irish RM* fame. Aunt Sylvia was one of the few people I consider really remarkable.' She felt that many families would only entrust their children to homes known or recommended to them.

Her British friends included Ambrose Coghill, who became Sylvia's London agent. One of her American circle of friends was Henry B. Cabot, whose mother cabled English cousins offering to take any children of their common ancestor, Russell Sturgis. Seven children came, one of them a great grandchild, Tim Sturgis. 'An amazingly generous offer,' he says.

More than 45 years later he wrote to his American school, Milton Academy, 'We were evidence of a marvellously generous wave of concern which swept New England at the start of the war. Getting children out of England to the safety of America, and looking after them once they were there, was something many Bostonians could do to show their passionate support for the British cause, whilst they were frustrated at a national political level by isolationist feelings.'

The Warren Committee, as it became known, was incorporated on 9 October 1940 so that it would be in a position to receive funds to help the children. Because she had earlier been in touch with so many people in England including Mrs. Coghill, who had an office in London to carry out the work required there, the US Committee gave its sanction to the Warren Committee. Sylvia, together with Cabot and James H. Perkins formed the Executive Committee.

Most of the Warren Committee evacuees were placed with families who paid the childrens' full support and expenses but where families were unable to do so the committee made up the difference. Most of the money came from committee members and their friends. Large family groups or groups with mothers were placed in homes run by committee funds. Two such houses were

Mr. and Mrs. Donald's house in Milton, opened in September 1940 and the committee's own house in Westwood, opened in August 1941[28]. The committee's work was so effective that the *Milton Record* could note on 31 August 1940 that Milton 'proved to be one of the leading communities in child refugee work'.

Gerald and I were two of Sylvia Warren's 'cases'. And in the Hinchmans, from Milton, she could hardly have found a family in America more sympathetic to the British cause. As will be clear from Mr. Hinchman's letter to our parents, quoted later, their cultural affinities were all with Britain. The Hinchmans had six children of their own, Hildegarde, Richard, Mary, Dody, John and Peggy. Only Peggy, known to us then as Daisy, was still living at home. Peggy was actually at boarding school when she heard the idea and thought it was a good one. 'That was the general consensus of the family. We looked forward to their arrival and hoped they would be nice kids.' Mary, married in 1939 to Hoel Bowditch, remembers how excited the family was to hear we were coming: 'We felt proud our family was doing something to help and most of our family was married and away by then so we felt Mother and Dad had plenty of time, space and energy to have Michael and Gerald and that it would fill in the gap left by the family leaving the nest.' They were particularly keen because Mrs. Hinchman had been a Henderson from England, and 'we felt they were sort of nephews who had come to live with the family'. 'We were all very enthusiastic,' says her husband, Hoel. He prepared a big surprise for us that first Christmas.

Mrs. Hinchman was indeed English, although born in New York in 1890. Her father had been head of the Anchor Line. Mrs. Hinchman had grown up in the old Gate House of Ludlow Castle but her forebears were Scottish. When Mr. Hinchman chided his wife for being a canny Scot she was always delighted to say she'd rather be that than a stingy Quaker. Her Hendersons were not related to us as far as we could ever determine but by a curious coincidence we discovered that our father was billeted in her old Birkenhead home for a time in 1940.

The Hinchmans had another reason at that point to have their attentions focussed on England. Mrs. Hinchman's brother, Malcolm, was one of the British troops rescued at Dunkirk. Malcolm had been 2 years in the French Foreign Legion and was later in the Royal Flying Corps, awarded his wings just before the armistice at the end of World War I. He had subsequently been apple farming in British Columbia. In 1940 he had been sent to North Eastern France in the Field Security Service.

Mr. Hinchman's long, handwritten letter, giving a masterly introduction to the family, is one of the few family letters preserved from that time. The letter is undated but was probably sent in July 1940.

Dear Mr. and Mrs. Henderson,

Mrs. Hinchman has written you already a lot about us and our home, and I understand that Miss Warren's committee says we're all right; nevertheless, you must naturally feel considerable apprehension in sending your two boys to us. In spite of anything we write, we must remain more or less blanks in your mind—merely Mr. and Mrs. X. All sorts of information about adequate room, adequate funds, etc., but what sort of people are Mr. and Mrs. X? If the situation were reversed, I should want very much to know.

Of course that's the sort of thing that Mr. and Mrs. X can't tell you about themselves; at least you could hardly be expected to believe them if they did! But I often feel one reads a good deal between the lines when the writer is talking about other things, so I add this letter to Mrs. Hinchman's in order that you may ascribe some sort of personality, however vague, to each of us.

First of all, who we are—how we came to be on this side of the planet. Mrs. Hinchman, as I think you know, was brought up in England. Her father is a Scot, her mother an American—now very old people residing in Victoria, BC. Her brother, a volunteer captain at present, somehow got his men and himself away at Dunkirk and is now somewhere on duty in England. Mrs. Hinchman's American connection, then, is partly through her mother's side; otherwise through marrying me.

My Hinchman people came from Northamptonshire in 1637 to Charlestown, Mass. That Hinchman, Edmund, was brother of the Humphry Hinchman who became Bishop of London under Charles 11. My American branch, or part of it, moved to Long Island after almost a century, then, soon after, to Philadelphia and neighborhood, where they became Quakers. My mother's people, Mitchell of Massachusetts, came from England, too, just before 1700; they were also members of the Society of Friends; and the family has remained so ever since. I'm afraid I'm not a very good Quaker, as I find myself able to believe in non-resistance only as between individuals. At all events, I could find no 'conscientious objections' in the Great War, and I can find them much less in this struggle for the very existence of civilization. I only wish more of my countrymen, who agree almost to a man about the issue, saw the need for immediate, aggressive action on our part. In time we shall cut red tape and send you materials and ships and raise the restrictions on American volunteers; I only hope it will be really 'in time'.

To return to my little biography—I was brought up in Philadelphia, went to Haverford College and Harvard University (class of 1901) and since then have taught English Literature at Groton School, Haverford College, and Milton Academy. On the side I have been a more or less unsuccessful author: *Lives of Great English Writers*, *William of Normandy*, editions of *Macbeth*, Mathew Arnold's poetry, etc., and for five years was contributing editor of the *Forum*. Perhaps more interesting to you, I am one of the few American members of the MCC. When I was a boy, cricket was in its American heyday in Philadelphia[29]. It's a joke now—even there. In 1900 I captained the Haverford team which visited England, I have been with the Gentlemen of Philadelphia to Canada, and in Philadelphia played against the teams Warner and 'Ranji' brought over. I have even played for the MCC *once*. I have declined on golf and gardening—inferior substitutes!

I am not sure how much Mrs. Hinchman has told you of our Milton home. Though Milton is only ten miles from Boston, it is far more rural than most of the suburbs, as the two rail lines in this neighborhood diverge to the East and West of us, so that we are in a fairly open area, with encroachments blocked off by the Blue Hills. Our place, about eight acres (chiefly woods, so that we have pheasants and quail, to say nothing of rabbits, groundhogs and skunks! Tell the boys), adjoins the school property, which covers about one hundred acres. The 'Academy' is really much what you would call a public school, except that it has its roots in an old day-school, so that, like Westminster, it takes both boarders and day-pupils. There are three divisions: a Lower School (ages 2-9), boys and girls together; a Girl's School (12-18) and a Boy's School (12-18), separate schools under one management. Almost 400 pupils in all. In addition, there are two good schools for small children (3-9) under the supervision of the Academy.

Mrs. Hinchman has told you about our children, now pretty well grown up, but we shall do our best to make your boys happy and comfortable and to regard ourselves, with rather more emphasis than usually attaches to the schoolmaster's phrase *in loco parentis*. Mrs. Hinchman's knowledge of English ways will enable her to ease your boys into our not very alien life, and I myself have been in England a good deal—in fact, taught for a short time at Westminster, to inaugurate our Milton-Westminster exchange of boys and masters—so I shall hope to be her not unworthy understudy. All this, I realize, doesn't tell you much about us—*really*; that is, what sort of people we are; but something may leak out between the lines. Perhaps I should add that there are many young children in the neighborhood, so your boys will not have to associate too much with fossils.

Mrs. Hinchman has written in detail about meeting the boys, so I won't do more than to assure you that all that has been gone into very carefully. Also, don't worry about the matter of funds. We can manage that easily; it is the least we should do.

Very sincerely yours,
Walter S. Hinchman

P.S. Forgive my writing 'Mr.'. We haven't been given first names or titles or ranks.

Our parents must have been reassured. Sadly, Mrs. Hinchman's letter was not kept.

The local paper, the *Milton Record*, had a headline on 13 July: 'To Harbor Children Fleeing War Terror Abroad'. It reported that a committee headquartered at the Milton Club was working closely with the Boston Committee for the Care of European Children and was appealing for names of owners of empty Milton houses which might be used for a few weeks in an emergency: 'It is conceived that it might become necessary to receive a boatload of children with little warning.' The American Unitarian Association said it wished to place 20 English children in Milton homes. A week later the paper reported that Milton Academy had responded with an offer of two buildings before the school opened and that the Milton Committee was going ahead with its plans: 'It was plain that, even without a perfected organisation,

Our American host at 18 (Philadelphia Colts vs P. F. Warner's XI, 1897)

Milton stands ready to receive and care for, even at short notice, at least fifty children.' A week later it reported that the town had been asked to handle not 50 but 100 children and had the headline: 'Milton's first little guests from bomb-strafed England arrive this week.'

That summer a major Boston newspaper, now defunct, the *Boston Transcript*, was taking the lead in encouraging area families to take in English children. Its August 1940 columns reflect its commitment and builds up the suspense. On 1 August the paper ran a photo of an Oxford family having tea at Yale and said that there were other children still in England 'who would like to have tea with you "for the duration". The *Transcript* will help you to help them.' The headline: 'Can you find a place in your home for a British envoy of goodwill?'

There was plenty of hype in the appeal. 'These young emissaries of good will, these juvenile Rhodes Scholars from England who are waiting to come into your homes until the war is over, will bring more than tea to you and to your children if you will open your home to them. They will bring the way of life of the best of England, the traditions of culture and gentility and the training of English schools. And from your children they will absorb the best of America, a sort of Anglo-American union of youth.'

The paper said that its plan to bring 500 British children to the United States offered an opportunity to further this exchange of culture. 'Already 173 homes have been assured them as shown in the accompanying table. There must be found 327 more if the quota is to be filled.' The sociological effect of a considerable influx of English children to the country 'invites speculation'. 'These children when they return to England will be bound to take something of America with them, just as they are bound to bring something of England with them to this country. And the impressionable age of the children will make the effects much more marked.'

It was also projected to the public as a sort of community competition: 'In the race among the communities for foster homes for the children the Newtons have crept into a clear second place with 16...Concord, still in first place and still moving up, Brookline is third with 14, and Cambridge fourth with 13.' The list of community workers who were finding homes was also growing and the paper gave a telephone number for those who wanted to help and also details of how to apply for a child. It announced that the number of private schools which were offering free tuition to the young British guests was also growing. 'Letters from England have recently hinted of more serious air raids. However serious the effects may be on physical objects, the effects on the emotions of children, who have not their elders' resources of courage and perseverance, must be tremendous. And the actual invasion will bring things infinitely worse. There is no time to lose. Some 350 children are sailing in August under the *Transcript* plan, possibly the whole 500. There must be homes for them here.'

Although the paper was allied to the United States Committee for the Care of European children, it had its own committee in London who were selecting children whose parents came from professional and business executive classes, children chosen 'to measure as closely as possible to the sort of foster homes that they will enter here under the *Transcript* plan'. One of the *Transcript* children, Charlie Fay, became my best friend at our school in Connecticut. Originally, his whole English school was going to be evacuated to Canada but at the last minute the Treasury refused sanction for the export of school fees. His father was to write later to Charlie's American hosts, 'If you'll forgive my saying so, I think the *Transcript* committee did a remarkably good job of finding exactly the right home for him.'

For the next couple of weeks a big story appeared every day stressing the urgency of the hour. 2 August: 'At the top of the page we reprint a letter from a mother in England that emphasizes the fear of so many parents there that even if the war spares the lives of their children it will leave indelible marks on their minds and emotions.' This letter, the paper said, explained something of the reason why British mothers and fathers wanted to send their children to America to homes of strangers—friendly and hospitable and child-loving strangers but still strangers. It explained why so many were opening their homes here. 'It is true that a generation of neurotics can hardly be expected to make a lasting peace after the present European mess is cleaned up. The effect of the previous war on young Americans is well known—and for many the actual fighting was far off. For those children in England who may find that England has become one immense battlefield, the effects can only be guessed. The need for more homes for these children grows daily more urgent. The first group may arrive any day, and the rest are close behind. We have assured the parents of 500 children that their sons and daughters whom they will entrust to the sympathy of parents in America will find here the homes they need. It is unthinkable that Boston and New England will fail them. If you want to defend a child against the cruelties, the privations, the terrors and the brutalities of war, fill out an application blank or call on the *Transcript* Child Director or one of the community leaders whose names appear in another column. It is the one thing we in this country can do to make war a bit less terrible.'

This is the letter:

Well, apart from old Adolph the Nasty we've had a lovely spring and early summer—lovely sunny days, lots of gardening, and incidentally we're having a bumper year for fruit—the trees are simply laden with apples, pears, plums and greengages and we have had so many cherries that we just gave them away to whoever wanted them. It seems a sort of compensation for the dreary business of war that goes on all around us.

I think the feeling of affection between our two countries has never been stronger and what really has put the final link on the bond between us is the marvellous way you folks have opened your doors to our children. Gosh, if we can only get them over to you it will remove the only real worry that exists as regards the war. I don't think it is fair or right that any one of them rich or poor should be exposed to these damned air raids. It would make your heart ache to see the poor little blighters being tumbled out of their warm beds and rushed down to a beastly damp cold dugout in the middle of the night. Apart from the risks of chills and other ailments can you imagine the effect it is going to have on their nerves? In twenty years time they'll turn out to be neurotics and that's just what we must avoid.

We're going to win this war but we want to hand on the peace to a generation that will know how to keep it better than we did. It is good to know that your homes are ready to welcome our children and you tell the people how much we women over here thank you all.

I've never been so proud of being English as I am now—you can't help being proud when you see the grand spirit that prevails everywhere—not a sign of defeatism anywhere just a steady, cheerful, preparedness on every one's part. That's where we've got Hitler and his mob beaten from the start—though I say it as shouldn't—the English have got guts and they never show it so well as when they're right up against it. Also it's rather a fine feeling that it really is up to us now, that we stand alone. Don't worry about us, we're all right—fighting fit and raring to go.

On 3 August the paper showed its first pictures of *Transcript* children. 'It was taken during that exciting day at the old skating rink at Grosvenor House in London when children and parents arrived for final arrangements before sailing. The children were examined by doctors, while the parents gave detailed histories of their sons and daughters which will aid in placing the boys and girls in mutually congenial homes in Boston and whereabouts. It may be that some of the children at Grosvenor House that day are at this moment crossing the Atlantic towards Boston. About 50 were expected to sail in the first boat, but their actual departure is of course blanketed under wartime censorship.' The paper reported, '194 homes as of last night—another community list, Concord remains in first place, Cambridge has begun to creep up and is now in undisputed second place.' Two new communities appeared on the list.

On 5 August: 'Homes here for British children hit 200 mark; response grows…An enthusiastic response has come from sponsors under the Harvard Committee for the Care of European Children…Despite the growing response there is still the rather alarming figure of 300 children unprovided for yet, and time is relentlessly speeding on toward the day when the final group of the 500 children will need their visas.' August 6 headline: 'Dedham, England, tells Dedham, Mass. what war means to English children'. 'School keeps all summer in England this year. It takes children off the streets where bombs are a new menace. School windows are covered with brown paper and cellophane—a protection against flying glass in an air raid—but children learn quickly the sound of enemy planes. They are getting used to nightly air raid alarms and sleeping in bomb shelters. And they are yet to know total war. Those who can be brought to America will escape that horror. By opening your home to one of the 500 waiting to sail you can enable another to escape.' There was another tabulation of responses and a photo of 'Two wee Britons getting a medical check up at Grosvenor House':

> In London today the full fury of total war is expected in a week or two. In that time the vast armada of bombers for which the recent raids have been but pale preludes may loose their cargoes on combatants and civilians alike. For children the ordeal will be terrible….The delay in the German invasion has been an unexpected blessing not only to England as a whole but to those children who are leaving as fast as ships and homes abroad are available. But there is no guarantee of further delay. War will not wait until parents here

return from their vacations and apply for a child. This is why we ask you to act now....

To take a child into your home, to shield him or her from the mental and physical wounds of modern war, is one of the greatest acts of mercy that can be performed. To you who have wished that you might in some way mitigate the agony of the innocents of war, here is the opportunity. But it is an opportunity that cannot wait. The child who is left behind because the lack of a foster home meant no visa is the child who may suffer the terrors of invasion, the flight from marching armies, and the fears of the unpredictable that scar the minds of the young even when they escape bodily injury. These children will bring a bit of British culture to New England: we have called them ambassadors of good will. And when they return after the war is over, they will take back with them something of America that will tighten the bonds between the two countries for generations to come.

The paper reflected the battle in Congress to smooth the sending and receiving of English children. August 8 front-page headline: 'Can you open your home to save a child's life'. 'With slight opposition the House yesterday voted a bill to send American mercy ships to rescue British children from war's frightfulness. Fully conscious of the implications of this move—the danger that it might indirectly precipitate the threatened crisis with Germany—the congressmen nevertheless were moved by the plight of the children whose lives may be a sacrifice to the ideals for which England is fighting. Signs multiply that the long heralded battle of Britain is soon to start and the slaughter of the innocents will be appalling.

'Homes are ready for 213 but there must be found homes for 287 of them before these can sail…If you can take a child into your home, you may be the means of saving that child's life, and you will certainly be the agency which can assure that child a normal, family life so essential for a satisfactory adulthood. Few in Britain will find a normal life possible when real war sweeps across the channel. For those over here who want to see England repel the German invasion, here is an opportunity to help, for England will fight better if it knows that many of its children are cared for over here against the time when they can come back to help in the reconstructed period after the war.'

August 9 front-page headline: 'Drive to complete home quota here for British children is speeded'. 'It is literally true that delay may be fatal for some of these. If they have no foster home, no visa may be issued and they cannot sail until a sponsor is found here. In the meantime the German attack may be launched in all its fury. It will not spare the children when it comes.'

Later in August the paper was continuing to run tables of the communities responding and then came photos of its '*Transcript* children' arriving. August 22 headline: 'Boston's own British children arrive'. On 26 August a group reached the city that had come on the *Duchess of Atholl*: 'Something of the city's repute had reached them in London and they were primed for a city of culture and propriety.' One of the children was Charlie Fay. August 28: 'British children attend esplanade concert; one group to see Red Sox game in afternoon.'

The US Committee enlisted the New England Home for Little Wanderers[30], which had been in existence for 200 years, as a staging post for some of the children often arriving in Boston with little advance notice. During the war this charity housed 255 British children on their way to finding homes. Its newsletter *Advocate* reported that summer, 'Under the eyes of experienced workers, who treat them as individuals, rather than as a group phenomenon, the children seem happy with the pleasant aspect of their green and quiet surroundings so similar to their own countryside. They are occupied with the rest and diversion to recover from the great emotional strain so recently undergone. In the meantime, their habits, taste, hopes, fears, talents and shortcomings are noted to prepare them for the homes where they will have the greatest chance of affection and success. No less exacting are the requirements for the future foster parents. Unhappy homes or families with grave problems of their own are discouraged and other alternatives for charitable instincts are suggested. Once settled, the children will remain in their new homes with occasional visits from the committee until the war is over...Psychologically these plucky children were well prepared for this sea-change in their lives. The courageous parents who have sent them far away out of danger, but also out of reach, have told them how to behave in a strange land. Contrary to the usual techniques of children as young as six or eight, no criticism or complaint has been uttered of the unfamiliar food or any other new and confusing aspect of their lives.'

In August an article by Evelyn Turner was widely reproduced. Evelyn, who left New York in 1939 to work with canteens in England, later did relief work in France, and when that country collapsed escaped to England on a coal boat from Bordeaux, wrote: 'This is a message addressed primarily to the boys and girls of America. Within the next few weeks you will be subjected to an invasion. It will be different from the one awaited in the British Isles. A little army will embark on your shores—but it will not carry arms! There will be a number of small boys. For the most part they will be dressed in gray flannels and some may have blazers of bright colors. Every private school in England has its own colors and usually this color scheme is carried out in tie, cap and blazer. There is much esprit-de-corps in English schools and as every boy thinks his school is the best, every one is naturally very proud of his colors. There will also be girls. Many of these will have different colored hat-bands and at first glance they will all seem much younger than American girls of the same age. Besides the boys and girls from private schools, there will be many who lived in poor streets and went to the council schools. Some of these have never had much chance to see even the English countryside. Think what it will mean to them to cross the ocean and see the New World.'

Referring to questions she had been asked about the United States, she wrote:

> The two remarks that made me write this message were these. A boy of 12 said to me: 'Last summer my American cousin said English boys were sissy because they had quiet voices and were polite. Will they think I'm sissy?' A 13-year-old cousin of mine, asked why she minded going so much, said vehemently, 'Go, and have them say I've run away, when I'd so much rather stay here and take it with daddy and mummy—that's what I mind.' If ever you are tempted to say 'sissy' to an English boy because his voice is lower, or his words seem to be more carefully chosen, will you remember this: Anything from seven to fifteen years ago England was full of gently-spoken polite boys like that. Today the skies are full of those same boys, now grown to be hard, keen, brave men, whose hourly deeds of heroism are one of the great epics of our time. Day after day, night after night, the seas are patrolled by men who not long ago were just like the boys you will so soon have as your guests. Remember that if the politeness of an English boy or girl still annoys you, it is second nature to them: they are not 'putting it on'; they are taught it almost before anything else. And if this is so in England, it is even more so in France. I shall always remember the big air raid over Paris because I happened to be sent down into a shelter reserved for a school. They were all marshalled in by a priest and a nun. The priest sat along the boys; the nun among the girls. They all smiled and said, 'Pardon, madame,' if

they brushed too closely by anyone, and during the raid, when we could hear the bombs falling, they never raised their voices because they had been taught that loud talking in a shelter is inconsiderate, as some people's nerves might not be strong. They talked quictly among themselves, said 'oh la la', when a particularly loud crash was heard, and, when it was all over, with smile and polite 'bon jours', filed out into the sunshine. None of these English child refugees has run away. In every case where a child has received the choice he or she has wanted to stay at home. One boy wrote to his mother from his school in the south, 'Of course I have decided. I want to stay and help defend England. We saw some lovely gulls over the cliffs today, wheeling and diving—just like the fight between the Wellington and the Messerschmidt we saw last week.'

Now to our part in that invasion.

4

Grosvenor House

You are going, for a little while, to a country where every child learns by heart at least one of the things in this book: the words of Lincoln at Gettysburg. They are grown-up words about a grown-up idea. But they are a token that we Americans, like you, have been dedicated to the great task remaining before us: that we too say that the things your fathers fought for shall not perish from the earth.
—The Token of Freedom

The spring of 1940 was the hottest in ten years and the summer was a particularly lovely one, with the countryside looking its best. There was an illusion of tranquillity. Vera Brittain wrote that May, 'The beauty of England increases as the news gets steadily worse.' According to Roy Jenkins[31] the atmosphere through which people lived their lives that spring and early summer was 'one of the most extraordinary, in some ways unreal, phases in the history of the nation'. The national mood was not so much defiant as impregnable. 'The prospects were awful, but people pushed the consequences of defeat out of their collective mind. It was not a question of bravery. It was more that they had chosen to believe the worst would not happen.'

We were fairly sheltered from the war, though the summer before we had spent our holidays at Woolacombe in North Devon and clambered over tanks on a field by the beach and even had to be pulled back from Morte Point as a Fairey Battle bomber, whose pilot's head I could distinctly see, was using the rocks at the bottom for target practice. A soldier gave Gerald a smoke bomb to handle and told him that if he turned it upside down it would ignite. At our Ealing day school, Durston House, we, along with all the other children in Britain, had been given our gas masks (38 million gas masks were issued). It was presented to Gerald as a sort of game of playing pigs 'for they had what looked like a pig's snout'. I remember the noise and the sight as I looked out from a window at a squadron of bombers that flew so low they seemed almost in touching distance. Even as a seven-year-old I had followed the fate of the submarine HMS *Thetis,* which had sunk in trials in Liverpool Bay as efforts over four days to raise it failed and 99 people drowned. We had not been bombed.[32] Both our parents were in uniform, our father in the Royal Engineers, our mother with St. John's Ambulance.

Gerald and I were sent from Durston House down to its sister boarding school, Ripley Court, in the Surrey countryside. I was by then seven, Gerald five. At Ripley we had air raid drills and trooped out of class to the newly built shelters. We drilled regularly on the playing fields. The older boys made model planes and there was always the smell of the paint as the models were camouflaged; I always wished I were old enough to cut out the intricate balsa wood sections. But apart from that, and bomber squadrons flying over and the presence of soldiers and vehicles pretty evident in the woods all around when we went for walks, and the fact that in May signposts were removed from many of the roads around lest they would help an invading force, war did not impinge much on the youngest of us.

Curiously, my own most vivid recollection of Ripley Court has nothing to do with the war and is exactly that of Thomas Merton, the American Cistercian monk who was there earlier. In one of his books he refers to the 'prickly woollen black and green striped jerseys' in which football was played and the line-up for church on Sundays. Merton describes the head of the school, Mrs. Pearce, as 'a bulky and rather belligerent looking woman with great pouches under her eyes'. He writes of 'the huge, dark green sweep of the elm trees where one sat waiting for his innings, and the dining room where we crammed ourselves with bread and butter and jam at tea time…On Sundays we all dressed up in the ludicrous clothes that the English conceive to be appropriate to the young, and went marching off to the village church, where a whole transept was reserved for us.' I certainly remember, less than ten years later, the line-up for church where we were all doled out pennies for the collection.

Being a lover of sport, of football and of cricket, I suppose what remains with me clearest is running back to the dressing room in the rain with the sharp hail on those prickly jerseys or lying out in the sun in the long grass at the side of the cricket field scoring and looking up occasionally at planes. I must have done some work as I have a green volume, a form prize. One older boy, Brian Boobbyer, with whom I was to work closely in later years, was setting school sporting records and went on to international honours.

From Ripley[33] we went up to Grosvenor House, London, which was the London headquarters of the US Committee and where children were being processed for travel to the United States. The hotel's Great Room, the largest ballroom in Europe, had been first an ice rink and the stage of many exciting ice hockey matches and galas and later was the scene of London's most brilliant balls and important banquets, motor shows, antique dealers' fairs and mammoth receptions. At this stage it was serving as an annexe to the US Embassy.

The main evacuation of children overseas, whether under the government scheme or privately, was to happen in the months of July, August and September 1940. But already in 1939 some groups and families had gone. On 3 September 1939 Oxford history professor Kenneth Bell, who had been an artillery officer in World War I, went to his garage roof and hauled down the Balliol College Boat Club flag which always flew at his home, Westfield, when he was in residence. Then he solemnly declared a personal war on Hitler and swore he would not raise the flag again until he, Kenneth Bell, had beaten him. Bell was invited by the University of Toronto where he once taught to send his children to Canada. He felt that they ought to be out of the way, that they would only be a nuisance in wartime and would eat food the soldiers needed. It was presented to Caroline and Eddie, 10 and 8, as 'a lovely summer holiday'. He helped get passports not only for his children but others from Oxford and for 20 boys and girls from the potteries and paid the fares of many who could not afford them out of his own pocket. His children wrote later[34], 'Of course he was anxious to have us in a place of safety but we think the reason he sent us ahead was not to get his own children out first but as a sort of evidence of good faith to all those fathers and mothers who were hesitating and fearful.' The children were photographed leaving by the press. Their mother commented, 'How disgusting to cheapen people's emotion by all this putting of pictures in the papers.'

By 1940 families all over England and in all sorts of circumstances and for different motives were preparing. The fundamental reason, of course, in all cases, was the imminent prospect of invasion. American foreign correspondent William Shirer wrote in his diary on 1 August: 'Everyone impatient to know when the invasion of Britain will begin. I have taken two new bets offered by Nazis in the Wilhelmstrasse. First that the Swastika will be flying over Trafalgar Square by August 15. Second by September 7.'

'All through this summer of 1940,' wrote Foreign Secretary Lord Halifax later, 'time moved with agonising slowness, as one by one we ticked off the days to the equinoctial gales of September, which for the British people became the accepted goal of comparative safety from invasion. For whatever may have been the best informed view at the time, and whatever we have since learned from German records, there was no shadow of doubt about the fact of the public expectation of invasion.'

On 19 July Hitler had given his orders for preparing Sea Lion: 'Since England, in spite of her helpless military situation, shows no signs of being ready to come to an understanding, I have decided to prepare a landing operation against England and, if necessary, to carry it out. The aim of this operation will be to eliminate the English homeland as a base for the prosecution of the war against Germany and, if necessary, to occupy it completely.' On 30 July he ordered Goering to prepare 'immediately and with the greatest haste' the German air force's onslaught against England. Goering's final directive for the pre-invasion air attack was issued on 2 August.

In the United States there was increasing activity on behalf of Britain. On 10 June thirty prominent Americans had met at the Century Club and formed a group which became known as William Allen White's Committee to Defend America by Aiding the Allies. In a 'Summons to speak out' they called on the United States to enter the war against Germany. With the behind-the-scenes encouragement of the President they urged the transfer of over-age destroyers to Britain. Later they formed the Fight for Freedom Committee, in the words of one of its leaders, Herbert Agar, 'to say much more than (Roosevelt) could dare to endorse and to ask for much more than he could hope to accomplish'. At the end of the month the Allied Relief Fund, renamed Aldrichs Relief Organization, announced that on 4 July they were launching a campaign to raise 5 million dollars to 'provide shelter in this country for European children who are now in Great Britain and facing the horrors of bombardment'.

Lord Lothian cabled London at the end of June[35] that he had been told that it was of vital importance that there should be no discrimination against foreign children sent over and that parties destined for the United States should include some German refugees and other foreign children otherwise popular criticism would become strong.

On 21 June half a dozen Yale faculty members met and formed the Yale Faculty Committee for Receiving Oxford and Cambridge University Children.

Dr John Fulton of Yale Medical School said that the Committee hoped to save 'at least some of the children of intellectuals before the storm breaks'. A few days later a thousand questionnaires were sent out with response cards and produced offers of beds for 247 children, with financial help promised by many who could not take in youngsters. A fund for expected expenses raised $10,000. Invitations to take 100 were cabled to C. K. Allen, the warden of Rhodes House, Oxford, and Sir Montagu Butler, Master of Pembroke College, Cambridge. Thankful replies were received from both universities. It soon became clear to the Americans that while Oxford was preparing to take up the offer Cambridge had asked for time in which to give the matter further consideration and Butler was telling them that a good many people were opposed to the idea of evacuation altogether as they thought it savoured of alarm. Members of the Oxford party recall that they had three weeks to decide. With much hard work tourist places were booked on the Antonia for 125 children and 25 mothers. Most places were taken up by Oxford. Historian A.J.P.Taylor called the move 'an unseemly scramble'. Canadian and American Rhodes Scholars accompanied the Oxford party, one of whom was Janet Baker[36]. Her father was a don, teaching geography. The family made up their minds in 24 hours. Janet was old enough to talk frankly with her parents about what should happen if they were killed or if her ship was sunk.

At a reunion many years later it was noted that among the party taking their seats in the train to the port of embarkation were a future government minister, a lord mayor, a judge, a knight, an orchestra conductor, several doctors and assorted dons and that 'for most it was the great adventure of their lives'. At the first train stop at Banbury, 5-year-old Susan Lawson asked, 'Is this Canada yet?' The party sailed on 9/10 July. On 11 July a cable was sent to Yale from Allen:

> GOODS DISPATCHED JAMES IN TOUCH WITH CUNARD
> ABOUT ARRIVAL CONSIDERABLE CHANGES IN LISTS
> FOR VARIOUS REASONS BUT ALL PLACES FILLED.

In all the accounts a few names of ships recur—between late July and mid-September nineteen ships carried evacuees, some of them taking two and in the case of at least one, the *Antonia*, even three trips that summer. Only eight of them were large enough to take more than a hundred children at a time.

Eleven-year-old Jim Baynard-Smith, who was at prep school in Yorkshire, remembers huddling all night under rugs in the cold stone cellars during air raids on Leeds and awaiting the 'all-clear' which they had forgotten to sound. Some of the 'older' boys like him were given pitchforks and fence staves, with an LDV[37] armband, to accompany a master into the adjacent woods in case of German parachutists. When informed he was to be evacuated he was very angry as his two older cousins were to be allowed to stay and in due course to join the fighting forces. He travelled on the *Duchess of Atholl*.

Yvonne Bowerman lived in Bournemouth which as it was opposite France was a particularly vulnerable part of the South coast. The Dunkirk evacuation meant that all the local schools were closed and taken over by troops who had survived that ordeal. Her childish memory is of their local park strewn with exhausted, bedraggled men lying on the grass in the sun. She, too, was on the *Duchess of Atholl*, where they were six to a cabin. On the trip she remembers being sent north because of submarines, and seeing icebergs and a spouting whale. In fact, historian Sir Martin Gilbert, then 3, was also on the ship and wrote later, 'Those icebergs, marvellous for a child to behold, are among my first memories.'

For Lord Montagu of Beaulieu, a 13-year-old, the sudden evacuation, was heartrending: 'Leaving school friends abruptly, not knowing where or when we would ever meet again, leaving Beaulieu and the dogs, leaving my mother and Anne, who, because she was the eldest, was staying on—all this was extraordinarily traumatic. Our last night at home had been rather overshadowed by the first bombing raid on Southampton. At least the sea voyage might be exciting and I might even see some action.'

He sailed on the *Monarch of Bermuda*, with two sisters, Mary-Clare and Caroline, with their governess. Their ship was simply known as 'Early July Special'. Its sister ship had already been torpedoed by U-boats. 'It was rumoured that our convoy was transporting the Norwegian and Dutch crown jewels to the safety of North America...I was in a small boy's heaven.'

Also Canada-bound was a party of 13 children and three teachers from Byron House School on the *Duchess of Atholl* on the ship's first trip that summer[38]. Senator Cairine Wilson in Ottawa had cabled an invitation to the school. The teachers, Mary Mason, Marjory Clarke and Leonora Williams soon became substitute mothers 'for the duration'. To Williams, the vice-principal, the 10-day trip was 'an awful muddle': 'There were about 800 on board, from schools all over England. We had a bucket in the gangway for the staff and as we went from one cabin to another we'd stop at the bucket to be sick ourselves.'

Also Ottawa-bound on the *Duchess of Atholl* was the Hutchison family from Glasgow, four girls with their mother. Ruth (Mackenzie) remembers mid-

Atlantic when their escorting destroyer turned to head back for Britain. The destroyer crew lined the deck, each sailor holding up his handkerchief by two corners in a farewell salute. 'The long line of little white squares receded behind us. We were on our own.'

On 13 August the *Duchess of Atholl* left Liverpool in a convoy of 28 ships of which 11 were sunk On board were twelve Quakers invited by Quakers in Philadelphia. The cost of the journey was L16, third class. They included two sisters, Blanche and Louise Lawson, who came from Plymouth which had already been bombed. Their parents were also apprehensive what might happen to them in case of a German invasion, as they had been active helping people flee from the Nazis and had taken refugees from Czechoslovakia, Germany, Hungary and Poland into their home.

Among the 900 on the *Duchess of Bedford* were children of Ford employees who were heading to Windsor, Ontario. The Ford President in Canada, Wallace Campbell, had cabled Dagenham offering homes for 25 children and then upping the offer for a further hundred 'if you can get them away at once'. Bob Turnbull, who was in advertising, was put in charge of getting the children to Canada. The Canadian authorities had said that they wanted footprints of the infants so all the children trooped off to Scotland Yard. 'We had a rather sticky time inking up their feet,' says Turnbull, before he discovered that it was only requested of children too young to give clear fingerprints.

Turnbull kept a log on the trip. An early entry: 'At last we were at sea, accompanied by two destroyers, and in convoy with the *Britannic*, *Duchess of Atholl* and *Viceroy of India*, together with aeroplanes flying so close to the ship that their occupants were clearly seen waving to the children. Needless to say, everybody was up early that morning and the convoy was very reassuring to the timid-minded folk. In fact, the whole of the 11-day journey was wonderfully peaceful. Not a submarine was seen and the biggest worry came near the end when the ship, dangerously close to icebergs, was slowed by fog.'

Martin Revis, a Ford evacuee who travelled with his brother, Peter, on the *Duchess of Atholl*, describes the atmosphere aboard ship as very much like peacetime and recalls a 'fancy dress evening in which we paraded through the first class dining room where one of the diners gave me a banana as we passed the table. I think they were all in evening dress.' He remembers his mother's unusual words to him as he left, 'I have a strong feeling we will meet again.'

Revis thinks that the decision, taken by the heads of Ford in Canada and Britain, put a burden on the hosts, as the responsibility was open ended, particularly if parents were killed, and also strict exchange control meant that they would be involved in additional expense when they had just become free of the anxiety of the depression. 'No ambitious executive could afford not to participate,' he says. Another Ford evacuee, Barbara Davis (Shawcroft), later a professor at UC Davis, agrees. To host a child was considered 'the right thing to do'. They were called 'war guests'. Barbara actually stayed first with Wallace Campbell, who according to Turnbull paid all the expenses of the children in Canada which must have cost him about $10,000.

Three other children, slightly older than we were, were preparing themselves also to go to Milton, our destination. Tony Moore, from Norwich, and his sister, Bridget, were 11 and 12. Their father, Harold, had been a regular soldier and their mother had died. At the end of May the father had been evacuated from Dunkirk. Tony was at a boarding school in Broadstairs and his sister in Swanage. Their father concluded that an invasion of England was imminent. Some friends with children of a similar age could not contemplate sending them abroad. They thought at first it would be better to stay together and await what might or might not come rather than risk disturbed education and upset personalities not to mention the danger of travel. The matter was settled, however, when a school friend of Bridget, Jennifer Clarke, was offered by relations on her father's side a wartime home in Milton. The family readily extended the invitation to the Moores.

To Jennifer the first sign of a war was when soldiers came and took over the house and a gun appeared in the garden. 'One night—it must have been before the war was really declared—the fleet came into Swanage Bay and we were all taken up into one of the top rooms in the house facing the sea and out of the window we could see all the ships lit up and lots of little boats scurrying to and fro—it was really a beautiful sight. Then the war really began and everyone went around looking worried and sandbags appeared everywhere and we were all taken to have our gas masks fitted, they were horrible smelly rubber things. People began to dig trenches madly in the public gardens, which were all muddy and wet, but we enjoyed chasing each other round and hiding in them. Suddenly one day I went upstairs and found that all the teachers were packing our clothes, so I asked what was happening and was told that we were all going home as it wasn't considered safe in Swanage but that I wasn't to tell anyone else as they didn't want to be bothered and they wanted to be as quick as they could. I immediately went downstairs and told one of my friends who told someone else and soon chaos reigned and eventually our parents arrived looking very worried and we were all driven off. We took home with us Bridget whose father was in the army and she had no mother. It was just the time of Dunkirk and no-one knew what was going to happen, there were soldiers everywhere.' Jennifer and the Moores went on one of the Empress boats.

Jeremy Thorpe, aged 11, was evacuated with his sister, Camilla, to stay with their American aunt, Kay Norton-Griffiths, in the USA. 'My parents took this precaution as my father was on the German blacklist, and in the event of a German invasion, which at the time was a real possibility, he and the family would have been at risk. My father was vulnerable because of his work (with Norman Birkett) on alien tribunals, which had the difficult task of determining who were genuine asylum seekers and who were under-cover spies.'

Similarly, Vera Brittain believed that her name and that of her husband were on the Nazi blacklist—her books had been burned at Nuremberg—and sent their children, John and Shirley. To have that surmise confirmed after the war 'brought a sudden spiritual catharsis'. After Dunkirk she felt she could face anything with equanimity, even the threat of a concentration camp, were it not for her children. They were her 'Achilles heel'. In 1938 they had been too young to travel alone, by 1940 they could. And so was added an even more acute moral quandary. Should she go with them? 'There seemed no right decision to be made; whichever course I took would involve bitter regrets.' On the train journey taking her children to join the *Duchess of Atholl* in Liverpool she met Jan Struther, the author of *Mrs. Miniver*[39], who was joining the ship with her two younger children. Jan had been invited by the Ministry of Information to be a propagandist for Britain in the US. Her book was a fictional account from wartime England. Vera recalls in *Testament of Experience* the scene:

> 'Are you going, too?' she inquired, and looked crestfallen when I answered: 'No, I'm only seeing them off.'
>
> 'I feel as if I were running away,' she said brokenly. 'But I thought if I didn't go I might never see them again.'
>
> I looked at John and Shirley, and felt sick at heart. In that inexorable speeding compartment, familiar words seemed to hang in the air between Jan Struther and myself.
>
> 'Lord, let this cup pass from me!'

Vera comments, 'Who was right, she or I? We had made different decisions, but so great was our mutual anguish of irresolution that neither could blame the other for her choice. As the days slowly passed, I became aware that I could not go on living if John and Shirley were drowned.' She hoped to visit them in America when giving lectures but her applications for an exit permit were turned down—because she was a pacifist. She felt then that she had 'parted with them for the duration without ever having decided to do so'. In gratitude for their safety she volunteered to work at CORB which was run by her cousin, Geoffrey Shakespeare.

Another parent on the black list was Maximilian Erwin Lobkowicz[40] from Czechoslovakia. He was an outspoken enemy of the Reich as was his friend Jan Masaryk, son of the first president Thomas Masaryk. The Lobkowicz sons were newly arrived in England. The reason for this was that their English mother had been visiting family in England and was returning via Belgium where a diplomat asked if her husband, Maximilian, and the children had left Prague. When she said no, he urged her to call him and tell him to leave. She did so. Maximilian said nothing would happen but she answered if that was the case the children could go home in a few weeks. He agreed and the children left the next morning. A day later and it would have been too late. In July the children left on the *Antonia* with their nanny, Elizabeth Kydd. Isaiah Berlin, the philosopher, who was also on the *Antonia*, wrote that the evacuee children swarmed over the ship 'behind, on, in, above, below every piece of furniture and rigging'.

Brian Proctor, then 8 years old, was with his family in York when the opportunity came for him and his sister Jean, 11, to be evacuated by CORB. Their parents were conscious of the fact that York as a key rail centre was a prime target for enemy bombers. 'I was asked by them which did I prefer, cowboys or kangaroos,' says Brian, 'so I chose Canada. I didn't realize I wouldn't see my mother and dad again for five years.' Later his school was to receive a direct hit.

Eric Hammond, later to be a national trade union figure, was living in Northfleet, Kent. His father, who was registered as 100% disabled after World War I where he had been gassed, had despite breathing difficulties become head timekeeper at Bowaters. Eric, then 10, was gardening when his father asked him if he would like to be evacuated to Canada. His mind was full of adventure stories from the *Wizard*, the *Rover* and *Hotspur* and so when he was being offered the chance of real-life adventure, his enthusiastic response, to his father's surprise and his mother's dismay, was, 'Yes, please, Dad.' The firm had a paper mill town in Newfoundland and people there had offered to look after the firm's British children for the duration of the war. 'I suppose my parents must have thought it was better to have at least one of their children safe. As I have told friends jokingly since, I was chosen to be evacuated by Churchill as Britain's best—the seed corn—just in case things went wrong and he needed to call us back to start over again.' He sailed on the company ship, SS *Corner Brook*: 'The crew treated us royally. At home, we always had something to eat, if only bread and jam, but because of our circumstances, it wasn't always enough to satisfy a growing lad's appetite. To be presented with the amount and quality of food we got on board was like entering an Aladdin's cave of delights.'

The idea of overseas evacuation was, as is clear, not universally popular. The Royal family felt that they should set an example to the country by not sending their daughters, Princess Elizabeth and Princess Margaret Rose, abroad. Queen Elizabeth said, 'The children won't leave without me. I will never leave the King, and the King won't leave.' Prime Minister Churchill disliked the idea because of the effect he thought it would have on morale. His wife, Clementine, learnt that Winston's great niece, Sally Churchill, was about to leave the country with a group of other children bound for the United States. In her biography of her mother, Mary Soames writes[41], 'Clementine, on hearing of the child's impending departure, realised at once the effect it might have if it became known that a "Churchill child" had left the country at such a time, and that no amount of reasonable explanations of the circumstances would erase the impression given. Although Sally was on the point of embarkation and the changing of her plans caused great inconvenience and some distress to those who had made the arrangements, Clementine insisted (to the point of having the child's passport withheld) that in no circumstances could she be allowed to depart.'

Duff Cooper, a cabinet minister responsible for morale, was attacked[42] for not letting his son, John Julius (Lord Norwich), share the dangers to which the rest of the population were exposed.[43] Some papers called those who went 'gone with the wind-ups'. One mother was sent a white feather. Shakespeare's children burst into tears at the suggestion and 'emphatically refused to go'. David Wedgwood Benn, whose father was a member of parliament, wrote a letter to his parents which was published in *The Times*[44] in July: 'I beg you not to let me go to Canada (I suppose you know that we are probably going?) A) Because I don't want to leave Britain in time of war. B) Because I should be very homesick. I am feeling likewise now. C) Because it would be kinder to let me be killed with you…than to allow me to drift to strangers and finish my happy childhood in a contrary fashion. D) I would not see you for an indefinite time, perhaps never again. Letters would simply redouble my homesickness. P.S. I would rather be bombed to fragments than leave England.'

We at our age, of course, knew nothing of all this. Our parents had no doubt that it was the right course to take. Our mother had grown up at the time of 'the troubles' in Ireland. She had experienced machine gun fights around her house and seen her Dublin school, the Rutland School, occupied by troops. In 1922 her father had been told to leave Ireland within the week or be shot. She wanted us to be spared war. She felt so strongly about it that she marched into the offices of shipping executives to try and secure places for us.

Our father could never be faulted on his patriotism. He had been in the trenches in the First World War. I still have a letter he wrote home from France in 1915, a letter quoted in Martin Gilbert's *A History of the Century:* 'I would not have missed doing my bit for anything, as after the war is over those that return will have a wonderful experience to look back on. I don't envy the feelings of those of my age who still hold back.' Even after those horrific experiences he was anxious twenty-five years later 'to do his bit'.

Apart from reasons of our personal safety they felt that they would be able to pursue their war responsibilities more effectively without us, our father becoming in the War Office an Assistant Quartermaster General and our mother in the Ministry of Information an Assistant Deputy Censor. Whether they would have been willing to go through with it if they had known that the separation was to last five years is another question which did not arise at the time any more than the question of whether host families would have been so keen to take in children if they had known how long they would have them.

Grosvenor House, London, was the first port of call for all us overseas evacuees. Author Alistair Horne remembers it clearly: 'Platoons of Americans, locally conscripted for the task, strained, but friendly, sat at card-tables asking hundreds of unhappy-looking parents the same questions, and writing down the answers. It was a matter of wait and shuffle, shuffle and wait, along barriers of white tape all that long, boring day. There was at least one air raid warning in the course of it.' Indeed, on the first anniversary of Charlie Fay's departure, his father wrote to his American hosts, 'A year ago today we took him to Grosvenor House where all the party were assembled, and watched him and hundreds of other children march out to the buses which took them to the railway station. We thought at the time they were giving us an extra long time at Grosvenor House for leave taking. It was not till afterwards that we learned that an air raid alarm had sounded outside while we were there. The Committee very wisely said nothing to the assembled parents and children and watched for the all clear before giving the signal to start. That was in fact the first daylight alert in London. Though we did not appreciate it the Battle of Britain was working up to its climax, and that day was one of the greatest days in the battle.'

At Grosvenor House we were each given a little 62-page book of sayings that Gerald and I still have. It was called *The Token of Freedom* and put together by 'The Americans-in-Britain Outpost of the Committee to Defend America by Aiding the Allies'. My copy is inscribed 'This token of freedom was given to me Michael Douglas Henderson when I was 8 years old by someone who loved these words and knew what they meant and knew why I must cherish them and hold them sacred so long as I live.'

The book contains sayings about freedom from 43 authors and ranges from the Bible to the Magna Carta, from Plutarch to Tagore, from GK Chesterton to Oliver Wendell Holmes. A foreword, signed B. L. W.[45] an American in England, reads:

> When you see the Statue of Liberty in New York's harbour, remember why she is holding up a light. It is what any brave mother would do, if her children were travelling a dangerous road in what Chaucer called 'the dark darknesses' of this world. The spirit of freedom is so dear to the Free People that they made her image enormous, strong as bronze, beautiful as a proud young mother.
>
> Remember, too, why she is holding fast to written words in a book. Milton tells you why, on page 33. Tyrants hate the very words Liberty, Liberté, Freedom, and try to destroy the very stones on which they find such words lovingly carved.
>
> But your British fathers and mothers are saying No to that. They have said that the name and praise of freedom shall not be torn down and mocked. They mean what they say. And you are their messengers.

Inside the back page are the words of Walt Whitman:

> Keep heart O comrade: God may be delayed by evil, but he suffers no defeat.
>
> God is not foiled; the drift of the world will is stronger than all wrong.

It was all far over the heads of the younger ones of us at the time and it was only much later we could appreciate the significance of this gift.

I was amused to read many years later a children's novel written in 1940 about evacuation by Alice Dalgleish. It was called *Three from Greenways— A story of children from England*[46]. It is about John, Joan and Timothy and describes the same experience at Grosvenor House, concluding:

> Just then a voice through a megaphone said, 'Will all grown-ups please withdraw and leave the children with their escorts?'
>
> No one kissed anyone, all the goodbyes had been said at home. No one cried, for every one knew that British children did not cry. The grown-ups went up into the balcony. Joan looked up. Daddy smiled and made the sign 'Thumbs up' and Joan smiled back at him.
>
> Then some one shouted, 'Are we downhearted?' And all the children shouted 'No!' The children kept shouting and cheering, the grown-ups waved. Then all the children formed in line, two abreast, and walked out with their escorts. Joan held John by the hand. Timothy walked with another little boy just about his own age. Peter was with a different group of children.
>
> Outside buses were waiting and the children piled in. In no time at all they were at Paddington station, on the way to Liverpool. The train was a little while getting started, so Miss Lester said, 'Let's sing'—and the children sang. John and Timothy didn't know all the words of the song but Joan was proud that she knew them to the very end—
>
> There'll always be an England
> And England shall be free,
> If England means as much to you
> As England means to me.

This song was sung frequently by parties being evacuated even if not all evacuees were English. Sometimes those from other parts of the British Isles made that distinction abundantly clear, altering the words appropriately as they sang. On one occasion when Geoffrey Shakespeare was seeing off the first contingent of Australia-bound evacuees at Liverpool docks, he led them all in a spirited singing of the song. The BBC recorded the occasion and the engineers noticed a distorted blurring of one word of the chorus. It soon became obvious that the word was 'England': 'By careful analysis,' writes Derek Johnson, 'it was also established that whereas one section of the group were dutifully chanting "England", another, made up of a highland draft, were dutifully substituting the word "Scotland". It seems that this particular group of nationalistic Scots had taken umbrage at the exclusion of their homeland in this stirring patriotic song. After suitable discussion it was agreed that in future renditions the title "There'll always be a Britain" would be strictly enforced.'

5

SS Early August

One more week passes and no British invasion. Germans boast war good as won.
—New York Times *Week in Review headline on 4 August*

Joy of joys, we all threw our gasmasks onto a big pile and went out into the open and walked along the dock.
—*Jennifer Clarke*

When it finally came time for us to depart for the United States Gerald and I went up to London from Ripley to stay with close friends, the Palmer-Jones family, 'Uncle and Auntie PJ', in Pembroke Walk as we prepared for our trip. I remember our last night, at the Sloane Court hotel, probably because a hotel stay was a new experience for us. Gerald recalls his brand new striped pyjamas that he was taking with him and wore for the first time and also going out in the street to post a letter and seeing barrage balloons on their long steel wires[47].

Jennifer Clarke also thoroughly enjoyed being in a hotel where she and Bridget rang everybody up on the room telephones and went up and down in the lift until they 'drove the lift man mad'. She was sure there was a spy in the hotel as whenever they talked about Liverpool, the ship, and when they were going, there was a man who always edged near. 'Once we caught him listening intently to us with his newspaper held upside down in front of him.' Bridget's father reported him to the police. Certainly all of us young children were brought up at that point with posters with the slogan 'Careless talk costs lives,' usually illustrated by Fougasse or David Langdon cartoons, perhaps of Goering in a luggage rack listening to train passengers talking beneath him.

We assembled in the Grosvenor Ballroom to meet up with all the other children who were sailing on the same ship. We were introduced to our travelling companions, Egerton (Toby) and Faith Coghill and our South African escort, Ann Walker. Faith remembers going for a walk round a lake and being told by her mother, 'It'll only be for a year, darling.' Had she not contracted mumps, she and Toby would have gone on an earlier ship with the Lobkowicz family.

'I felt no sorrow in parting,' says Gerald, 'only excitement and expectation, thanks to what must have been a remarkable degree of restraint on the part of our parents, who quite genuinely thought they might never see us again.' The actual moment of departure from our parents has gone from my mind. But it must have been a wrenching experience for them as we waved goodbye, labelled, our national insurance number on a chain round our neck, in our black and green school caps, with Gerald clutching his small koala bear, which our father had brought back from a business trip to Australia two years earlier. Apparently I called out the latest grown-up phrase I had picked up, 'See you after the duration.'

Angela Pelham,[48] who was also to travel on the same ship, noted in her diary, 'I was glad the aunts had asked people not to come and see us off because there might have been tears, as it was we all looked upon it as a great adventure and a holiday in America. The smaller ones have no sense of time, and the older ones were excited about sleeping on the train and going on the boat. The train was packed with children and as it moved out there was a great shouting from them all echoed by people down the platform.'

Our destination was Glasgow where on 10 August we boarded an impressive grey-painted[49] ocean liner, armed with two 5-inch guns. Geoffrey Shakespeare tried to be at as many sailings as he could to see off the children and so he was there to shepherd the Canada-bound CORB children up the gangway.[50] The night before he had spoken to them in the hostel where they were staying. His message, repeated at the different sailings, was 'When things go wrong, as they will, remember you are British and grin and bear it.' He told them, 'Be truthful, be brave, be kind and be grateful.' In his autobiography[51] he writes, 'I was amused to hear on several occasions that some of my advice had borne fruit. Across the other side of Canada, at a railway station in the early morning, an escort found a small girl of seven weeping bitterly. Suddenly a girl of eleven went up to her and said, "Stop it at once and be British." And the escort recorded that the child immediately pulled herself together.'

Shakespeare's exhortation is also reflected in a book, *Pilgrim Children,* written two years later by Jean Lorimer about the overseas evacuation and our own Atlantic crossing: 'Britain has 3,500 unofficial ambassadors. They carry no diplomatic passports, nor do they claim any diplomatic privilege. They work not in the limelight of officialdom, but insidiously in the very heart of the country in which for the time being they are at home. They carry no instructions in sealed envelopes, for their instructions are simple and easy, even for the very youngest among them, to remember. "Be truthful, brave, kind and grateful" are the words written in their hearts. Six simple words accepted with childlike faith as sufficient to enable them to meet any situation they might have to face in the country far from home where now they work for Britain. For these are the children of Britain who during the months of July, August and September 1940 sailed from the threatened shores of our island fortress to the kindly welcoming lands of our great Dominions and of the United States of America.'

We were not supposed to know the real name of our ship. SS Early August, was the name we were given. But enterprising youngsters swarming all over the ship soon discovered the name badly painted out on a bell—the *Duchess of York*. How many hundreds of children were on board is disputed. The book *Canadian Pacific, the Story of the Famous Shipping Line* says 1,100 children, while an unpublished work on the wartime activities of Canadian Pacific ships puts the figure at 500. As the figure for Canada-bound CORB evacuees on the ship is reliably given as 494 perhaps that is where the 500 come in and doesn't take into account those evacuated privately. One thing is clear: there were a lot of us roaming about the boat!

The *Duchess of York* had been launched on 28 September 1928, the first time a merchant vessel had been launched by a member of the royal family. She was the last of four duchesses to join the company's North Atlantic service. They were known as 'the drunken duchesses' because of their ungainly progress through water.[52] In 1930 the *Duchess of York* had made a record crossing from Liverpool to Saint John in six days, 22 hours, 14 minutes, the first time such a crossing had been made in less than seven days. By the outbreak of the war she had made 132 Atlantic voyages and in March 1940 was requisitioned. On 1 June she sailed from Liverpool to Ana Fjord to rescue 4,000 troops and civilians from Norway. After her return to the Clyde she carried a group of French Foreign Legionnaires to Brest and then made her way to St. Nazaire where she was bombed all day, fortunately without being hit. After embarking 5,000 British troops and nurses she returned to Liverpool. Leaving Merseyside for Canada on 21 June, her entire passenger list was made up of German prisoners of war and their guards.

The *Duchess of York*

The Canadian Pacific history of the liner tells an unusual story:

As there were only 250 armed guards to look after the 3,000 prisoners, a request was made that the ship's officers should be allowed to carry side arms, but this was turned down by the authorities. The prisoners virtually had the run of the ship and were allowed to visit the canteen to buy cigarettes and soft drinks and could take the bottles away. However, this privilege had to be stopped when one of the prisoners threatened a guard with his bottle and had to be shot. As a precaution after this incident, it was decided to flood light the decks after dark. An amusing result of this defensive measure was the noisy protests from the POWs who thought this would make the ship too good a target for their U-boats. However the *Duchess of York* reached Quebec without being attacked and then had to lie offshore for 24 hours because no prior arrangements had been made to receive the prisoners. The official mind works in curious ways. On the next voyage from the United Kingdom the York carried 1,100 children being evacuated to Canada to escape the bombing; and for this voyage each officer was issued with a .38 calibre revolver.

The departure from our berth on Saturday 10 August at 4.30 pm and moving down the Clyde, towed by tugs, in broad daylight was an exciting experience. We saw a sunken ship and discovered later that it was the wreck of the French destroyer *Maille Breze* which sank in the Clyde with heavy loss of life after an explosion and fire on board. I remember sighting HMS *Cossack*. The first morning we woke and looked out of our portholes at an impressive sight—ships as far as the eye could see in all directions. We were at the Tail of the Bank in the Clyde Estuary which was the assembly point for all Clyde shipping outward bound and the dispersal point for inward bound ships waiting for the tide to go up the river, and the anchorage for warships based on the Clyde.

Another part of the convoy sailed a day later from Liverpool and we joined up off Rathlin Island. We were known as convoy ZA and consisted of the liners *Duchess of York, Empress of Australia, Oronsay, Antonia*[53], *Georgic, Samaria, Orion* and HMS *Asturais* which was serving as an armed cruiser. We had a Royal Naval destroyer escort of *Ashanti, Griffin, Watchman, Vortigern, Hurricane* and one other ship of unknown name. And, to our great joy, just across to port from us was the battleship HMS *Revenge*. At one point a signaller from the battleship came over to us by what is called jackstay transfer, a system of blocks and tackles which enable personnel or stores attached to a running block, to be pulled across by ropes. He probably brought across orders or signals too lengthy or sensitive to be sent by the Aldis light which we saw in constant use. I was very pleased to secure his autograph.

'I felt awfully proud that I was British,' noted Angela Pelham. She also wrote, 'What do you think happened this morning? I woke to a strange sound of lapping water and for one dreadful moment I thought we were sinking. I jumped out of bed straight into icy cold water right over my ankles and found the cabin was flooded.' They weren't, however, sinking. 'They went into our bathroom and found that the taps had been left turned on and the bath was overflowing. Helen, 10, had gone to have a bath the night before, not knowing that there is never any water for baths before a ship has properly sailed, and she must have left the taps on... Poor Helen was weeping because it was all her fault, but James, 2", who is always in on any excitement was highly delighted and wanted the steward to come and paddle in the cabin so that he could sail his new boat.' She found the worst part of the night was going to sleep with no portholes open. It was awful: 'They are all screwed up now because some foolish person showed a light and the battleship signalled to our captain and everyone was furious and said we might have been hit.'

Seasickness was a common experience of evacuees on the different ships. Certainly by Wednesday, the sea was very rough and most people on our ship were sick, with the dining saloons half empty at almost every meal. Certainly that is for me a powerful memory of the trip. But as what I threw up was distinctly chocolate in colour it may have had as much to do with the sweet shop as with the rough seas. Felicity Hugh-Jones believes that there will be few who were on the *Antonia* a month earlier who will forget the day the ship hit exceedingly rough seas to the west of Ireland. Only nine people were at lunch in the large dining room which usually served two sittings. She remembers singing

> My breakfast is over the ocean
> My luncheon is over the sea
> My tummy's in such a commotion
> Don't bring any supper to me.

The *Antonia* was four days out in the Atlantic when an enemy submarine fired two torpedoes at it. They both missed, but the escape was narrow for one of the 'tin fish' passed within six feet of the boat. Depth charges were dropped. But as a ship's engineer said, 'There was only one thing we could do—cram on speed. We certainly made the boilers wheeze.' BBC broadcasts were relayed in first class but important items were printed out and stuck on the third-class notice board. Felicity noticed the fact that the German invasion of Britain was expected to begin on Friday and thought this was 'a bit optimistic of the Nazis'[54]. Third class was so deep in the bowels of the ship that she feels steerage would be a more apt description. She wrote home to her parents, 'The amount of room for moving about the cabin is about as much as there is in the china cupboard.' Janet Young remembers being 'very, very nervous' when they were pursued by the submarine. The conditions in steerage were so bad none of them would have survived a sinking, she says. Her parents had no idea of the conditions.

Thirteen-year-old Brian Joseph was also on the *Antonia*. In letters home he gave a running commentary on his new experiences. For instance: 'I have played all the deck games now that there are to play, the best is one in which you shove round wooden disks. I never hit hard enough. And the disc goes on the minus 10. Tonight a Sir Charles Morgan-Webb is giving a talk on "Why we are at war"—as if we didn't know. I will be missing then….We saw the captain for the first time yesterday. I always mistook him for the chief engineer. They both have four rings on their sleeves, but the chief engineer has red or purple between his rings. They are both fat.'

Life on board the various ships was also pretty much the same for most evacuees travelling out. This meant new experiences. Harry Collins, from Stockport, who was on the *Duchess of York* and his older brother were confronted in the dining saloon for the first time with a menu. His brother solved that dilemma for him. 'I'll start from the top,' he announced. Collins recalls the fact that they would close their cabin doors at night only to find later that someone had come round and put all the doors on a chain. Asking why, he was told that if they were torpedoed the doors might jam. Each of the first four days began with a lifeboat drill. Angela Pelham noted about the younger children in her party, 'We all have to carry our life-belts wherever we go and they are a good deal more awkward than the old gas-masks we grumbled about. The little ones are completely swamped in the big cork things and the first time we had boat drill was too funny. Simon and James fell over immediately they had theirs on, and rolled down the alleyway; we set them on their feet but when the ship rolled down they went again like ninepins. It is very difficult to bend and pick them up when ones own chest sticks out a mile in front of one. Tessa insisted on being carried as soon as hers was on and Aunt Amanda had to try and explain not as man to man but as life-belt to life-belt it was impossible. The decks are piled with rafts, the Aunts say that they did not realise what they had undertaken until they saw them. We have been told that there will be 6 short blasts on the hooter if we are hit or in any emergency, if the hooter is damaged they will rattle or bang any-thing that is handy, as we are leading the convoy, and blow our whistle every time we change course, we are constantly pricking up our ears to count the number of blasts.'

A few times in our convoy depth charges were dropped. I don't know if the echo-sounding devices, ASDIC or SONAR, had located submarines or whether it was just practice. For Jim Baynard-Smith, who was en route to Canada and then to New Zealand and was also in the peacetime steerage class below water line on the *Duchess of Atholl*, 'It was all a colossal adventure so we children didn't mind the discomfort as day after day we played the popular board game "Smash the Nazi Navy".' Similarly, we sat on our bunks playing Battleships, not the expensive extravagantly packaged version of the game you can buy today but simply sheets of graph paper on which we plotted our ships. There we were, trying to sink each other's ships, quite oblivious to the fact that submarines were out there looking to sink us. Harry Collins, looking back on the journey, says he did not realize how lucky he was to be so ignorant of the very real dangers around us: 'We ate well, played happily all day and got up to mischief—even throwing the rocking horse overboard—how lucky we were to arrive safely.'

Nina Laville, a CORB evacuee to Saskatchewan, travelling in the *Anselm*, looks back at her experience as an 11-year-old with the comment, 'I cannot believe how brave I was.' David Brown, who went on the *Duchess of Richmond* and stayed with two Rotary families in Montreal, recalls his reaction as one of excitement: 'I had no sense of the dangers of staying or going.' But then we were very young. Our ignorance of the reality is captured in the words of 5-year-old Heather Turvey on the *Hilary* seeing a distant attack on her convoy, 'Isn't this exciting, it's just like firework night' and of a young teenager Ellie Bourdillon, from Oxford, who was quoted in a newspaper, 'Wouldn't it be fun to be torpedoed[55].' Ellie was on the *Antonia* on its earlier voyage: 'Our ship was rather old, very crowded and noisy. Our quarters were low down, no portholes. The crew were very kind, as indeed, were a group of homeward-bound Rhodes Scholars. They entertained us good-naturedly with sing-songs and games in the evenings, enduring our teenage attentions and autograph seeking.' Several evacuees found their way through to the first class and managed to obtain the autograph of one of the leading actresses of the day, Elizabeth Bergner. Also on the *Antonia* with the Oxford party was Ann Spokes. She writes, 'Towards the end of the journey some of the girls started a craze which might have shocked North Oxford. They staged wrestling matches, which soon brought enthusiastic audiences of adults who viewed them from the upper class deck above. Boys and girls wrestled against each other with the girls usually winning.' It became a popular sport and Ann, though proud of the fact that it had all been her idea, was not quite sure whether her parents would have approved of mixed wrestling.

Another shock to the Oxford academic community at home if they had witnessed it, according to some of the travelling party, were the conditions of shipboard living. Ethelwyn Goodwin wrote her husband, 'Oxford would certainly collapse at the sight of D deck—lines of nappies—suitcases in piles outside cabins around the square—mothers bathing and feeding babies in each corner, children playing snap in groups, toddlers pushing animals and engines in and out of the mob.' They were also tickled to think what Oxford society would have made of its wives helping out with the stewards in the pantry.

Anthony Thwaite, the poet, writes, 'There were quite a lot of other unaccompanied kids of about my age, or a bit older, on the boat, and we had a high old time running about, sneaking into the First Class quarters and watching films, staying up half the night, drinking black coffee. My aunt Nora used to recall that when she met me in New York two weeks later I had a huge hole in the seat of my short trousers—and my skin was absolutely filthy—I don't think I'd had a bath or shower the whole time. Very much *Just William* stuff.' He was sent to Nora who had married an American political economist living near Washington, DC. They had cabled his parents, 'Send Anthony to us.' 'A great deal of agonised discussion must have gone on but I wasn't aware of it. I've always felt guilty—or maybe I should say as an adult I've always felt guilty—that I wasn't worried, didn't miss my parents, apparently took to the whole new situation without a murmur or qualm.'

Many years later he was to develop that thought in a poem:

Evacuation 1940

Liverpool docks. The big ship looms above
Dark sheds and quays, its haughty funnels bright
With paint and sunlight. As slim sailors shove
About with chains and hawsers. Mummy's hand
Is sticky in my own, but I'm all right,
Beginning an adventure. So I stand
On a deck piled high with prams, the staterooms shrill
With mothers' mutterings and clasped babies' cries.
I squirm and tug, ten years impatient, till
Loud hootings signal something…the surprise
Of hugging her, feeling her face all wet:
"Mummy, you're sweating." They were tears; not mine.
She went away. I was alone, and fine.

Pleasure and guilt. Things you do not forget.

The hundreds of CORB children were not so closely attended as those of us who went privately. In fact, Margaret Wyatt, aged 10, on the *Duchess of York*, remembered no supervision at all because the ladies assigned to look after them were sea-sick and kept to their cabins. The children roamed everywhere and went to bed when they liked: 'When we were bored, a favourite game was to play "dentists". We made little holes in the warm tar between the planks on deck and filled them with silver paper.' The CORB boys were somewhere else. She looked for her younger brother, Stephen, and found him once in a washroom in a lower part of the ship. He was trying to wash a pair of socks in a hand basin. 'Bless him, he was only 8, so big sister washed his socks for him and showed him where to dry them, poking them into a wire fence near the warm ship's engines.' Brian Joseph on the *Antonia* writes of the CORB children: 'On Friday night after dinner the children from the government scheme had a sing song on deck. It was very good. We listened to them from the deck above.'

On the *Samaria* was a group of Kodak children. One of them, about nine, was noticed to be giggling frequently at lunch when there seemed nothing in the conversation to giggle about. The matter was resolved when a lady supervisor realised he was thoroughly tipsy. His trick, according to Martyn Pease, was to slip into the cocktail lounge after the gong had sounded and polish off the heeltaps in the abandoned glasses. 'If he avoided alcoholism,' comments Martyn, 'he probably made a fortune.'

On the *Samaria* a contest was held on board ship with a ten-shilling prize to see who could best recite Lincoln's Gettysburg address. First prize was won by a 13-year old girl, Tryphaena Alchin, who with her 12-year-old brother was one of a party of about fifteen arranged by the *Boston Transcript* Another young *Transcript* evacuee, Claire Stephen, on the *Duchess of Atholl*, remembers that each of her party had to learn a piece from *The Token of Freedom* on the eight-day journey. 'Being ten years old and crafty with it, I learnt the shortest I could find, after the seasickness wore off.' It was *King John*, v 7 (Shakespeare):

> This England never did nor never shall
> Lie at the foot of a proud conqueror.
> Come the three corners of the world in arms
> And we shall shock them. Nought
> Shall make us rue,
> If England to itself do rest but true.

Margaret Hanton had a wonderful time on board her ship whose name she cannot recall. It included playing cards with a group of lumberjacks returning home. Nine-year-old Alys Acworth was on the *Monarch of Bermuda*, with a party from her brother's school, Abinger Hill, in late June on their way to Ashbury College in Ottawa. She thinks that they must have driven the poor sailors demented by their escapades: 'First the girls battled with the boys in the saloon, missiles flying through the air. Then we climbed up the empty middle funnel. Finally we went down to the hold and saw behind bars gold ingots. After this we were told that if we didn't behave ourselves we'd be put into the cells!'.Also in the Abinger Hill party was the later TV personality Daniel

Farson who says, 'We raced around the decks, upsetting the passengers, convinced we saw a polar bear on a passing iceberg, taking a midnight boat drill as a real disaster' until finally 'exuberance was brought to heel'. On Jennifer Clarke's ship 'there was a very film starry looking young man who used to leap about on one of the covered hatches, fencing, surrounded by admiring small boys, and he was very disappointed one day, while lounging on the deck sunbathing, as he said to us very pompously, "Do you know who I am?" and much to his disgust we said, "No" very innocently. I still don't know who he was but he may have been Errol Flynn.' Patricia Backlar who was on the *Monarch of Bermuda* says, 'There wasn't much done for us. We ran wild with a pack of children, everything a giggle and freedom.' She and other children were convinced that their ship was carrying the crown jewels: 'The story was that they were in the swimming pool.' She had been told she was coming for 'the summer holidays'. On the *Oronsay* each child was given by the chaplain a copy of the New Testament. CORB evacuee John Bland still has his.

Tony Moore and his sister had both travelled by sea before, four Atlantic crossings to Jamaica where their father was stationed, so subconsciously felt they knew the ropes. He says, 'The child's eye view of the eight day crossing was centred on the steward in charge of our cabin and the waiter at our table, a splendid fellow who showed us pictures of himself manning the ship's auxiliary gun. For the rest the journey passed with memories of the sweet shop where mars bars were obtainable unrationed and where we probably ate too much.'

One visiting professor who was on an evacuee ship that summer gave a rather romantic view of the trip in a letter to the *New York Times*[56]:

> The convoy was a perfectly beautiful thing to watch. The six liners without extending or diminishing distance, were continually altering their positions. One liner acted as leader and made the signals. It would hoist a pennant, and then the whole argosy would swing into their new positions without altering speed, without losing distance. It was a lovely, slow, kaleidoscopic movement, performed with perfect seamanship.... In the most terrible war in history some nine hundred or a thousand persons sailed on our ship in complete liberty and comfort, without let or hindrance from any external force. Except that we carried life jackets wherever we went on the ship and showed no external lights at night, this solitary sailing was just the

same as in time of peace. We enjoyed excellent if plain meals, were admirably served by table and stateroom stewards, read, slept, walked the decks, chatted with sailors in their off time, listened to the orchestra and had the usual concert for the seamen's charities. As we passed the Ambrose Lightship we saw ships which had been originally in the convoy and which had disappeared converging toward us out of the blue. They, too, had been travelling for many miles alone, upheld by the unseen arms of the British Navy.

Obviously for some children, particularly those who survived torpedoing, the experience was traumatic. A US Committee report on the children in their care stated, 'To some it was an adventure tempering their homesickness with the thrill of excitement and landing them in America in buoyant spirits. To others it was a long drawn out nightmare of seasickness and fright, which showed up in their drawn pallid faces.'

Also with the Oxford/Yale group on the *Antonia* were Meggie Milne and her sister Eleanor. Their father was Professor Milne, a distinguished astrophysicist. While lecturing in the US he had earlier met Dr. Theodore Dunham, an American astronomer, who when the war came invited the Milne children to stay with him and his wife. Dr. Dunham visited London during the Blitz, to fly with the RAF, advising them on gun sights in his capacity as chief of the optical instruments section of the US Office of Scientific Research and Development. Meggie was then a seven-year-old and revelled in the freedom to roam over the ship's passageways and decks. A few days out from Liverpool, however, just when she felt confident that she knew her way around, she heard an announcement over the address system which put a stop, at least temporarily, to her chasing about the ship. Children were either to go below or remain stationary on deck; there was to be no moving about. Eleanor elected to go below while Meggie waited in urgent expectation. The gun next to which she was standing had its cover removed by a sailor and he waited, too. After a bit Meggie asked him what was going to happen. His reply, she remembers, was 'a masterpiece of reassurance'. He told her that he was going to fire the gun to blow up an iceberg which surely she could see on the horizon. Accepting this explanation but waiting eagerly with childish expectation she was disappointed that he didn't get on with it. Why not fire, she asked. At last, in response to further enquiry he said that we had now gone by the best position for blowing it up, and with that he replaced the gun cover. 'What a feeble way to behave,' thought Meggie. It was only five years later when she returned to

Oxford that she learned the true reason. The ship was threatened by torpedoes. More than fifty years later she wrote, 'I revised my opinion of the kind unknown sailor, who had so sensibly diverted my attention and had made up such a plausible story for a child.'[57]

Meanwhile back home during the very days we were at sea the decisive Battle of Britain was being fought over the skies of England. Indeed, the air campaign over southern England in August 1940 has been called 'one of the most decisive military engagements in history'. At the beginning of August Goering informed his commanders, 'The *Fuehrer* has ordered me to crush Britain with my Luftwaffe. By means of hard blows I mean to have this enemy, who has already suffered a decisive moral defeat, down on his knees in the nearest future, so that an occupation of the island can proceed without any risk.' To the Germans 12 August was *Adlertag*, the Day of the Eagle, the start of their two-week assault on RAF Fighter Command's aircraft, airfields, and installations as a preliminary to the invasion of the UK. On 17 August Hitler announced the total blockade of Britain and gave the order to sink all but Irish ships. Unbeknownst to us of course 18 August, when we were still four days out, was the day of the *Luftwaffe*'s greatest attack on Britain. Every fighter squadron in the country was engaged that day with 34 aircraft lost against 76 German attackers brought down.

And while we were en route decisive battles, legislative ones, were also being fought in the United States, duly reflected in the pages of the *New York Times*.

On 8 August there was an editorial in the paper saluting the passage through the House of Representatives of a bill which permitted the use of American ships to rescue British children: 'The House has simply recognized and shared an overwhelming public desire to get the largest possible number of these children away from the dive bombers.' The paper urged the Senate to act and to act promptly: 'The British now warn their people that the present air raids are pin pricks compared to the coming onslaughts. Marshal Kesselring, the chief of Germany's air fleets, says it will come with "the unpredictability of lightning"—we will be stirred to our depths by pity and horror, and by the normal American impulse 'to do something," but it will be too late. The British roads and railways will then be reserved for military traffic; the ports may be closed or wrecked; thousands of children whom we might have saved will be lying in hospital wards or morgues. Thousands more of those who survive may never become normal children again, after the sights and terrors they will have experienced. The time to save them is now. The way to save them is for the Senate to pass, without a day's delay, the bill which will make their rescue possible under the American flag.'

The next day the paper reported that women volunteer workers were mailing out petitions to all states about the Senate Bill and quotes Mrs. Raymond Gram Swing: 'Many people, including some of the Senators, were under the impression that the Women's Mercy Ship Committee is interested only in rescuing British children. That is distinctly not the case. We want American ships to rescue children who are in danger, without regard for race, creed or nationality. We want these ships to go to ports in the war zones in which they are assured of safety. We want to do a rescue job which is no less important than the work of the Red Cross or any other humanitarian agency.'

The paper that day also carried an appeal to Mrs. Roosevelt from a mother in Yorkshire: 'Hearing your name mentioned on the wireless in connection with the refugees, I feel I must write and ask you to hurry and get the children on their way as soon as possible. We are willing to stand any suffering, bombing, starvation, anything so long as our children are safe. You, yourself, being a mother will know how hard it is for us to part from our children—like taking our hearts from our body. As night falls we pray to God to keep them safe until another day dawns. Each night we put our few belongings together in bags with enough food to last for two days to take with us into shelter, which in our case means the cellar. But we can stick this, we will live in cellars before giving in so long as our children are out of the way, because we mean to win this war for justice and freedom for all. To all American mothers who take our children at this terrible time I want to say "thank you, and may God bless you".'

On 14 August Roosevelt agreed to give Britain 50 American destroyers in exchange for the use of British naval bases in the Caribbean and West Atlantic, the famous 'lend-lease' agreement. His folksy rationale: 'Suppose my neighbour's home catches fire, and I have got a length of garden hose four or five hundred feet away; but, my heaven, if he can take my garden hose and connect it up to his hydrant, I may help him put out his fire....I don't say to him before that operation, "Neighbour, my garden hose cost me $15; you have got to pay me $15 for it"....I don't want $15—I want my garden hose back after the fire is over.' Isolationist Senator Taft's response, 'Lending arms is like lending chewing gum. You don't want it back.' But when the deal was concluded on 3 September, the anniversary of the war, it had, in the words of Foreign Secretary Halifax 'a profound moral effect throughout the world'. He said this arrangement 'was evidence of a growing identity of concern between the two countries with what was happening in the world, that was later to be the world's salvation'. Lend-Lease showed the extent to which 'an unprecedented act of generosity to a foreign nation could serve the enlightened self-interest of his own'.

Prime Minister Churchill in a speech at the Mansion House in London referred to 'the majestic policy' of the President and Congress of the United States in passing the Lend-Lease Bill through which about L3,000,000,000 was 'dedicated to the cause of world freedom, without—mark this, because it is unique—without the setting up of any account in money.' The Prime Minister went on, 'Never again let us hear the taunt that money is the ruling power in the hearts and thoughts of the American democracy. The Lease-Lend Bill must be regarded without question as the most unsordid act in the whole of recorded history.'

The Oxford party had by then already arrived safely much to the relief of parents. Janet Young's mother told her later that after she had left and during the period while the boat was at sea 'nature came to the rescue and she ceased to feel anything until the cable arrived'. Mother's last word to her and her sister when she set off had been, 'Whatever you do, don't get separated.' On the first night they were and her sister was in tears. Fortunately, they were then put together.

When the Oxford party arrived by train from Canada where they had first landed reporters boarded the train and, as one observer wrote, 'The Dragon school boys in particular, had no trouble in answering their inevitable question: What do you think of America? This despite the boys having only seen it from the train windows for about an hour or so. Experience of Hollywood films enabled them to give what the boys assumed were perfectly satisfactory accounts.' Occasionally, precocious British children commented adversely on American accents and actions. One reporter retaliated by saying that British boys were more adept at conjugating Latin verbs than in keeping their necks clean.

After four days at McGill University the Oxford children rode to New Haven on a special 3-car train loaned by the New Haven railroad. Hundreds came to the station to welcome them. The New Haven *Evening Register* captioned two photos: 'Refugees find new haven in land holding promise of peace' and 'England's new generation here to live as Americans'. Many of the children remained at the Divinity School for about two weeks under measles quarantine before they went to faculty homes.

Yale Chaplain Sidney Lovett, who was chairman of the Yale Faculty Committee for Receiving Oxford and Cambridge University Children, wrote in the *Yale Alumni Magazine*, 'A heat wave of unprecedented torridness in these parts, routine physical checkups with added inoculations, the limitations of quarantine regulations, sporadic cases of measles, failed to break the morale of our overseas friends or to check the rapid growth of Anglo-American cordiality, marked even by the free exchange of British and Yankee slang. The fine courtesy and patience of our English guests under conditions not only new but often embarrassing, excites one's unqualified admiration in retrospect. Within a month all were established in foster homes.' The Youngs went to the New Haven home of Yale professor Robert Calhoun and his wife, who soon became Uncle Bob and Aunt Ella to them. The Yale Committee had forestalled financial problems by raising more than $30,000 to pay for transportation, to offset costs for the poorer host families, and to enable mothers who had come with their children to set up housekeeping for them.

For security reasons departures and arrivals were often shrouded in secrecy. Sometimes this meant that hundreds of children often landed unannounced at Canadian or American ports. Sylvia Warren enlisted the help of Travellers Aid to meet the boats and look after the children. In August Sylvia wrote to Mrs. Coghill, 'If it is a tremendous satisfaction for you to get little white-faced children off, and I know it is, you can imagine the satisfaction that you should feel when I get the little white faced children at the train here, holding their hands over their ears if the train whistles, and cringing at first when the passenger planes go overhead.' She was working hard to place children in homes that approximated to the background they came from 'not only for success here but for repatriation later on'. She was competing for space with the US Committee.

On 13 August the destroyers departed from our convoy and at the same time HMS *Asturais* and the liner *Orion* left to go south. Angela Pelham: 'The destroyers left us after three days and I must admit that I can't help wondering what the battleship could do if we were attacked, but strangely enough I find myself forgetting that we might be in danger, it is all rather fun.' The *Samaria* left the convoy on our last day, the 19th, heading for New York. HMS *Revenge* remained with the convoy to Halifax, from where she was to return with a convoy of Canadian troops. According to the report of the captain of the battleship: apart from foul weather, there were no incidents on the passage.

The sight of land, on 21 August, as it has always been for sea voyagers, was an exciting moment for us, and no doubt for our escorts a great relief. 'This afternoon about teatime we saw land, Hurrah!' noted Angela Pelham. 'What a thrill, a sea-plane came out to look us over, we knew it was a friendly one and every body cheered like mad. It swooped quite low and we saw the pilot waving back at us. The sun was shining and gradually the land took shape and there were rugged cliffs and all trees just like one imagines Canada.... We watched the lights go on in the town and around the harbour. How funny it was to see lights again and the rain made them twinkle all the more. They seemed to be laughing at us, and wishing us welcome. I am sure they were saying to the captains and crews of all our convoy: "Well done, you've made it again." Every one walked round and round the deck watching the reflections of our own lights in the water. It was funny how we talked so much more loudly than when the ship had been blacked out.'

'Coming into Halifax[58] was like fairyland,' says Patricia Backlar. Joan Collister, who also travelled on the *Duchess of York*, wrote home, 'We sighted silver sands on the Nova Scotian coast and after three or four hours in a very calm sea, we saw the harbour mouth, a beautiful place surrounded by forest-clad hills rather like a bristly doormat at the gates of a new land. On a point jutting out into the sea, there was a beautiful little white lighthouse surrounded by fishing-nets drying in the sun, and just inside the entrance was a huge oil refinery, Imperial Oil Ltd. The warship and the *Oronsay* entered before us and we could see them lying in dock, but it was not our luck to land that night. Instead we lay in the middle of the river to wait until the quay was clear and the trains ready. The river was full of the strangest craft of all colours, shapes and sizes and nationalities, from the tiniest boats with outboard motors to destroyers, cruisers, liners and houseboats. All this was wonderful, but I think the nicest part of it all was to see the millions of unshielded harbour lights that night. We were all very tired and excited so you can guess we didn't sleep well that night.'

The lack of blackout struck all of us. Indeed, Jim Baynard-Smith, steaming into the St. Lawrence Seaway recalls being very puzzled and indignant that 'the whole place was ablaze with lights on all sides' in such contrast to the blacked-out port and river they had left. Likewise the 210 children on the *Samaria* had the same experience entering New York harbour. The *New York Times* of 24 August wrote, 'A small pyjama-clad figure hung at the ship's rail looking towards the lighted skyscrapers and the rose-and-yellow glow the distant city cast against the summer sky. The youngster was a British refugee. He had passed the border of the blackout.'

The Coghills' Boston host, Mrs. Farley, had come up to welcome us as she was Canadian from Sydney near Halifax. I retain two things from the arrival at Halifax. The immigration officers had glasses of ice water—I had never seen ice in a drink before—and the loudspeakers were blaring out a new hit, 'The stars at night are big and bright deep in the heart of Texas.'[59] Toby enjoyed chewing the ice and Faith remembers Mrs. Farley saying to him, 'Over here we don't eat ice.' Harry Collins recalls the newsreel photographers and reporters coming on board while Faith remembers lining up in the smoking rooms where Mrs. Farley found us and, with a certain flourish that seemed to cut red tape, ushered us off the ship. Telegrams were sent off from Halifax announcing the safe arrival of Hendersons and Coghills and must have been received with much relief and joy.

Canadian Press news agency sent out a story datelined from 'An East coast Canadian port', a euphemism for Halifax. It stated, 'Youngsters by the hundreds waited beside a pier tonight for their landing in Canada from Britain as officials struggled to complete the greatest water-borne migration of children in history. Of the 2,000 who arrived here yesterday to find new homes in the Dominion, 429 slept tonight aboard the liner that had brought them across the Atlantic.' To Ellie the sight of a 'mountie' in full uniform at the dockside meant 'we really had arrived'.

As we disembarked from our ships, Canadian troops were waiting to board. The *Halifax Herald* reported, '"There'll always be an England" and other songs popular since the outbreak of hostilities were sung by the youngsters as they left shipboard and tramped through the sheds to immigration headquarters....The children were tired but happy....A few showed traces of homesickness but the majority were keenly enthusiastic at the prospect of new things that lay ahead.' Some, like Diana Cran, were on board SS *Hilary* where a child had contracted measles, and had to stay on board until quarantine was over. As a star-struck 13-year-old 'keen for adventure' and offered the chance of a CORB passage she had opted for Canada as her destination as 'the nearest I could get to Hollywood'. 'I am sure,' she writes, 'most of the children on board, like me, wondered if we would ever see our homeland again.'

Even when it was to family that evacuees were going, they often did not know of the children's arrival. Grace Baldock and her brother, who sailed on the *Oronsay*, went from Halifax to Toronto and were at the university for two weeks: 'While we were there a cousin saw my picture in the paper holding my black doll. He rang my aunt and uncle and that was the first they knew we had arrived.' Likewise, it was an *Oronsay* crew member who told the parents of Malcolm Joyce, 7, of his safe arrival. Other Canada-bound evacuees boarded trains to Montreal and places further West. At each stop crowds would gather to hand the children candy, gum and apples. At Saskatoon, for instance, three thousand people, along with the mayor, were at the station to welcome twenty-five evacuees. Some evacuees, particularly those who came with CORB, had to endure long medical examinations and the ordeal of waiting to find families who would take them. Some were split up with siblings and mother being in different towns.

In Vernon, British Columbia, the civic authorities and a brass band were on hand to welcome 'a motley group of dishevelled travellers', as John Eden[60] describes his mother's party, made up mostly of girls from the school she ran in the New Forest. Vulnerable to attacks on Southampton, his parents had decided that the school, his four sisters (one of them three weeks old) and he and his cousins should be sent to Canada. Sight unseen they had purchased a large house in Vernon. They arrived at the end of June 1940 having travelled in the *Duchess of Richmond*. 'It was a very bold decision of my parents,' he says, 'to risk sending the entire family on a very hazardous trip, with ships torpedoed in our convoy.' He adds, 'We weren't strictly evacuees but self-imposed voluntary transferees' and, in an understatement, 'The Vernon Preparatory School was something of a change after Eton.'[61]

Our party, who were going to the US, took a quieter route by train to Yarmouth. We stood in the observation car—another first for us—and watched the Bay of Fundy as we headed south. Then there was another short boat trip to Boston. Gerald says, 'I remember standing at the rail when we docked looking for the white hat which we were told Mrs. Hinchman our guardian would be wearing. Sure enough we saw her very quickly.'

The various Boston papers had photographs and stories about our arrival. The *Evening American* had the headline 'More war children arrive, meet hosts' and reported that 'all four were friendly and talkative—but wary of disclosing military information'. The *Christian Science Monitor* had a front-page photo of Faith and Egerton (Toby) and Gerald and me. My brother has his tongue out at the photographer and the caption reads, 'Gerald's impression of the proceedings seems a bit questionable.' 'Four smallish English "guest children" walked down the gangplank of the Steamship *Yarmouth* at Boston this morning with all the confidence of world travellers,' wrote the paper. 'Gayety was the keynote of the landing. Michael and Gerald explored part of the pier while Faith and Egerton answered questions. They were "glad to be here". They "expected to like it". There was "no reason to look upon them with pity". They were world travellers on a lark.' The paper reported that on questions concerning their passage across they maintained a discreet silence. 'Once when Faith had spontaneously answered a question about their convoy she quickly said, "I shouldn't have told that. Please cross it out." As to the name of the boat that brought them across—they were quite prepared to tell them what her name was. Early August, they cried in chorus, that's what she was called. Early August—anyway that's what we call her." It was a good joke on the reporters and they made the most of it. Egerton clutched a half-size violin case in his arms but he said he only played once during the voyage and then, with a twinkle in his eye, "Only to annoy somebody", and he looked roguishly at his sister.'

CHRISTIAN SCIENC

AN INTERNATIONAL DAILY NEWSPAPER

BOSTON, FRIDAY, AUGUST 23, 1940—VOL. XXXII,

On New World's Doorstep

By a Staff Photographer

London Evacuees Reach Boston to Stay for 'Duration of the War'

Introducing, left to right, Gerald Henderson, Egerton Coghill, Faith Coghill (Egerton's sister), and Michael Henderson (Gerald's brother). They are shown as they lined up for the benefit of immigration inspectors today. Gerald's impression of the proceedings seems a bit questionable.

The author, right, brother Gerald, left, and Toby and Faith Coghill at the immigration in Boston. A front-page photograph in the *Christian Science Monitor*.

The Coghills went home to the Farleys[62] in Needham where they were to stay for two years, then moving to Canada. Gerald and I were whisked away by car to join the rest of the Hinchman family at Rockywold camp on Squam Lake in New Hampshire, a world away from the London Blitz. Our only casualty was the loss of Gerald's koala bear.

The fact that a large number of children arrived in July and August at holiday time meant that many went to camps or summer homes, making the transition from wartime England easier. Janet Young speaks of the clever way Yale hosts arranged invitations to tea or outings to the beach. She too went for two or three weeks to Squam Lake. 'It was a wonderful summer holiday,' she says. Homesickness did not hit her until she returned to New Haven and school 'and it swept over me that we were not going home. What had seemed like the holiday of a lifetime had come to an end.'

6

Closing the Door

Tony Quinton, later Lord and President of Trinity College, Oxford was one of only eight out of 23 passengers and crew in his lifeboat who were still alive when picked up. Endowed with an unfailing sense of humour, he always made light of it, claiming that, on returning to his grandmother's house in England, she barely looked up from weeding the flower beds and remarked, 'Good heavens, are you back already?'
—*Told by Alistair Horne in* A Bundle From Britain

There's something quite exciting, it gives you quite a thrill,
About a fast destroyer and her own free will.
But dead still children on a storm-tossed sea
To greet you when you get there is an awful thing to see.
—*From a poem[63] by Lt Cdr Hugh Crofton Simms, RN, captain of HMS* Hurricane

We had arrived safely, and the next few weeks brought more children to North America. But some were not so fortunate.

Newspapers kept up the momentum of reports and advocacy. On 1 September the education section of the *New York Times* reported that 425 American schools were ready to receive English boys and girls. The list included 'all of the best known and highest standing schools in the country'. Seventy-five of them signified their readiness to accept at least 25 pupils each and were offering almost everything from free tuition and actual overhead costs to the establishment of individual school units in their midst. An editorial the same day was entitled 'A way to save children'. It said that at a time when British children were 'being killed and maimed almost every day by German bombs', the executives and workers of the Hoover vacuum cleaning company and the Eastman Kodak company had set a fine example of bringing to the US the children of employees in their British factories. Their example was worth studying by other great American businesses which have branch factories or affiliated plants in Great Britain. 'The pioneer work has now been done by two progressive American companies; it is now all the easier for other companies here to follow their lead.'

In early September the Milton paper reported that there had not been much activity in the local branch of the US Committee for the Care of European Children as it was apparent that sentiment in England was now less enthusiastic about letting people leave. The paper told the story of a Milton woman who had seen the English children who had been living in the Wellesley College dormitory while awaiting homes: 'As she approached a group of children, one little boy who was running fell down. She knew he must have hurt himself, but he did not even whimper, so she said, 'You must be a very brave boy not to cry when you are hurt.' And the quick reply from the little fellow was, "It's all for England."' The paper comments, 'There are many of us here who are learning new lessons of courage and self-control these days.'

On 3 September a British report of the torpedoing of a ship bearing refugee children to Canada was dismissed by informed quarters in Berlin as having the earmarks of 'another Churchill canard designed to win sympathy in the United States and rouse Americans against Germany'. It is strange, it was said in Berlin, that neither the name nor position of the vessel was mentioned by the British, 'while reports that the children sang the Beer Barrel Polka give the story a certain air of incredulity'. One official was quoted as saying that 'the whole story smells. It was undoubtedly designed for American consumption. There probably never was any such ship or any children.' If such a vessel were really damaged, the Germans claimed, it could easily have run on a mine and been 'irresponsible frivolity on the part of the British government'.[64]

The ship was the *Volendam* which was torpedoed on 30 August off the north coast of Ireland with 320 children among the passengers. The attack occurred at ten o'clock at night, with the ship being hit twice. The order was given to abandon ship and the children who had been well practiced in boat drill found their way, even in darkness, to the point of assembly and took their place in the boats. One escort said later that it was the most moving experience in her life to hear in the darkness, borne on the wind, the voices of the children singing 'There'll always be an England' and 'Roll out the barrel'. A major tragedy was averted when three ships from the convoy succeeded in picking up the survivors, including all the children. There were two fatalities, the purser and a cabin boy. One nine-year-old boy, Robert, unnoticed in the confusion, was inadvertently left in his cabin on board the sinking ship. At midnight he went on deck, could not find anyone and so went back to his cabin and slept. In the morning the ship's list had increased and she had almost capsized. Robert at this point found the nucleus engineer crew and felt less lonely. When the destroyer came alongside they had difficulty persuading him to leave his command. He finally returned to Gourock decorated with innumerable badges and buttons and carrying part of the German torpedo. Shakespeare wrote later, 'To be on a big ship of 15,000 tons in company with others is sometimes a frightening experience. For a small boy to be quite alone must have been a nightmare. Robert, however, was Scottish, and of the same race that has provided leaders in every part of the British Empire.' The ship was towed to land and beached.

Mary Justham, 9, was one of the children rescued from the *Volendam* and returned to relieved parents: 'I was very happy to be home again. I really had no idea at all of the implications of what was going on.' As a family they were very close but she does not remember ever talking about it. More than sixty years later she finds that quite strange. 'How times have changed, haven't they?' she reflects.

The *New York Times* responded to the sinking of the *Volendam* with an editorial 'Our ships for children' in which it said that there was no reason one near disaster at sea should interrupt the effort to bring as many people as possible from Great Britain to the safety of the new world.

Over the next couple of weeks American papers continued to carry reports on the evacuee front, from adventures at sea ('200 evacuee children escape from a submarine attack that sank five ships in their convoy') to the reactions of evacuees on arriving in America ('Child refugees tell "homefolks" of delights of new homes. Interviewed by Bob Emery, director of WOR's Rainbow House, they voted New York the most impressive sight. Baseball received a vote of approval although this was qualified when compared with cricket.') While the arrival of sisters Jean and Margaret Moore on the West coast was greeted with the headline in the *Pasadena Star*, 'Refugee English girls enthusiastic about beautiful trees in Pasadena.' The paper wrote that the children's instructions regarding giving out information must have been thorough for both are impressed with the idea that 'they mustn't talk too much'.

However, on 23 September came the first public word of the tragedy that was to bring the whole evacuation of children to America to a halt, the sinking of the *City of Benares*. Propaganda, said Germany again. An official statement issued in Berlin said, 'German naval and air units attack only armed merchantmen. That is our only answer to the British report, which is a brazen lie for squeezing the tear-glands of the world and contributing to bringing the United States into the war on the British side.' An official in Berlin asserted that no German U-boat was operating 600 miles from the British coast. The wireless bulletins declared that the announcement of the sinking of the liner carrying children to Canada 6 days afterwards was suspicious and one semi-official broadcast said that if the ship was really sunk the sinking could only be regarded as another 'typical Churchill case'. The British Government alone was responsible for sending children into the danger zone. In many cases children had been taken on board ships so that the vessels—even though actually auxiliary cruisers—might be described for propaganda purposes as children's transport vessels. The German News Agency said that if the ship really had been torpedoed with the loss of children's lives 'then the murderer's name is Churchill'.

Seventy-seven children were drowned when the *City of Benares*[65] was sunk. US Secretary of State Cordell Hull[66] called the sinking 'a dastardly act'.

The *City of Benares* had sailed from Liverpool on Friday 13 September. On board were 400 passengers and crew, among them 90 children and 10 adult escorts. Four days later on 17 September she was sunk six hundred miles out in the Atlantic. Until that very morning her convoy had been guarded by HMS *Winchelsea* but the destroyer had to leave to meet an incoming convoy carrying stores and ammunition.

The torpedo struck the ship below the quarters where the children were asleep and thirty CORB evacuees were killed instantly. She sank within twenty minutes. Some passengers and crew managed to get into lifeboats. But, inadequately dressed, with no coats over their pyjamas, some perished in the next hours, while some boats were never seen again, and of the 400 passengers and crew just over a hundred were rescued. Two were CORB escorts and seven were CORB children. Two child survivors, Elizabeth Cummins and Bessie Walder, clung to the keel of an upturned boat all that night and the next morning and were picked up by HMS *Hurricane*[67]. Peter Collinson, who was the ship's medical officer, writes, 'It was a moving experience—we rescued

14 children but 3 could not be resuscitated in spite of the valiant efforts of the Petty Officer's mess. They were buried at sea next day with full naval honours.' Nearly sixty years later Bess said, 'I knew we'd make it. We weren't in the business of giving in.' The casualties were particularly high because of the rough sea and because the two nearest ships which might have been expected to rescue survivors were themselves torpedoed at the same time. Twenty sets of parents lost more than one child.[68]

On the day the news of the sinking was in the papers the King made a speech condemning the inhumanity of the action and announced he was instituting a new award for gallantry, to be called the George Cross.

To everyone's amazement, eight days after the sinking a lifeboat was sighted by a Sunderland flying boat. It contained 46 survivors, among them 6 CORB boys and an escort, Mary Cornish. The moving story of their ordeal and bravery, particularly of music teacher Mary, fired the imagination of the country. Her story was told in a book, *Atlantic Ordeal*, published the following year, and she was awarded the British Empire Medal. The tragedy upset the public as much as any single incident thus far in the war. Fethney writes, 'People saw the evacuation of children to safety abroad as an act defiance against Hitler. So, mixed with grief over the disaster, there was anger, and there was also inspiration derived from the bravery of the survivors. As a result, the affair proved an even greater source of anti-Nazi propaganda than the torpedoing of the *Volendam*, giving rise to an even stronger resurgence of the Dunkirk mentality.'

One father, J.E. Grimmond, who had five children drowned when the *City of Benares* sank and who in addition had been bombed out of house, wrote to the *Sunday Dispatch* at the end of the month as one of the many thousands of people who had already had their loved ones killed in the war and 'have the right to fight on until we have avenged them'.

One of the last ships to leave Britain before the *City of Benares* was the *Antonia* on a third trip across the Atlantic with children that summer. On board were the Mathews children, Clifford, Sheila and Dinah. Back in England the Mathews parents were horrified, not having heard anything from them or even knowing what ship they were on, to see a picture in a newspaper of a little girl, wrapped in a blanket, having been rescued from the sea after the sinking of the *City of Benares*. It was a false alarm for them but it was to be another month and a half before they heard that the children were safe and living with families in Ohio.

Likewise, Norman Bonham Carter and his younger brother, Gerard, were booked to travel to Canada on the *City of Benares* and were switched at the last moment to the *Duchess of Richmond*. Their parents were not told of the change. Their ship was some fifty miles from the *City of Benares* when it was sunk but was instructed to proceed at full speed, it being too risky to stop. It was a relief to the worried parents to discover their children had not been on board.[69]

When news of the *City of Benares* broke in the British press a friend of mine, Athalie Warren, now in her eighties, was a schoolgirl. She remembers the effect the sinking had on her and the other girls at her school in London. Sitting under the stairs of her house during evening air raids she wrote this poem:

Lost "77" Children

Dreaming of the ranch house low,
Of cowboys and Indians
Of wild horses' hoofs
Thundering, thundering nearer—
Finding themselves waist-deep in water,
It was the blow,
To find friends dead
That were lying with mothers;
The surging seas and the dread,
Of the open boats.

A memorial service for the dead children was broadcast on the BBC Children's Hour. Hearing one speaker, deeply moved, read the text—'And God shall wipe away all tears from their eyes'—was for many others, their own children safe at home or in reception areas, 'the saddest moment of the war'[70].

On 28 September Churchill told the Defence Committee, 'In view of this recent disaster to the ship carrying women and children to Canada, the future of evacuation overseas of children must cease.' At that point the US Committee still had 3,500 children on its registry and had already engaged sea passage for 1,000 of them. It was left for those still in transit to arrive.

On 30 September the *New York Times* had a headline '"All's well"salute to NY as British children arrive for the duration' and the subheads 'Child refugee bombed 16 times/not a nervous case among 118 whose train and ship were attacked repeatedly/joyful on arrival here.' On 3 October, a day two shiploads of children arrived in New York under Committee sponsorship, evacuation came to an abrupt end with the British Government's formal withdrawal of encouragement. Four groups of evacuees waiting to embark were sent home. On the same day the Canadian government announced the end of evacuation for the winter. Nine parties totalling 1,532 children had arrived in the Dominion.

The organisers of one privately sponsored group who were already embarked decided that they should stick to their plans. This was a group of boys and girls from the Actors' Orphanage in Chertsey, Surrey. In early July they had been assembled and told by the Actors' Orphanage Committee Secretary Peter Jackson, 'Noel Coward and the committee consider it advisable that all the children under the age of 15 be evacuated to Hollywood in California. . . . We have written to all your parents and guardians to seek their consent. Noel Coward is on his way to Hollywood to make all the arrangements.' It was decided that fifty-four children would travel, with ten too old and the parents of ten others declining permission. A news story in the *Evening Standard*[1] announced that they were to be duration guests of Douglas Fairbanks, Jr, who 'has already posted a cheque for $6,000—as "bond" for the children—to the British Embassy in Washington'.

Children from the Actors' Orphanage when told they were going to the USA.

The Orphanage party was due to sail in early September in the *Empress of Australia* but departure was postponed for a week. Granville Bantock, who was then 14 ″, remembers, 'As the coaches made the journey to Euston station we could hear the guns and bombs. It was to be the last day of the battle of Britain and the Germans had sent over a huge force of bombers. The boy sitting next to me remarked, "We may never get to Euston, let alone Hollywood."' Because it was a private evacuation the ship could travel unescorted.

Although many children, particularly those younger ones like us, were unconscious of the dangers, some children on ships that came through unscathed were not untouched by the realities. Sheila Christine, 12, and her older sister Pat and younger brother Jock McDougall were in a convoy of some forty ships that went via Newfoundland to Halifax. Under attack by submarines the convoy had been forced to disperse. On embarking it had been difficult not to feel a little nervous, Sheila remembers, but she was greatly encouraged when she saw the long, shining white passages of their ship *Newfoundland* that led to their cabins and could not imagine them at the bottom of the sea. One evening as she was saying goodnight to Jock and his friend William Paterson, they heard a strange, metallic bump, as if the ship had hit something hard. A stewardess told her not to worry about it. In the early morning she saw a ship sink before their eyes without survivors, and they spent a lot of time standing by the lifeboats. Richard Price who was in the same convoy remembers people sliding down their sloping deck and asking his mother why they didn't stop to pick them up. They would be 'sitting ducks', she replied, and the escorts would come back. But their destroyer escort had already left to shepherd an East-bound convoy. Five ships had been sunk that night including the *Clan McPhee* which Sheila had earlier waved to as it had sailed along besides them. The bump had been a torpedo that failed to explode.

'Fear remained with me for several days,' she says, 'the fear of an awful metallic bump which would explode instantly into chaos and death.' As no second bump came they gradually regained confidence, unaware of course that submarines lurked all the way to the North American coast.

Several hundred children came privately as late as mid-October sailing from Glasgow on the *Cameronia*. A young Texas-bound Scot, Ian Skinner, says that before arrival the Scottish children in the party were encouraged to wear kilts if they had them: 'Most of us did and I have a faded cutting from a New York newspaper describing the sensation we caused. I recall leaning against some wet paint while looking at the Statue of Liberty and making a mess of my tweed jacket, being rushed below for the application of turpentine and missing the actual docking.'

The evacuation project was officially 'held in abeyance' for the winter but by the end of the summer it had anyway become evident that Britain did not possess enough ships or enough escorts to carry and protect the nearly 200,000 children preparing for safety overseas. The sinking of the *City of Benares* made it clear that the whole endeavour was too dangerous.

Following CORB's decision to stop and after consultation with the United States Committee, the American Committee decided 'to suspend its activities in sending children to America during the winter months'. On 8 October Lawrence Tweedy, who was chairman of the US Chamber of Commerce in London, wrote on behalf of the American Committee to Shakespeare, 'I regret exceedingly that we have had to close down our operations, but in view of all the dangers on the high seas these days we had no option but to come to the same conclusion as that reached by HMG and your organisation.' Marshall Field, Chairman of the United States Committee, cabled:

THE UNITED STATES COMMITTEE AT MEETING THIS MORNING EXPRESSED ENTIRE UNDERSTANDING OF AND SYMPATHY WITH DECISION OF BRITISH GOVERNMENT AS TO TEMPORARY SUSPENSION OF EVACUATION OF CHILDREN FROM GREAT BRITAIN DUE TO DEMONSTRATED RISKS THE UNITED STATES COMMITTEE WILL CARRY OUT ALL OBLIGATIONS FOR CARE OF CHILDREN ALREADY IN THE UNITED STATES AND WILL KEEP ALIVE ALL NECESSARY MACHINERY FOR RESUMPTION AT SOME FUTURE TIME WHEN CONDITIONS MAY PERMIT.

Considering the risks involved it is fortunate that more ships were not sunk and more children not drowned. On 17 August, while my brother and I were still at sea, Hitler had lifted all restrictions on U-boat targets. Neutral as well as enemy shipping would be sunk on sight. Tonnage lost rose from 382,000 in July to 394,000 in August and 442,000 in September. The fact that some merchant ships who carried children were armed, as was the case with our *Duchess of York*, led Goebbels to defend sinkings, commenting that 'the device of putting children in auxiliary cruisers and calling them children's export ships might be extended to munitions factories; through the presence of a few children they would acquire the status of orphanages.'

The first sinking of ships with evacuees had not been enough to dampen the enthusiasm for evacuation by sea either in Britain or the United States, particularly as all the children were saved. The *New York Times* in an editorial supporting evacuation pointed out that only about one seventh of one percent of convoyed British ships had been sunk in the war and the percentage of passengers lost was far smaller: 'There is no reason why one near-disaster should interrupt the effort to bring as many children as possible from Great Britain to the safety of the New World.' A Gallup Poll taken in the US after the *Benares* sinking showed that Americans were now far more ready than before to risk their neutrality to help Britain.

The first sinking, however, was to bring home to parents in Britain who were going through with evacuation of the real dangers to which they were submitting their children, even with escorted convoys. It also increased the sense of urgency in the United States of the need to find homes for the children. The second sinking convinced the authorities in Britain that the exodus had to stop. Over the next months only a trickle of evacuees crossed the Atlantic.

On the morning after the disaster Shakespeare's first concern was to disembark all children who might have already boarded ships. He phoned Glasgow and 600 children, bitterly disappointed and many in tears, were landed at the last moment. Fortunately, for one of the ships from which they were disembarked was torpedoed and sunk within 12 hours of sailing.

7

In a New World

By this time, as the war in Europe went on escalating, English children were pouring into the United States to seek refuge from the falling bombs. My father took on an entire nursery of fifteen children and their teachers, rented a large country house near Warrenton, Virginia, furnished it hastily, and lodged them for the duration of the war. It was called Clover Croft School.
—*Katherine Graham,* Personal History

Right across the continent evacuees had landed in a variety of homes and situations, a few of them exotic. Peter Isaac, later a documentary film maker and author, found himself in Hollywood, taken in by film producer Hall Wallis. To him evacuation was five idyllic years at poolside, watching 'an endless parade of celebrities and sycophants'. One of the film stars he remembers best was young Ronald Reagan. The later US president taught him and his sister to swim. 'He was really very, very nice.' Chris Eatough lived with his mother's sister in New York. He spent the school years at Phillips Andover Academy in Massachusetts. Enlisted in the high school soccer team, his captain that first year was a skinny senior, George Bush. A retired construction supervisor, he recalls Bush as a friendly, athletic guy who was well liked. At Princeton an evacuee had an old man help her with her math homework—it was Albert Einstein. In Dayton, Ohio, Anthony Bailey went trick or treating one Halloween and was rewarded with a silver dollar by Orville Wright, the pioneer of flight. The silver dollar was a precious possession he would later take home to England. Ann, Venetia and Oliver Gates were three children taken in by the

Felix Frankfurter family. Their father, Sylvester Gates, had studied and worked with the American justice system. Soon the justice was regaling Washington with stories about the children. President Roosevelt remarked that he would like to meet them. So, accompanied by their nanny, the children called at the White House. Later the justice called the president to thank him and tell him that he had made a marvellous impression on the children, except that is on Oliver, who seemed a little reserved in his reaction. 'Send him over and give me half an hour with him alone,' said Roosevelt. It really troubled the President, commented Frankfurter, 'that someone held out against his charm'.

British children, including the author and his brother, Gerald, and Faith and Toby Coghill at Sylvia Warren's home in Dover (MA). Also in the photo Dominik and Oliver Lobkowicz, Richard Price, Margaret and Tim Sturgis, Michael and Jennifer Hankey, Jane, Ann and Julian Seymour.

The 54 children from the Actors' Orphanage faced a big disappointment when they landed in Canada. They were told that they were not going after all to Hollywood but to New York where they would join the Edwin Gould Foundation. But, as Granville Bantock observed, 'Soon realising that we were away from the food rationing, blackout and bombs of the war, we quickly settled in, grateful for now being guests in the United States. Going from blacked out England to a New York ablaze with light was an incredible experience, as were the generous, kind people all around who helped us. We were, of course, very worried about our families back home facing the mighty German army poised across The Channel.'

Not long after arriving at the Foundation Granville received a letter from Hollywood. It was from actress Dame May Whitty introducing herself as his sponsor but saying it would be impossible for her to travel to New York to see him. Instead she asked her daughter, Margaret Webster, a theatrical producer involved with the Shakespeare Foundation in New York, to act for her. The list of Hollywood sponsors for the children included most of the British actors and actresses living in California and they would visit the children at the Foundation whenever they were in New York. Charlie Chaplin came several times and so did Cary Grant and Douglas Fairbanks. 'When Joan Fontaine visited I fell madly in love in spite of her husband Brian Aherne coming with her,' says Granville.

Brenda Lorden, another of the students, who was later to marry Granville, still has an autograph book containing many of the visitors like Charlie Chaplin, Ronald Colman and Boris Karloff. Gertrude Lawrence wrote in the book that it was wonderful to have the children safe in America with these generous and helpful people, and ended ' "There'll always be an England" so "thumbs up".' Brenda was quoted in the *New York Journal American*: 'Brenda Lorden, 11-year-old refugee, likes toys, too—but the one gift she asks for is *Peace*! "That would be the very best present," says Brenda. "Next would be—*going home!*"'

Boris Karloff arranged for all the boys and girls to see *Arsenic and Old Lace* in which he was starring and when Chaplin came to New York he had them bussed to a huge cinema to see his latest film *The Great Dictator*. 'We were asked to sing "There'll always be an England"' remembers Granville. 'I was a little embarrassed by this but thoroughly enjoyed the film.'

Many Americans likewise did what they could to make the evacuees feel at home. Mr. Griffin, principal of the Foundation, had heard that a British warship was under repair in Brooklyn naval dockyard and contacted the ship's captain who immediately invited all 54 children on board his ship—the cruiser *Phoebe*—for a real English tea. 'It was a welcome taste of home to hear the English voices of the crew as they told their stories, entertaining us and making us feel welcome,' says Granville. Another time Griffin came into the playground and asked if anyone would like to ride in his big Buick car. About ten pupils squeezed inside and he drove them to Pelham Sound and there, anchored a short way off, was a large merchant ship flying the Red Ensign. 'I thought you'd like to see the flag,' he said.

First days in an American school were a challenge to all evacuees. Again, it depended on age and the kind of preparations made at schools how we all responded. Few can have had the variety of responses that Granville Bantock ran into at his school in New York where twenty English children found themselves surrounded by 6,000 Americans. They marched in to their first homeroom to Land of Hope and Glory. 'Great,' thought Granville, 'a gesture to us English kids. Not so, I quickly learned from the boy sitting next to me who exclaimed; "It's the finest American patriotic song ever written."' Like many of us they had to pledge allegiance to the flag, and in their case to sing God Bless America and listen to readings from the Gettysburg address.

'We only had to say two words,' remembers Granville, 'to be immediately recognized as "Limeys".' Several of the English boys were still in short trousers which was even worse: 'Where's the other half of yer pants?' At his first history class he was introduced to the teacher, Miss Reynolds. 'When all the students were settled, the teacher stood up so we were expecting the lesson in history to start. Instead, she began with, "Now class, I am going to tell you all about the British and the way they've treated the Irish."' She was of Irish extraction. For what seemed an age she delivered a tirade of abuse about Britain and the British, hardly pausing for breath. When Granville didn't answer back a girl next to him stood up and told the teacher to shut up: 'Don't be abusive, get on with American history or I'll take the matter up with the principal.' Miss Reynolds then apologized. And there was no repetition. 'In fact she helped me as time went by. The girl who came to my rescue was Mary Ann, my first American friend and someone who was to set me on course for the wonderful world of music.'

His first English class was entirely different. Again he introduced himself to the teacher. After a while she said, 'Class, we are extremely fortunate to have one of the English boys join us—please stand up Granville.' There was a chorus of 'Hi, Granville'. Then she said, 'I'm going to ask him to read a page from this book, please come up here Granville.' 'I was acutely shy; we had never done this at Silverlands[72]. There were thirty-five strange faces staring at me. I read out the whole page and when I had finished she asked me to sit down, saying, "Thank you, we all enjoyed that."' 'Now class,' she continued, "before Christmas I want every single one of you to speak just like that, with no slurring—just good, solid English.' A boy at the back immediately stood up, 'Please, teacher," he said, 'I didn't understand a single word.' It became a weekly event for the students really did like to hear him speak.

Accent exposed the children in Canada as well as the United States to ribbing[73]. On a warm autumn day someone asked for a classroom window at

Shelburne Academy to be opened. 'Oh, yes please, could we?' said Sheila Christine. 'It's jolly hot.' And every kid turned to his or her neighbour and repeated, 'Oh, yes, it's jolly hot!' Sheila says, 'I wished I could die and I resolved not to say anything again until I had acquired the Canadian accent.' Jock and William, in their kilts, experienced a similar embarrassment when, arriving in Newfoundland, they were made fun of by the local youth for wearing 'skirts'.

Ten-year-old Jean Phillips found the first few months with an aunt and uncle in California 'very strange'. 'On my first night,' she says, 'I thought I was still at home when I was woken by sirens which sounded just like the air raid sirens. They terrified me at first, only to be told it was the fire brigade, ambulances or police. The second thing to upset me was the search lights used for advertising that reminded me of the night back home when we saw them picking up two planes in a dog fight over the Wirral as we were running to our air raid shelter in the garden.'

As we started school a year earlier than in the United States, many of us found ourselves either with comparatively easy work or put in with those a year older. One evacuee commented, 'It is simply lovely going to school again. You don't do hardly any work at all.' George Forester, whose father, author C.S.Forester, was working for the British Information Services in America, found that the school didn't believe his birth certificate 'because England couldn't have as good an education system as California'.

Wilkinson, who was moving in an older circle than I was at Milton, found that as soon as his English accent was heard, heads turned, and the question came, 'How do you like America?' This enthusiastic response was followed by, 'How's the old country?' 'This usually floored me,' he writes, 'as I was unable to serve up a concise piece on England's perilous situation. Often many uncomplimentary comments were made about George III, though not too unkind, and being Massachusetts, heavy jokes about the Boston tea party. In self-defence, I developed a strong American accent.'

Lord Montagu was enrolled at Ridley College, Toronto. At the time there were strict currency controls imposed on money leaving Britain and it helped greatly that Ridley agreed to waive payment of fees of evacuees until after the war ended. An editorial in the school magazine commented: 'A stroll through the Lower School dormitories this year will convince any visitors that, without question, "there'll always be an England". A considerable representation from that island has invaded Ridley and consolidated its forces. Should more follow, this peaceful invasion will already have done its work of improving further the understanding between Canada, England and the United States.'

In October, two months after we arrived, Princess Elizabeth, then 14, made her radio debut in a broadcast to child evacuees abroad. The *New York Times* report from London stated, 'It was the first time the 14-year old heiress apparent to the British throne ever had spoken publicly. Her fresh, clear voice, which many listeners here thought resembled her mother's, carried a message of hope around the world, as well as through this country, where she and ten-year-old sister, Margaret Rose, have remained despite the menace of German bombs. While she was speaking there was no air raid going on.' Princess Elizabeth said: 'To you living in new surroundings, we send a message of true sympathy and at the same time we would like to thank the kind people who have welcomed you to their homes in the country…. I can truthfully say to you that all we children at home are full of cheerfulness and courage. We are trying to do all we can to help our gallant sailors, soldiers and airmen, and we are trying, too, to bear our own share of the danger of sadness and war….And when peace comes, remember, it will be for us, the children of today, to make the world of tomorrow a better and happier place.' Princess Margaret spoke a few words at the end. One British paper commented, 'Her voice came as a surprise, the secret that she would join in the broadcast had been well kept.'

Earlier that day Shakespeare had made a broadcast to British children evacuated to Canada and the US. He told them they had a war duty to perform and said they had to show their new 'parents and friends' Britain's gratitude for providing them with safe shelter from the dangers of war and sending aid to this country's war against its enemies. He invited evacuee children in Canada to write him letters explaining 'why I love Canada'. Prizes would be awarded for the four best letters.

At various times starting in 1941 opportunity was given for evacuees in the US to exchange messages with parents through the radio. In January, for instance, young John Spooner, in Winnipeg, was one of seventeen British war guests, eight in the United States and nine in Canada, who spoke by transatlantic radio to their parents. The *Winnipeg Tribune* reported that he chatted with his father in the RAF and his mother, in Chelmsford: 'John spoke from the CKY studios, told his father and mother he now weighed 90 pounds, was learning to ride a pony, and that it was 28 degrees below zero in Winnipeg. "Pardon", said father, "That's a long way down".'

In December 1941 the Mathews children in Ohio had their chance to broadcast home. Their American hosts filmed them doing so and sent the film to the parents. John Mathews thanked them: 'I eventually managed to hire a projector and screen, and the film was shown after tea on Xmas evening to an audience of seventeen. I had never used a projector before but I had a private tryout and then it ran three times on the night. You should have heard the children scream with delight when they recognized their cousins. We recognized you, Jean, using the typewriter and especially enjoyed the bit where Warren got all tied up with the presents at the birthday party. I have shown the film fifteen times now and kept the projector a week, but however much they sting me for the rental it will be worth it to have seen a filmed record of our children's stay in America.'

Vivien Brawn and her brother David in Wellesley Hills went early on for their first radio broadcast. 'It was difficult,' she says, 'as we had to make statements instead of holding a conversation. The second occasion was much easier as our mother was in a BBC studio and we were in a Boston studio and we were able to speak to each other.' In a letter her mother had written that she was thinking of getting a goat so they would have their own milk supply. Their house had its own gateway into a large park in Wellingboro where the goat could be pastured. With her love of animals this idea fascinated the 11-year-old. To her disappointment her mother did not want to talk about goats but about what clothes she was wearing. Her mother later explained to her that each mother had been assigned a topic to speak about so all the conversations would not be the same. Unfortunately she had been given 'clothes'. 'This insistence on clothes added an air of unreality to the proceedings and knocked me off my stride. After the broadcast we were given vanilla ice cream cones as our reward. Newspaper photographers gathered us together for a group picture but they wanted our dalmatian in the front of the group. They insisted that I give my cone to the dog so he would stay there, promising me another cone if I would do so. They got their pictures but I never got another cone and left feeling I had been unfairly treated. That's life.'

This structured broadcast was a little like the cablegrams which Canadian guest children could send home each month. They could choose from a list of messages provided by CORB. These ranged from 'I am having a good time chins up love' to 'thanks for lovely presents writing', from 'parcel received many thanks love' to 'have left hospital and am quite well again'. Though rather restricted in content they proved useful.

In a BBC series, *Hello, Children*, in April 1943, broadcasts were limited to 30 seconds each. When the idea of broadcasts was first suggested it was thought in the United States that the children might be too upset, that 'the parents would find the pain of separation accentuated'. But it didn't work out that way. 'The children thought it was wonderful,' reported the *New York Times*, 'and now clamor to speak over the air. With parents it is the same. It's only the listeners-in who do the weeping.' Twelve-year-old Ann Brunsdon in

Stamford (CT) did well in her broadcast and the local station offered her a job on Saturday mornings. She so took a liking to radio at that time that years later she found herself working for the BBC Overseas Service.

For Henry Jacobs, who was evacuated with his mother and sister Ann to Pittsburgh to his mother's cousin, the opportunity to broadcast was 'a major event'. He recalls that he and Ann were taken by bus to the radio station in downtown Pittsburgh along with a dozen or so other evacuees to broadcast messages home. 'Gracie Fields was the host and I remember her singing "The White Cliffs of Dover" and "Tomorrow Just You Wait and See" and all the moms crying and maybe we did as well—because our mums were!'

One of the songs that Gracie Fields sang early in the war 'with a tender thought to all evacuated children' was

> Goodnight children ev'rywhere,
> Your mummy thinks of you tonight.
> Lay your head upon your pillow,
> Don't be a kid or a weeping willow.
> Close your eyes and say a prayer,
> And surely you can find a kiss to spare.
> Tho' you are far away, she's with you night and day,
> Goodnight children ev'rywhere.[74]

Ruth Hutchison found the broadcasts a 'kind thought but proved to be painfully emotional'. The family were told the date and gathered round the set as message after message was read out by parents in Britain. Many parents broke down. Then came her father's cheerful voice: 'Hullo, Anne, Ruth, Janet and Lesley—this is daddy speaking.' 'I was thrilled, but it was the voice of a stranger, with a strange accent.'

By then, too, most children had picked up traces of a Canadian or American accent and the BBC began to caution parents against commenting on their children's accents as it often upset them. Our experience was a little upsetting but for a different reason. We went round to the home of the Morrisons, to hear our parents broadcast to us. Gerald and I were worried that we wouldn't recognize our parents' voice. And we didn't. Because the wrong parents were put on to broadcast to us! Later, the broadcast was rescheduled. 'I can still hear the tears in your mother's voice,' Jinny wrote me more than fifty years later. 'I remember your mother being so choked up she could hardly speak and then your father spoke while she collected herself.' We also recorded disks that were then sent to our parents. I recited two poems that I can still remember in part and Gerald sang the song, 'Oh dear, what can the matter be, Johnny's so long at the fair.' Jinny claims I recited *Gunga Din* but I don't remember doing so. The BBC has not kept the recordings.

We, like other evacuees, were quickly caught up in American rituals like Halloween and Thanksgiving and with them new foods whether it was hamburgers or hotdogs, corn on the cob, sugar on tomatoes, or peanut butter and jelly sandwiches. Brian Joseph, who was in Norfolk, Virginia, wrote home, 'Since my arrival I have done many things. Mostly the thousands of new foods I've tried. I've tried corn on the cob which was not so bad and much else. What surprises me is that I actually like most of these new dishes. You would faint if you knew what I now can eat, I'm getting over my nervousness of trying new food.' Angela Pelham also in Virginia, explaining to her parents the significance of Thanksgiving to Americans, added, 'Thanksgiving Day is usually the third Thursday in November but for the last year or two Mr. Roosevelt has made people keep it earlier because it comes rather near Christmas and the shop people would do a better trade if it was put earlier, so it was the first Thursday in November this year, but lots of people in the Northern states wouldn't agree to the day being altered, and some of them are even keeping two Thanksgiving Days.'

Christmas 1940 seems to have been special to all evacuees. Richenda Pease's only disappointment was that 'nobody gave me a book'. Twelve-year-old Caroline and ten-year-old Eddie Bell in New Milford wrote about their first Christmas away from home: 'It was a lovely, frosty night with no moon but lots of stars…. As we got near the village we began to pass little lighted Christmas trees in front of the pretty white houses. We had never seen any before as there are none outdoors in England…. We wandered around the village green looking at the lighted trees and candles in the widows. Then we decided to walk all the way home, singing carols as we went…We bellowed out: "Good King Wenceslaus" and other familiar English songs. When we ran out of carols, we started on hymns…It was a peaceful sort of walk….Of course we thought of England, and the blackness over it, and the people we loved there. But we all hid from each other what we were thinking, and at least the Germans had promised not to bomb that night….When we go back we think the thing we will love most and remember best about America is this Christmas, and especially the little lighted Christmas trees. They make you feel that Americans don't want to keep their Christmas happiness just to themselves, but wish everyone to have a part of it. That gives you a warm and happy feeling.'

Many children and families were involved in helping with 'bundles for Britain'. Mrs. Hinchman and Jinny Rorstrom, who had come to help look after us, knitted sweaters. 'We used royal blue yarn,' remembers Jinny. 'I must have knitted three or four.' Younger children sometimes found this sort of thing an ordeal. Jennifer Clarke, also in Boston, remembers, 'Every Saturday morning we sat at breakfast dreading to hear Aunt Helen say "Well, girls, I think you'd better come down to the Red Cross with me this morning" and groaning inwardly Bridget and I would be driven by Aunt Helen down to Governor Hutchinson's house.' This was the Red Cross headquarters. Immediately they got there they had to put on 'a ghastly pale blue gauze affair over our heads to keep our hair out of the bandages and white overalls' and then spend the whole morning in company with lots of old women folding and making pads and bandages on 'a specially marked out bit of cardboard showing which way to fold the stuff'. Some British children modelled in fashion shows to benefit aid programmes. Eleanor Roosevelt invited the more than 100 British evacuees in the Washington, DC area to an indoor White House party during the traditional egg rolling on the lawn.

Lord Montagu found himself in the position of sending food parcels to his family at home in Britain: 'The 1940 Beaulieu Christmas cake was made from the unrationed butter and sugar I sent from Canada. I sent preserved fruits, sweets and biscuits as well.'

In the summer of 1941 Colonel Wedgwood came to the United States. A biographer writes,[75] 'He sailed for America chiefly to speak for Zionism but no doubt he was also hoping to do as much as he had done in the previous war to bring America in on the side of democracy. For what the United States had already done and was doing for children evacuated from Great Britain he felt a profound gratitude which he expressed in the warmest terms on all occasions. He certainly also looked on his journey as an opportunity for giving thanks in person for "the limitless generosity of American people".'

His local paper, the Staffordshire *Evening Sentinel,* saluting his commitment, published a poem:

> From Europe's last bastion of freedom we send
> To God's country of promise, the underdog's friend;
> Whom the world disinherits, their battle he shares,
> Though his only reward is a place in their prayers.

I think that all of us were, as Janet Baker whose father was in air force intelligence recalls, 'intensely patriotic'. She would cut out clippings from the newspapers about the war and put them up on her wall. Lord Montagu, with the help of his music master, composed a song called 'Good luck to the boys in the RAF' which was played on the radio in Toronto. Like Anthony Bailey, and I suspect most evacuees, we saw our role as ambassadors for our country. He writes, 'Whether because of wartime patriotism or the Portsmouth naval tradition, perhaps transmitted in a school history lesson, I had taken to heart Nelson's flag signal flown on the Victory before Trafalgar, "England expects every man to do his duty."' That child's concept of representing country is captured in a book-length poem published in 1941 entitled *Timothy Taylor— Ambassador of Goodwill*. Timothy Taylor is seven years old. Here his RAF father breaks the news of evacuation to his son:

"Tim, old chap," his father began,
"Our mother has thought of a splendid plan.
We've decided it might be wise for you
To go away for a year or two.
Aunt Lee has invited you over, you know,
And we really think you ought to go."
"That might be fun," Tim started to say,
When he suddenly thought, "Why, I can't go away
Just now in the very midst of war.
Well, really, what is an Englishman for?
To run off now would be real disgrace.
Who'd see to things and look after the place?"
He tried to explain but his father said
An Englishman's job was to use his head,
And do the thing that would help the most,
Even if off at some distant post.
And certainly England's present need
Was friends she could count on in word and deed.
An airman couldn't possibly go
To America now, as Tim knew, and so
They'd thought that perhaps he'd fill the bill
As England's Ambassador of Goodwill.

I am not sure that I would agree with some of Alistair Horne's assessment that 'we were generally odious, supercilious and often arrogant, complaining of American food (I never had to go to a dentist before I came over here), decrying American educational standards (Why, I was doing Virgil before I left England), and ridiculing their national sentimentality (That awful hymn "America, America"), scorning their apparent toughness (We don't wear helmets to play rugger, or gloves and masks to play cricket)'. He writes, 'It was almost a mystery why most of us were not massacred within a week of arrival. On the whole we were accorded that warm, spontaneous and unquestioning friendliness which only Americans seem capable of. "After all" as one very small boy explained to me in my first week, "I guess you're just Americans with funny accents."'

But then Horne was quite a bit older than I was. I do agree that we tried to excel at everything and I was rather proud of the fact that English boys at my later school won top prizes in the classroom and on the playing field. I very consciously studied reference books so that I could say with authority that this or that Englishman was the inventor or discoverer of this or that. Miss Reader Harris who was in charge of a group of Sherborne School girls who spent the war at the Canadian Branksome Hall School, reported that an influx of energetic English girls meant that some of the prizes for work and games had passed to the English girls but that 'the ready generosity of those who but for this influx would have gained the prizes has been very marked'. Her girls were 'able to be loyal and enthusiastic members of two schools at once'.

Daniel Farson was perhaps asking for trouble when he wrote in a letter seen by one of his host's family that American men were so weak they would not fight to defend their country. When told, 'Dan, you know that isn't true,' he replied, perhaps showing his bent for later media success, 'Yes, but it's much more dramatic.'[76]

The *New York Times* had a headline[77]: 'They don't like boiled eggs in cups.' Obviously differences of food and language were remarked on by visitors and hosts alike. One young evacuee said, 'Our "aunt" asked if we would like crackers with our lunch and we looked for those very English treats—to discover that in America crackers were something rather dull to eat with soup.' One child noted words like icing (frosting), biscuits (scones), sausage rolls (pigs in the blanket) and welcomed new foods like hamburgers (which hadn't yet crossed the Atlantic), Popsicles, fudgsickles and Eskimo pies. Another noted differences at school: prep called assignments, prep time called study and break called recess. Ann Spokes observed, 'No one stands up when a teacher comes into the room or opens the door and we always go out before the teacher and never stand up when we want to say anything.' Louise Lawson's happy discovery, 'What a joy to have no uniform or corporal punishment.'

In most cases there were visits from the various host organisations to see how we—and our hosts—were getting on. 'Our scheme was very well done,' Janet Young says of the Yale committee. 'It was almost as if designed by a social worker.' She particularly singles out 'Aunt Ella'. 'My amazing foster mother had four children and looked after elderly parents. This marvellous woman got up at 6 am every morning and did 6 packed lunches.' She was shy but wrote well and in her letters to Janet's parents reported on all the good things and troubles. Her sister had been knocked down by a car the first winter. 'The way my mother described the accident my mother knew no matter what she would get the whole story. It was a reassurance.' Although very religious, she never sought to impose her views on the English children.

The US Committee, investigating how evacuees were faring, wrote, 'Some children found their first days at school particularly painful, but gradually learned to distinguish between warm-hearted friendliness and idle curiosity....Before a year was out, some families on learning that even an English child can be annoying as well as charming, began to regret their impulsive hospitality and to look for acceptable ways of getting rid of their little international responsibilities.

'The differences in British and American schooling were a great worry to the parents. The younger children, thriving under the freedom and lack of "canings" in the American schools, did not bother much about the fact that they were not getting any foreign language; while the older children tended to worry about missing subjects needed for further study back home, but found the self-discipline required in an atmosphere where "nobody *makes* you study" difficult to maintain.'

Between the time of our arrival in August 1940 until the entry of the United States into the war in December 1941 many influences conspired to change US attitudes to the war. The daily coverage of the war and the broadcasts like those of Edward R. Murrow from London, the books and films of the time, possibly even the presence of so many refugees and evacuees helped bring home the reality of the situation. By May 1941, 73% of Americans in one poll expressed themselves in favour of fighting if that was the price of continuing to help Britain. An example of the powerful influences is the poem 'The White Cliffs' by Alice Duer Miller which went through eleven editions between 16 September and 12 December 1940. Its last verse reads:

I am an American bred,
I have seen much to hate here—much to forgive,
But in a world where England is finished and dead,
I do not wish to live.

8

501 Randolph Avenue

We should all be enthusiastic to see thousands of English schoolchildren gathered here because not only will they be preserved from damage and death, but they will grow up to return to their own land with a great love of America in their hearts, a deep and grateful feeling for the people who saved them; and thereby they will become a strong ingredient of a better understanding of America among the English people.
—Dr. Vivian T. Pomeroy, Minister of First Parish, Milton, July 1940

We felt proud our family was doing something to help.
—Hinchman daughter, Mary Bowditch

501 Randolph Avenue was a large family house with five acres of grounds that included wide stretches of grass, a croquet lawn, flower gardens, greenhouse, an orchard and woods. Its animal life lived up to Mr. Hinchman's introduction. Its flowerbeds and rose garden with a small pond were beautifully laid out and tended by him. In winter it was wondrous to tramp on snowshoes in the woods and follow animal tracks to holes and burrows. There was also the new experience for us of poison ivy as well as of the skunks[78] we had been told about. Before the winter snowfalls, stakes had to be put out round the drive so that visitors to the house knew where cars should go.

501 Randolph Avenue

The house was built shortly before World War I by a German called Haas. He, it turned out, was later arrested as a German spy. His party in the house in 1915 to celebrate the sinking of the *Lusitania*, according to Hinchman daughter Mary, may have tipped the police off to his loyalties. The house stood empty until the Hinchmans came in 1923. Soon after they moved into the house there were great plumbing problems and they discovered that the septic system was filled with ammunition which they surmised was dumped by Mrs. Haas when the police came in at the front. Behind the panelling in the room which Mr. Hinchman was to use as his study was a secret compartment where Haas had kept his papers.

When the Hinchmans first arrived the whole front circle was covered with dark, straggly evergreens so Mr. Hinchman cut them down leaving just a few hemlocks at the end. He also created all the gardens and the lawns at front and back. He enlarged his greenhouse while we were there, teaching us how to plant and weed. I was to earn my first cents by weeding the flowerbeds; how I disliked the spiders in the peonies. He was at pains to point out the ginkgo trees and their Chinese pedigree as one of the world's oldest. He employed a craggy gardener, Hiram Pfyffe. Mr. Hinchman wrote in one of his books about gardening as an avocation: 'Lots of people like to have gardens; they condescend to pick flowers and to do a little weeding—even enjoy getting their hands and shoes dirty...but what do they know of gardening. Ask the son of Adam who works for them. He knows what it is to toil till the "hinge in his back" rusts fast; he has crooked wireworms by the thousand and squashed cutworms by the million (quietly, methodically, courageously, as part of the God's work he is engaged in); he reeks gloriously of a strange mixture of sweat and whale oil soap and tobacco and sheep manure....And he understands what indeed is the chief of gardening joys—to gather seed and to plant it, and to transplant the seedling, and nurse it through its babyhood and guard its adolescence, till he sees it, through his creative energy, live gloriously in a flower.'

The house had a guest wing that downstairs had a billiard table where at a young age we became quite proficient at snooker and billiards. It could also be converted into a table-tennis table. Behind the house was a tree we loved to climb and from which son John had suspended a swing for us. Nearby was the sandpit where with my lead soldiers and dinky toys from England and my newly acquired American soldiers I would enact the defence of Britain. No matter that the soldiers were different sizes and the British ones were in their dress uniforms. If the wind was in the right direction the air was sweet with chocolate. Another evacuee to Milton, John Wilkinson also remembered that later: 'Away from Milton, I fondly recall such trifling things as the delicious aroma of chocolate drifting up from the Baker's chocolate factory below as I bicycled by in the sharp air of a late afternoon in the fall.' The chocolate factory started in 1765 when Dr. James Baker, a minister, a medical doctor and a Harvard alumnus, financed James Hannon, an Irish immigrant who was learned in the ways of chocolate making. The product was first called Hannon's best chocolate. Hannon disappeared in 1780 while on an expedition in warmer climes to find the perfect cacao bean.

The Milton Academy buildings were on the adjoining property, just a short walk along Randolph Avenue from the Hinchmans'. You could go along the road or through the woods. The Academy was founded in 1798, in the words of its charter, for 'the promotion of piety, religion and morality'. The school motto was 'Dare to be true'[79]. It has always been closely linked to Harvard University. In the early part of the 20th century almost all Milton boys went to Harvard—at least thirty, and usually more like forty, out of a class of about fifty. Even as this century began 19 were headed for Harvard. In fact it is probably the only school which can boast that one year eight or nine Milton boys started the Harvard-Yale football game in their senior year at Harvard. J. Sinclair Armstrong CBE, when chairman of the English-Speaking Union of the United States, wrote me, 'Thrilled to hear that you refugeed in 1939 to the Hinchman home. "Wally" (as we boys called him behind his back, Mr. to his face) Hinchman was my English teacher in 3rd and 2nd class years (grades 10 and 11). He was an inspiring teacher, and motivated me to take English as my field of concentration at college.'

A history of the school[80] written after the war in 1948, its 150th anniversary, stated:

> World War II was hard for an educational institution to meet. The world of 1939 at its outbreak was restless, unsettled. Some could see and more could feel that something would happen soon, but almost none could foresee what did happen. Under this strain different people reacted differently. Some masters planned ahead what war service they could give; others planned how to hold the school together in the coming crisis. Some boys felt the wave of isolationism of that time, and gave expression to a feeling that America must not fight Europe's wars. Others felt that since we must get into it sooner or later, we had better get into it sooner. As early as 1937 one graduate, Frederic Faulkner, acting on that belief, gave his life with the Loyalists in Spain. With minds so divided, it was hard to keep ahead of the situation. Yet, when concrete problems appeared, Milton was quick enough to be among the leaders in acting:
>
> For example, just after Dunkirk, when plans were bruited for a mass evacuation of English children, the Academy acted quickly. Planning started at the end of June 1940—the files contain a letter of June 22 that seems to have provided a starting point. At the end of a month and a day, on July 23, the Executive Committee of the Trustees put those plans into effect. In part because of personal connections, Milton Academy was one of the first to receive children from Europe—they came from Poland, Czechoslovakia and France as well as England—and had one of the largest proportional enrolments, at one time forty-one of the six hundred in the three schools.
>
> The Academy's life was enriched by these visitors. Not only did they give it an opportunity to serve, they taught Milton much. To this day the faculties of the three schools use the experience they have had of teaching overseas students as a criterion for judgment. Milton is proud of the accomplishments of the students it sent back across the Atlantic, the records they subsequently made, and above all the friendships so begun.

Milton Academy had first communicated with Westminster School in London, with which it had exchanges for many years, offering to take its boys. By 22 July, however, Milton had word that Westminster did not contemplate an organised renewal and so the school announced that it was in a position to act on inquiries from persons in the Milton neighbourhood. Headmaster Cyrus Field wrote, 'The Academy is desirous of co-operating in every possible way with persons in its neighbourhood who plan to take into their homes boys and girls who in the existing emergency have been removed from English schools and brought to this country.' Depending on space the school was ready to enrol supernumerary pupils 'and to defer or abate tuition charges'. The Milton headmaster saw the welcoming of evacuees as 'a unique opportunity for a personal contribution to the Allied cause...not only do we feel that your cause is ours, but our admiration for the British resistance is unbounded.'

I attended the Milton Academy Junior School, the Margaret Thacher School, Gerald a primary school next to the Episcopal Church. Sixteen British children including the two Coghills joined the Junior School that September. The school magazine, the *Milton Bulletin*, using 'English' for 'British' as many accounts did, wrote in November, 'The English pupils are making a real contribution. They are earnest in their endeavor to enter into all activities. They have a purposefulness in their attitude towards work, and a willingness to accept responsibility, both for their own tasks and for the group, that bids fair to set a "new high" in the school standards for these matters.' I enjoyed art classes with Miss Saltonstall and was proud that a picture I painted of a Spitfire or a Hurricane over the channel was hung in the assembly hall. In music lessons I don't think I progressed beyond the triangle. The songs we sang included 'D'ya ken John Peel', 'Oh no John, no John, no', and the 'British Grenadier'. When I was later in the sixth grade I went across to the upper school for Latin lessons, a concession by the school as they knew I would need to know Latin when I returned to England. In my Latin book a previous pupil had written, 'Latin is a dead language, as dead as dead can be; it used to kill the Romans and now it's killing me.' School friend George Chase's clearest memory is 'the way you and Francis Darwin used to run circles around the rest of us during recess football'. I was also made Speaker of the House of Representatives, but can't remember what responsibilities that entailed. All I can recall is taking my food on a tray to a separate room to meet with a few others.

To Betty Buck, who was in charge of the Junior School, the presence of British boys and girls during the war added much to the sympathy and respect for what was going on in England at the time. She wrote me nearly sixty years later, 'We, in America, were so remote from all the horror and the agony that was going on across the Atlantic at that time and gave us a perspective that we badly needed. I think that our students were tremendously impressed by the fact that you boys and girls had come because of the dangers and fears that you had gone through and that you had had to leave your homes and parents to come to a perfectly strange place and were able to put up with all that. It was a very "positive" time for all of us.'

Sylvia Warren was able to write to Mrs. Coghill, 'We are not having the slightest difficulty with any of the children, and they seem to have settled down happily, and foster parents are delighted.' Medical expenses, she told her, are covered by White Cross and Blue Cross 'so you must make British families feel that the schools, the hospitals and doctors, everyone are doing their part for the children who come, so that no very heavy burden falls on individual hosts and hostesses'. She added that the children were not perturbed: 'It's a mercy, isn't it, to be very young.'

One of our first activities soon after arrival at the house in Milton was to help Hinchman son-in-law Hoel build and fly a huge box kite. Later we became quite expert at kite making. The box kite was to publicize Wendell Willkie's campaign against the encumbent Roosevelt for President, the Bowditches being Republicans. The election was that autumn after we arrived. Somehow when the kite was maybe two thousand feet up—we were on one of the school's playing fields—it broke loose and we never saw it or its trailing string again. We were in the crowd when Willkie drove along Brook Street. Both Willkie and Roosevelt told the electorate that they wanted to safeguard national unity, to aid Britain to the utmost and to keep the country out of foreign wars. Willkie, urging immediate aid to Britain, said, 'With Britain and democracy imperilled this is no time for third-termers to play politics with the possible delivery of equipment.' He praised Churchill for telling the people of England the truth and calling on them for sacrifice. In his speech accepting the Republican nomination he had promised that by returning to those American principles that overcame German autocracy once before both in business and war, to out-distance Hitler in any contest he chose in 1940 or afterwards and to beat him on American terms in their own American way. He would dedicate himself to making the American nation strong; but he would lead them down the road of sacrifice and service.

Roosevelt had initially not wanted to run for a third term unless 'things got very, very much worse in Europe'. On 15 May Assistant Secretary of State Adolf A. Berle wrote that the question of whether Roosevelt would run 'is being settled somewhere on the banks of the Meuse River'. In late May or early June Roosevelt decided to. Both he and his opponent wanted to be as supportive of Britain as the public allowed them to be[81]. But as historian Joseph Lash wrote, 'That autumn, the detached observer sensed the truth of the Churchillian view that democracy was the worst system of government except for all others. The last weeks of an election campaign present democratic politics at their shabbiest....A momentum takes hold in which victory becomes the paramount consideration....The pressures mounted on Roosevelt to emphasize his desire for peace, not his defiance of the aggressors.' Two weeks before polling day Roosevelt made a decisive intervention when he gave a pledge in Boston that American boys were not going to be sent into any foreign wars. On 5 November Roosevelt was re-elected for a third term with 449 electoral votes to 82 for Willkie, a vote of confidence which was to give him greater freedom in conducting foreign policy.

Mr. Hinchman was very Republican and naturally not a great supporter of Roosevelt's 'new deal' even if the president was a graduate of Groton where Mr. Hinchman had taught for twenty years. The Works Projects Administration (WPA) was known around the house as We Putter Around. Mrs. Hinchman was, however, a staunch Democrat. Mr. Hinchman used to say that there was never any point in his voting, as his vote would always be cancelled out by his wife's.

Peggy, or Daisy as we then knew her, still lived there when she was not away at boarding school at Concord Academy. Hildegarde, the eldest, was married to Herwin, an academic, Mary was married to Hoel, an engineer, and Dody was engaged then or shortly after to Mal Barter. We were taken out on his sailboat on Boston Harbor. He was a reporter on the *Boston Globe* and later covered that terrible fire at the Coconut Grove, where in twelve minutes 492 people died or were dying because the exits were blocked. I remember that he put in a claim for his suit which had been singed as he covered the fire. The fire generated calls for better fire safety. Dody's wirehaired terrier, Teddy, was great company for us and it was a tearful day, with protests on my part, when he had to be put down.

John, like Hoel whom he had got to know at Haverford College, was very good with technical things. He loved repairing watches. At a young age he had impressed the family by mending a clock that wasn't working by boiling it! He was attending the Massachusetts Institute of Technology (MIT) where he was incidentally an expert fencer. We went up to MIT to watch him fence and he came back with a huge trophy.

As with our first interview on arrival we children were very conscious of security. We had been warned not to describe what we saw on the trip out. So we were guarded in what we wrote[82]. Every letter coming out of or into Britain in those early years was opened by the official censor. Our mother was a censor. Soon after we arrived one of the family gave us a typewriter to play with. I enjoyed creating a sailing boat with x's and included this in a letter home. This caused some concern in the censor's office and actually landed up on my mother's desk and she was able to confirm that this was no secret communication. On one occasion she told our father that she had a very vivid dream about something we were doing in the United States. Some days later a letter from us arrived describing this very activity. Our mother had to own up that she had actually read the letter earlier.

Our first Christmas with the Hinchmans was special. To Gerald it was the happiest memory he had of his time in America as a child. He lists the excitements: 'The opening of stockings on Daisy's bed first thing and the poem "The Night Before Christmas"; the carols around the piano; Hoel and Mary's lovely voices (I remember deciding that if ever I had a daughter I would call her Mary); listening to the King's speech over the radio; turkey and cranberry sauce; snow and building igloos—and toy soldiers as presents. I do not know if it was the first or second Christmas that I created the evacuation from Dunkirk across the bedroom floor with toy soldiers, model boats and the like.'

The *Milton Record* of 14 December reported, 'No special group entertainment is being provided for the Christmas season for the nearly 40 refugee English children, who are living in Milton. Each child, however, will participate in the holiday festivities of the family where he, or she, is resident, and the families have assured the committee on refugee children that special efforts will be made to make the days pleasant for the youngsters so far away from home.'

Christmas in those years was enjoyable for the family, says Peggy, 'as it was fun buying toys and games for children'. It was at that first Christmas that Hoel unveiled his present to us, a magnificent model of the British battleship HMS *Rodney*, about six feet long, with one gun turret that actually fired metal slugs and searchlights that worked. The 33,900-ton Rodney was at the time one of Britain's biggest and newest battleships. The model was on little wheels so it could be moved around, and by putting dry ice in the funnel we could produce smoke. The Rodney became an important fixture in the enclosed sun porch where we had our toys, dressing up box, building blocks in the shape of logs, and on occasion some vicious hornets.

On the way to the school you passed the pond where every afternoon in winter Gerald and I would be out skating and the hill where we would toboggan. Hockey skates were a very welcome annual Christmas present as my feet grew. Those wartime winters seemed to have heavy snowfalls and with John's help we built an igloo. Sometimes we went to school on snowshoes or on skis. By the time spring and summer came round I had picked up baseball and had learned to stop swinging cricket-style at balls that didn't come over the plate and to drop my bat as I ran to first base.

Some evacuees, often depending on age or the habits of particular parents, soon took to calling their American hosts uncle or aunt or some affectionate names, even in a few cases mother and father. To us our hosts, even after five years, and later after the war, remained Mr. and Mrs. Hinchman. Mr. Hinchman, as perhaps was fitting for an intellectual, sometimes liked to call my brother Giraldus Cambrensis, the name of a Norman-Welsh chronicler in the 12th/13th century! To Gerald, Mr. Hinchman 'was always a distant and revered figure, whom one respected'. Mrs. Hinchman made us feel very much part of the family in an openhearted way, while at the same time wanting to make sure that their care enhanced rather than detracted from our love of our own parents. 'I wonder,' says Gerald, 'if because of that she might have, quite selflessly, not wanted in any way to draw us too closely to her. There is no doubt that the Hinchman's exceptional care gave me a profound love for America.' The Hinchmans did not want us to become too American. This was possibly one of the reasons they did not let us read American comics. We loved our visits to the barbershop downtown as we could read them there!

A college friend of Dody, Ginny Rorstrom, from Framingham, took on to live in the house and look after us for the Hinchmans and no doubt played an important role in helping make our transition to America so easy. 'In terms of affection,' says Gerald, 'I was almost closer to Ginny than to Mrs. Hinchman, partly because she had the daily care of me.' Neither my brother nor I remember much disciplining perhaps because it was still an age when discipline and obedience was taken for granted. Though Gerald was heard to say on occasion after being punished for something, 'Mummy and Daddy wouldn't have done that.' Our aunt, Kittie Carpenter, visiting us later in the war, returning from Burma to England, wrote home to our parents, 'There did not seem to be many restrictions of any sort, and what rules there were the boys seem to obey without any fuss and certainly no frustration.'

Jinny describes Gerald as a mischievous rascal: 'He kept me on my toes. I'll never forget one night. He had been in the habit of prolonging the goodnight routine. Thinking up ways "not to get in bed yet". Mrs. H said I needed to spank him so that he would know that when Jinny said time to get in bed, it was time! It was not to be love pats either. So I picked up Gerald's soled slipper, put him across my lap and slapped him hard about four times, put him in bed, covered him and kissed him goodnight. I went down to the kitchen afterwards to have a cup of coffee and wept a few tears. Marita commiserated with me. The funny part of this episode was that the biceps of my right arm were quite sore for a few days. I had forced my right arm to do something it didn't want to do.'

Michael and Gerald with Jinny and terrier Teddy.

Mrs. Hinchman had a cook, Ruth Bolster, to be followed by Elizabeth Gustafson, and also a maid, Marita Barter, who later married Carl Lundin. She had come over from Sweden to work and had worked in one of the 3-storey apartments on Beacon Street where one of her jobs there was to polish wood floors with milk to make them shine. She couldn't get over the horror of wasting food that way. When she served at table at the Hinchmans she would be called by a little silver bell with Mr. Micawber on it. Also a bell under the carpet which could be activated with the foot. Sometimes when the table had been moved because new leaves had been added you could see Mrs. Hinchman obviously trying to feel with her foot the way to the bell. In a cabinet on the side was Dresden china and above the sideboard at the end a large black and white etching of the Roman Forum and on the sideboard usually cod liver oil pills and mints. By the window was the upright piano.

Jinny recalls the Hinchmans as very reserved. 'I can't remember Mr. Hinchman even putting an arm or hand on Mrs. Hinchman's arm or shoulder, or using the expression "Hello, dear" when he came back from school to join us for lunch. They were not very demonstrative. We all called them Mr. and Mrs. Hinchman.' Jinny wrote me recently, 'I know Mrs. H gave you boys hugs when she was proud of something you did—like some activity at school or reciting that long poem you memorized—was that "Gunga Din"? Or when you returned from camp—I'm sure you got hugs from both of us. You were more reserved and seemed not to want kisses—but you got some hugs. Gerald got hugs but we showed our love for you in a more reserved manner with an arm across the shoulder.

'When I looked after "my boys" and said "it's bedtime", you would go up to your room to finish your homework and get your PJs on while I'd read a story to Gerald after he'd put on his PJs. Then we'd share a hug and goodnight kiss. Then I'd go up to your room. We would talk about your homework, and then play checkers and at one time you taught me chess. I never played well enough to beat you at chess, but I was glad to learn the game. After our game I would give you a hug and you would pop in bed, and I always gave you a kiss as I tucked you in. Gerald was young and more impulsive and probably got more hugs during the day. There was no favoritism there—just that he was the baby—only six I believe when I started. Golly, it must have been so hard for your parents to put you on a great ship in a great big ocean sending two little boys off to people they had never met.' Jinny took us to Sunday school each Sunday at the Episcopal Church down Randolph Avenue towards the town. She would attend the services while we were at school. 'I don't remember talking to you about your Sunday lessons. Looking back, I feel badly that I didn't say prayers with you each evening. But back in those days I was not comfortable saying personal prayers out loud.'

As Jinny underlined, Gerald was very young. One incident Peggy and other family member still recall sixty years on. There was a question about an elm tree. Gerald insisted they were called 'elves.' In spite of many efforts to persuade him otherwise, he remained unconvinced. 'In England we call them elves,' he said.

For us it was a rapid switch from English songs to American ones. From

> Underneath the spreading chestnut tree
> Mr. Chamberlain said to me,
> 'If you want to get your gasmask free
> Join the bloomin' ARP[83].'

and

> Whistle while you work, Hitler is a twerp
> Hitler's barmy, so's his army
> Whistle while you work

to less politically attuned popular numbers like 'Little Brown Jug', 'You Are My Sunshine', and 'America the Beautiful'. It was a switch, too, from current English jokes:

> 'He was told to keep calm, cool and collected during an air raid.'
> 'And did he?'
> 'Yes, he kept calm and cool and he's still being collected.'

to

> 'When Roosevelt went up in a plane, why didn't he want to come down?'
> 'Because he was afraid of landin' (a reference to Landon who had opposed him in the previous election).

The pedigrees of some jokes I still remember escape me. Like 'Why did Hitler keep his boots on in bed?' Answer: 'Because he smelt de feet.'

133

In the nursery, Gerald's room, was a Victrola, an old wind-up gramophone. Patriotic records got a lot of play. They included 'Tramp, Tramp the Boys Are Marching' and 'We're Going to Hang Out the Washing on the Siegfried Line' and of course 'There'll Always Be an England—Red, White and Blue, what does it mean to you, Britons are proud, shout it aloud, Britons awake....' Another record had the 'Maple Leaf Forever' on one side and 'Oh, Canada' on the other. Others were of Caruso and Chaliapin.

Ginny and the Hinchmans must have put in a lot of thought in how to keep us occupied when we were not at school. I was introduced to photography and in my room was a walk-in cupboard which served as a dark room where I did my own developing. The results came out brownish. Many evenings we would play cards, the favourites being hearts and 'Oh, hell', a sort of German whist. And we had interminable games of monopoly which would be continued evening to evening with us usually having to settle on a figure how far you were permitted to go into debt. If Mr. Hinchman was free we would get the card table out downstairs and I would play with him—cribbage, bezique or Russian bank. I had brought with me from England my stamp collection and that absorbed hours of my time, soaking, sorting, mounting, swapping. Mary Gill, sister-in-law of Milton's headmaster, Cyrus Field (who retired in 1942), gave me some wonderful mint early-American stamps (1893 Columbian Exposition in Chicago) which really encouraged me. Stamp collecting was a hobby I was proud to be involved in because I knew King George VI (and King George V before him) was a stamp collector ('King of hobbies, hobby of kings'). It was also an invaluable way to learn history and geography. Certainly that is how, for instance, I knew about Bosnia-Herzegovina, long before the modern tragedy there. I used to get stamps on approval through the post. I had to enlist Mr. Hinchman's help once when a company was accusing me of keeping stamps I had returned.

Miss Gill, a delightful older lady, spent a great deal of time making us feel at home with imaginative games in her home. She also shared with the local paper some of the letters she received from correspondents in England, which, as the *Milton Record* wrote 'gave an intimate picture of the courage with which the British are carrying on under bombing raids and wartime restrictions'. The issue of 11 January 1941 carried extracts from three letters. One London suburbanite wrote, 'After three weeks of very heavy raids— nights of noise, taking what rest was possible behind the oak sideboard on mattresses with books, till 5:30 a.m. when I retired to bed after seeing people pass along the road with their mattresses from shelters—I come to a relative's here, but not until the gas is cut off. I was called back by the police, because the house had been broken into. I had a horrid journey—two bombs had fallen in my path—one on the railways, causing everyone to get out of the train and have a country ride till the next station; and one on the High Road. By the time I reached my housekeeper for the keys, blackout was upon us. So I went to a friend's and spent the night under her oak table, the warning for the night's raid having gone off as soon as I was off the doormat. It was most sad that the loss and destruction goes on.'

Jinny would help us with our weekly letter writing home: 'As I remember many Saturday mornings were spent writing letters to mummy and daddy. I often sent a letter with theirs, telling their parents of the boys' activities and little things parents would like to hear about. Mrs. Henderson's letters to me would bring tears to my eyes, as I knew how difficult it was to have her boys across the Atlantic so far away.'

We used to go on outings to Chickatawbut and to the Blue Hills (Our phone number was Blue Hills 3820) where, when we had climbed to the top, we would eat chocolate chip cookies, and drink a mixture of ginger ale and Welch's grape juice. From time to time there was a visit to Quincy to buy shoes or to Milton Lower Falls for a haircut, with possibly a stop at Hendries for ice creams. I even accompanied the Hinchmans to a lecture and thought inwardly what odd things gave pleasure to grown-ups. We must have been pretty healthy. Gerald had an ordeal with croup and I had a large wart taken off my thumb and went to the Boston children's hospital to have my tonsils out and can still recall the sensation of sitting in a large room that had a panoramic view of the city and then being given gas and feeling I was falling.

One of the strands of the Hinchman family was the Mitchells and Walter Hinchman was proud of his great aunt Maria Mitchell, the first woman astronomer. Mr. Hinchman's mother was born in Nantucket in the Vestal Street home of the Mitchells. They were related to the Starbucks, Coffins, Gardiners and Macys, the old families of the island. From his mother he inherited the view 'it never occurred to me as a boy that we were anything but "plain people"—in no class, just members of the American democracy'. In 1908 an observatory was built as a living memorial to Maria Mitchell. Twice, I think it was, we visited Nantucket at Easter and were able to visit her observatory. I was well prepared by reading the Stacpole books about early whaling adventures on Nantucket boats. It was on Nantucket that I learned to ride a bicycle. I used to go for long rides battling with the wind. We visited what was described as the world's largest cranberry bog. And at one part of the island had to contend with ticks and I can recall the embarrassment at one house we went to when we had to absent ourselves from the dinner table to dislodge them. It was also fun to search for Indian arrowheads.

As befits the home of a teacher, our meals were learning experiences. We would often play spelling or geography games where one person would come up with a word and the next would come up a word beginning with its last letter. If you got an 'h' then 'Halifax' was a good follow-on to stump the next person. You could be challenged on a word if you were trying to pass one over on someone. From time to time at table Mr. Hinchman would get us to fetch the *Encyclopaedia Britannica* from his study to elucidate some point. It had to be the eleventh edition which, he maintained, was the best ever and that succeeding editions were lacking in scholarship. In his autobiography[84] he notes that one of the rewards of old age is that he could 'waste' his time on a crossword puzzle or on irrelevant scraps in the encyclopaedia—'one of my private passions'—without any sense of guilt.

In September 1941 his latest book, *England, a Short Account of Its Life and Culture*, his eleventh, was published. I was proud of being given some of the text to proofread though then rather chastened by the fact that I had missed typographical errors he thought I should have picked up. In its last chapter it gives something of his views which we heard from time to time at lively meal times. He felt that Roosevelt's great virtue as a war leader had somewhat blinded Americans to the unreliability of his domestic administration in the thirties. He wrote, 'My personal feeling—I don't suppose it has great value, but I had known him more or less since college days—my view is that he was a curious combination of idealist and adroit politician. After all, much the same combination appeared in Abraham Lincoln. The main difference as I see it, is that Lincoln had thought his ideal through and understood its implications. Roosevelt on the other hand frequently confused ideals with expediency, indulged in "breathing spells" when the adroit politician found them wise, and like most reformers viewed honest opposition as contemptible. He was as sensitive as a *prima donna*. The result was that businessmen (good boys as well as bad) had no basis for long-range planning; they were kept jittery for a decade; while labor and the academic theorists continued to applaud and vote unwittingly for continued confusion.'

On foreign policy Hinchman wrote of Roosevelt, 'His great defect was his persistence in assuming that he was dealing with gentlemen; his inability to see, as Anthony Eden and Winston Churchill did, that Hitler was merely bluffing England into concessions and was making promises he had no notion of keeping.' Throughout the pre-war period few people understood clearly, he went on, what was now easy to see in retrospect, that the issue was not solely one of conflicting nationalisms, but that it was, at bottom, a conflict between free nations and totalitarian despots. 'Many, however much they disapproved of Hitler's methods in his own country, believed that Germany was the chief bulwark against Russian communism. It was only when the methods of external aggression, as of internal tyranny, bore an identical ugly mark, that people realized the real threat to an orderly world of free men. Cajolery, coercion, broken promises, invasion—the method was much the same in Ethiopia, Czechoslovakia, Finland; it made little difference whether the shirt was black or brown or red. To this conflict, unlike that of the Great War, there was little question of power politics. It was, and is, starkly an issue between orderly government by free peoples and government by enslavement of the world to the dictates of ruthless autocrats.'

9
Pride and Prejudice

The common denominator of the nation's idealism has remained the same.
—Arthur Bryant

Over the fireplace in the Hinchman's living room was an old map of London and the Thames. Under the window on the right was an oak table on which sat different magazines like the ever-familiar, yellow-covered *National Geographic* and the *Illustrated London News*. By the side of the window were shelves of 76 albums of symphonies and other classics, including Prokofiev's 'Peter and the Wolf'—the Hinchman children were very musical and all played instruments—and next to it the radio where I could plug in and could listen on a head set without disturbing the family. Every day I was allowed fifteen minutes except Saturday, I think it was, when I could listen to the Lone Ranger which was half an hour. Programs were broadcast by WHDH from the Hotel Terrain in Boston and WBZ. They included *Superman*[85], *Terry and the Pirates* and *Jack Armstrong, the All-American boy*, 'brought to you by the makers of Wheaties, breakfast of champions'. The wind in the rigging, the storms, the creaking doors and 'Hio Silver' were probably more real to me than any television programme could have been.

Angela Pelham wrote home from Virginia, 'The radio in this country is strange to us, each programme is advertising something and a man will suddenly interrupt a lovely piece of music and gabble off about soap or cigarettes, but on Sunday the Ford Symphony orchestra plays some really good stuff, which we all enjoy listening to, and I am sure you will never believe it but

Carter's Little Liver Pills do a most exciting mystery play, real blood and thunder, and then at the end a man says, "Are you sluggish or constipated, do you need two way relief etc." They don't seem to mind what they say.'

All over North America British evacuees were acquiring a taste for American music and programmes. Lord Montagu was near the Canadian border and so it was easy for him to receive American radio. 'Not only did I tune in to NBC concerts from New York, but I also discovered the delights of jazz. Listening on my "cat's whisker" radio under the blankets after lights out, I first heard artists such as Tommy Dorsey, Artie Shaw, Harry James, Duke Ellington and Glenn Miller. This youthful enthusiasm for jazz later bore fruit at Beaulieu in a way that was not far short of sensational[86].'

My favourite room at 501 was, however, a large by then empty bedroom at the top of the house—favourite because of what was on the shelves in a large wall cupboard. There were stacks of back numbers of two magnificent British publications which between them could keep any young person or a grown-up occupied for hours. They were an education into the past and the present if with somewhat imperial dimensions. They still awaken happy memories and I reach for them when I see them at auction sales or second-hand bookshops. I refer to the *Boy's Own Paper* and the *Illustrated London News*.

In those days the *Illustrated London News* had a familiar red masthead with a view of St. Paul's and the Thames and the rest of the front cover was advertisements in blue. It was full of photos with the latest news from around the world and had a magnificent stable of artists. It had, too, what to me were the most wonderful colour photographs of members of the Royal family. 1937 was my favourite year as it had specials to mark the Coronation of King George V1 and Queen Elizabeth. The Coronation week double number had a colour portrait of the Queen and a 4-page pullout of the new cruiser HMS *Southampton*. There was also the naval review of the fleet at Spithead that month, perhaps the biggest peaceful array of ships ever seen together then or since. G H Davis, an artist who did the most detailed sectional drawings, had before the coronation done drawings of Westminster Abbey inside and out and Bryan de Grineau had exciting drawings of the latest Nazi aircraft and of the 'scourge of the Luftwaffe'—Hurricane and Spitfire aircraft. I would pore over these sectional drawings; I remember particularly a four-page pullout of the aircraft carrier *Ark Royal*, also by Davis.

There was always a regular article on 'The art of the postage stamp' and reproductions of the new coinage for Edward VIII and then George VI.

Looking at those old issues from pre-war years recently a few things jumped out at me—a description of Singapore's 'impregnability' from attack so soon to be proved untrue; an article on harbours on the high seas, a concept similar to the Mulberry Harbours used effectively in the invasion of Normandy; and a feature on Pantelleria 'Italy's strategic island base between Sicily and Africa', which of course played its part in the move of the Allied armies from North Africa to Italy. It is also interesting to see 'the world's most delightful cruising liner', the *Arandora Star*, mentioned earlier in the book, advertised with the words 'make a date with happiness now'. It was sunk on 2 July 1940 with the loss of 714 lives.

The issues covering the first years of the war occupied me for hours. The official Admiralty artist, Sir Muirhead Bone, did dramatic war drawings, for instance of Dunkirk. The magazine's masthead proudly proclaimed, 'The war completely and exclusively illustrated.' At the end of June 1940 there were double page spreads of King George V1 as Admiral of the Fleet and as a Field Marshal, complements to the one the year before of him as Marshal of the Royal Air Force. Thanks to depictions of the different ranks of officers in the three services I felt fully informed about uniforms and could later recognize comparative ranks.

The *Boys Own Paper* contained exciting adventure stories often with the accent on service. The BOP was, as Roland Huntford, biographer of the explorer Shackleton, says, 'a British institution'. Every Saturday, he writes, 'It dispensed an inimitable blend of escapism, practical advice ("How to tame a snake"), moral uplift, true adventure, first class fiction, patriotism and blood and thunder serials like "Nearly garrotted, a story of the Cuban Insurrection."' And if it was 'exactly calculated to inspire a late Victorian schoolboy like Ernest Shackleton' its copies still had me under their spell sixty years later. With hindsight it is clear that they reflected an attitude of superiority to other races and nations but this was tempered with an emphasis on duty and sacrifice and service to others. Years later I was to come across some words of Arthur Bryant which mirrored as well as anything I have seen the basic philosophy I imbibed through my young wartime reading: 'From Philip Sidney passing the cup to the dying soldier to Captain Oates walking into the blizzard to save his friends, from Richard Coeur-de-Lion forgiving the archer who shot him to the men of the 43rd standing motionless on the deck of the sinking *Birkenhead* while the women and children were lowered in the boats, the common denominator of the nation's idealism has remained the same.'

I was already a voracious reader before I went to the United States, working my way through the usual fare for a young English boy like *Rupert* and the *Just William* stories and fascinated by the exploits of World War I pilots in their biplanes in the Ace series and the battles with the Hun and the Red Baron in which I imagined myself participating.

Saturday mornings in those first years in Milton before I went later to boarding school used to include the letter home, some handicraft work on a little loom, or wood blocks or leatherwork and poetry to be learned, much of it patriotic. American classics like 'Barbara Frietchie', 'Paul Revere' and 'Old Ironsides' and British poetry like 'Drake is in His Hammock', the 'Charge of the Light Brigade' and 'Tommy Atkins'. There were epics like 'Horatius at the Bridge' and 'How They Brought the Good News from Ghent to Aix' and occasional lighter fare like Tennyson's 'The Brook'. From all these poems I can still recite verses. But it was only many years later that I realized that it was often only a part of a poem I had learned. Each had to be neatly copied out in an exercise book.

One of my favourites was 'The Yarn of the Nancy Bell':

Oh, I am a cook and a captain bold
And the mate of the Nancy brig,
And a bo'sun tight, and a midshipmite,
And the crew of the captain's gig.

For those unfamiliar with this piece by W.S.Gilbert, the elderly man who recites his experiences could indeed be said to be all these people because the desperate and hungry shipwrecked crew had drawn lots, as I remember it, and one by one been eaten by the others. He was the only one left at the end!

I don't know how many hours I would be absorbed in books. In the newest guest wing of the house there was downstairs the billiard room. At one end it had children's bookshelves where I could find the books the six Hinchman children had grown up with. The top shelves had George Macdonald titles like *The Back of the North Wind* and *The Princess and the Goblin* and *The Princess and Curdie* and great seafaring tales from Stacpoole and Dana and the mystery of what might have happened to the crew of the 282-ton Mary Celeste in 1872 and one of my favourites, Nordhoff and Hall's *Mutiny on the Bounty*. I can still remember the frisson of the story of Captain Bligh and of Fletcher Christian and Pitcairn Island. I was drawn into the trial of the mutineers and I can't forget the passage where the hero of the tale, Roger Byam, is found guilty and sentenced to be hanged and then at the last minute saved: 'I found myself at the end of the long table, facing the President. The

midshipman's dirk was lying on the table before him. Its point was toward me.'
Also great adventures like *The Count of Monte Christo* by Alexandre Dumas
and *Michael Strogoff* by Jules Verne where I was first fascinated by the
name Nijni Novgorod and *The Complete Sherlock Holmes*. I still have an
edition of James Fenimore Cooper's *The Deerslayer*, with illustrations by N
C Wyeth which was given me as a present by Herwin and Hildegarde and Carl
Sandburg's *Abe Lincoln Grows Up* by the Farleys, the Coghill hosts.

The Hinchmans had a number of Henty novels on one shelf. These are
unknown to more recent generations but in the second half of the nineteenth
century and the beginning of the twentieth they were staples for young boys
in England, like my father. By the 1950s 25 million copies of G.A.Henty's
books had been sold and in the view of writer A. N. Wilson he had probably
more influence perhaps than any other writer in shaping the way the British
thought about the other peoples in the world. They were also widely read in the
United States and used in schools in both countries. Jon Meacham, in his book
Franklin and Winston, says that both the president and the prime minister
would have read them.

Historical stories mainly of the British Empire, Henty's novels wove
personal sagas into actual events. Published by Blackie and Sons they predated
any political correctness. Henty titles ranged all over the red-coloured world
map and included *With Allies to Pekin—a Story of the Relief of the
Legations; With Roberts to Pretoria—a tale of the South African War;
Under Wellington's Command—a Tale of the Peninsula War; With
Cochrane the Dauntless—a Tale of His Exploits; With Buller in Natal—
or, a Born Leader; Through Three Campaigns—Story of Chitral, the
Tirah and Ashanti*; and *At the Point of the Bayonet—a Tale of the
Mahratta War.*

A synopsis of *By Conduct and Courage—a story of the days of Nelson*
gives some idea of the approach: 'It is a rattling tale of the battle and the breeze
in the glorious days of the three-decker. The hero enters the navy as a ship's
boy, but is soon raised to the dignity of a midshipman. He is a born leader of
men, and his pluck, foresight and resource win him success where men of
greater experience might have failed. He is several times taken prisoner; by
mutinous Negroes in Cuba; by Moorish pirates, who carry him as a slave to
Algiers, and finally by the French. In this last case he escapes in time to take
part in the battles of Cape St Vincent and Camperdown. His adventures
include a thrilling experience in Corsica with no less a companion than Nelson
himself.'

Reviewers captured the spirit of the author. *Spectator*: 'A boy could have no better guide to that story of British pluck and energy'; *Saturday Review*: 'As rousing and interesting a book as boys could wish for.' *Christian World*: 'Full of every form of heroism and pluck'; *Dundee Advertiser*: Gives animation to recent history, and its confident art and abundant spirit will greatly satisfy the intelligent and spirited boy.

In addition my parents kept me updated with successive Arthur Ransome books like *Swallows and Amazons, Swallowdale, Peter Duck, We Didn't Mean to Go to Sea*, and *The Picts and the Martyrs*. I was entranced by the sailing, fishing, swimming, camping and piratical exploits by children on an uncharted lake that had a certain resemblance to Windermere in the Lake District. I was interested to learn that sixty years later they still have their appeal, with Ellen Macarthur, the British solo round-the-world sailor modelling herself on the heroine of Arthur Ransome's tales.

All of this I have found of value in later life, even the pride and the patriotism, provided it is with an acknowledgement of your country's shortcomings and evil deeds as well. It was an education in love of country. It may have been a world of unreality but no more so than much of today's entertainment. Many of today's young people, with imaginations slightly deformed by television, have sadly little idea of the pleasure that reading can give.

I was always very keen on the series of books about Dave Dawson and Freddy Farmer, an American and a British airman who served together in the RAF. Sentences from the opening paragraphs of *Dave Dawson with the R.A.F* give some idea of the content:

Dave Dawson lay on his back, fingers laced behind his head for a pillow, and lazily watched white patches of cloud tag with each other at some eighteen thousand feet over England. It was the tenth day of September 1940, and the most glorious summer the British had experienced in forty years was still very much in evidence....A beautiful summer day, and the people of the greatest empire on earth were waiting, ready to fight and die to the last man that their empire might continue to survive.

'Well, Pilot Officer Dave Dawson, of His Majesty's Royal Air Force,' a voice suddenly spoke in Dave's ear, 'I'll give you a penny for your thoughts. No, wait, let me guess. You were thinking about your home in Boston, Massachusetts, back in the States?'

Dave sat up and grinned down at the good-looking, sun-bronzed youth sprawled out on the grass at his side. He shook his head and held out his hand.

'Wrong, Pilot Officer Freddy Farmer, of the same Royal Air Force,' he said. 'So pay me the penny. I was thinking that it sure is one swell day. And I was wondering if we were going to get a little action, or if Hitler had found out we were now regular active service pilots, and had decided to call off the war.'

'Hardly,' the English youth said with a chuckle. 'True, he's probably scared stiff now that you and I are in the RAF. I fancy, though, he isn't that scared. But it's pretty wonderful, isn't it? I mean, to be in the RAF.'

If that doesn't indicate the sentiments of the story, how about the last paragraph of the book:

Air Vice-Marshal Saunders looked at Colonel Fraser and smiled.

'I ask you,' he murmured, 'what chance has old Adolf got when he's up against chaps like these two?'

You are, I believe, what you read, just as you were when radio was supreme what you listened to, and you are in a television age to a certain extent what you watch. The modern computer phrase is 'garbage in, garbage out'. But the other side of the equation that must equally apply is 'character in, character out'. I cannot help thinking that my love of country and belief in the human capacity for sacrifice and selflessness must have been strongly influenced by what I read in my preteen evacuation years perhaps as much as it has been association over the years with men and women from many countries and different faiths who have been working with Initiatives of Change for reconciliation and greater understanding between nations.

10
After Pearl Harbor

Our two nations are now full comrades-in-arms.
—President Roosevelt to King George VI

The seventh of December 1941, the Japanese attack on Pearl Harbor, Hitler's declaration of war on the United States, and the US entering the war against both countries changed the mood of the nation overnight. John Wilkinson was in the Milton hospital recovering from pneumonia and remembers most vividly listening on his bedside radio as the events of Pearl Harbor poured forth 'and the first stunned 24 hours as the news of the attack sank home—and then the unforgettable crescendo of the national response as mobilization started'.

We at the lower school were taken down to the room below assembly hall to hear President Roosevelt's broadcast to the nation. 'At last we really knew that America was at war,' says Jennifer Clarke who was in the class ahead of me. 'We evacuees, as foreigners, were taken across the road to the upper school to be fingerprinted.'

Richenda Pease in her weekly letter home commented on 7 December, 'We got back about 3.30....Kay suddenly said, "We've declared war on Japan, that is, about to." I felt queer but being an "old" hand at hearing war declared and did not feel quite the same as when we declared—or were about to.' A week later she wrote to her parents, 'We had an air raid alarm on Tuesday. In the morning everyone had been very calm towards the war, not all het up or anything. And then we had an air raid; everybody got excited including us English (at the thought of a little excitement and showing these A's how to behave)...and at last it has got into some of the thick American heads that to help America is to help England! Sorry I mean the other way round; I was getting so het up myself that I was just writing down what came into my head.'

Angela Pelham wrote her parents, 'It seems rather more serious now, and I have never seen so many people in a dither as on the Monday morning, heaps of them were crying or going about with red eyes, and saying "I can't speak to you this morning I am so upset." I went to the bank for the teacher in "recess" and found the Aunts, Mrs. Finlay and Mr. Knight talking cheerfully together outside the drug store. Mrs. Finlay's face was the first cheerful one I had seen on a grown up; she had won her bet that America would be in the war before the New Year, but that wasn't why she was looking cheerful, she said that she knew it had to come and that now we might be able to finish it all the sooner.'

To the Woods, hosts of Louise and Blanche Lawson, and the other Quakers of Moorestown, New Jersey, America's entry into the war was a shock. Moorestown was established by Quakers as a settlement in the 17th century and the first Quaker meetinghouse was built there in 1700. 'To the Quakers of Moorestown for whom war was totally abhorrent it was a very bitter blow,' writes Louise. Dick Wood was joint editor of *The Friend*. 'Uncle Dick, who spent a great deal of time preaching peace and reconciliation, it was enough to make him feel quite ill and he went about in a sort of dazed condition after he heard the news.' He and others soon became involved in helping conscientious objectors and other pacifist groups, setting up camps where they could do work other than militarily contributing to the national welfare.

In New York Granville Bantock found that 'no longer were we just "Limeys" but fully fledged allies; the patriotic fervour was almost unbelievable. All the English children were making firm friendship with the American students: It was now "our war" and there were more invitations than we could cope with.'

Many younger evacuees missed the significance of what had happened. On 7 December Harry Collins was roped in to sell extra editions of the *Winnipeg Free Press*, receiving five cents for every 25 papers sold: 'Together with my other mates, I roamed the snow-covered streets yelling "Extra, extra, read all about it. Japs bomb Yankees at Pearl Harbor." We sold hundreds of copies and my share of the kitty was 30 cents. That was all that mattered. I never read the paper I was selling and wasn't at all concerned about what had happened. I had thirty cents to spend on candy and soda pop, so hooray!'

Janet Matthews wrote to Grace and John Mathews, parents of Cliff, the evacuee who was staying with them, 'Many of the news commentators have said in the last few days that they have been struck by the similarity in the way British and the Americans have taken the news of actual war. There is no excitement, remarkably little hate, just a sort of quiet and grim determination to go through with it. There are certain advantages. The isolationists will be silenced.'

On 11 December King George VI wrote President Roosevelt, 'We are proud to be fighting at your side against the common enemy.' The President replied, 'Our two nations are now full comrades-in-arms. The courage which your people have shown in two long years of war inspires us as we join the struggle.' Churchill saw at last a fulfilment of his June 1940 pledge to go on to the end 'until, in God's good time, the New World, with all its power and might steps forth to the rescue and liberation of the Old'[87].

Three days later one of the English parents, Edgar Fay, father of Charlie Fay, wrote a long letter to his American hosts, Huntingdon and Betsy Thompson, which must have echoed the sentiments of many whose children were at that moment three thousand miles away:

> This is Sunday. A week today the Japs attacked Pearl Harbour.
> Since then you have suffered grievous blows, and we have lost our greatest battleship. Yet I think it has been the happiest week since the war started two years and three months ago. For it means that your nation and my nation are where they ought to be side by side, with no doubts, no reservations. The faintest hearted need not doubt the outcome now. Before all the mess is cleared up I hope we shall no longer be talking of your nation and my nation, but of our nation.
> I want to pay my own small tribute to two Americans. The first of course is the President. I expect you realise the great good fortune of the United States in having such a man in the White House at this time. We were not so lucky over here, and had to wait for the Norwegian fiasco to bring forth Churchill.
> I have never been one of those who complained that the U.S.A. should have entered the war before now. (You will forgive those who did complain: the man in the thick of the fight finds it difficult to take a detached view of circumstances). Rather, having my slight acquaintance with America, have I marvelled at the help you have given us and the speed with which you have been changed from the neutrality policy of 1939. It's Roosevelt's doing. I don't know which

to admire the more, his prescience, or the patience with which he has taken the public one step at a time towards their own salvation. There is the true function of leadership in democracy.

The other American is Raymond Gram Swing. His Saturday night broadcasts over the BBC have been listened to for years by all thinking people. The objectivity of his reporting has been magnificent, and I think he's done more than any other individual to help us understand you and appreciate that your viewpoint is not necessarily our viewpoint.

I wish I were less busy, so that I could think more about the epochal events of this last week, and submit myself more to the emotional tide it has released. When I was much younger I used to think it was reason that ran the world, and that people did things because they had reasoned them out and found logical cause for them. I have since learned how subsidiary a part reasoning takes in most affairs and how subordinated it is to emotion, especially in politics and more especially in international politics. Everyone may know how reasonable some closer form of Anglo-American union is, but it takes the emotional response to the impact of great events to move a nation towards such a goal.

You will forgive me for getting this homily off my chest. They are things I need to say, though they are not things I need to say to you. You know them already. You have been in the war longer than most of your fellow citizens. You started in advance to make the sacrifices that the rest of America will now have to make, and those fresh sacrifices will be correspondingly more heavy for you. I hope Charles will not make too much difference. And I hope that now we are in the war together some way will be found of easing the dollar-sterling situation so that we may be able to contribute.

Some parents in our situation are now wishing their children were back home. Perhaps those with sons in Bermuda or Australia have some justification. But we have never regretted sending Charles and I see nothing in present events to make me alter that opinion. Over here one never knows when the bombers are coming, and invasion is always either a possibility or a probability. I reckon that the chance of warlike action in the Berkshires is remote.

Nor is Charles ever likely to run short of food, whereas we, as you know, are dependent on the Atlantic lifeline for a good proportion of ours. Which reminds me of something I have been meaning to say for some time: how the Lease-Lend shipments are easing our life here. We are smoking Lease-Lend tobacco, our buses are running on Lease-Lend petrol, and the larders are full of Lease-Lend canned stuffs. 'Spam' and 'Mor' and such like hitherto unknown products are now household words. England must never forget that monumental piece of legislation.

We are all well. Our last letter from Richmond was from Charles dated Nov 1st, and it brought on acute attacks of nostalgia to read his vivid description of the Halloween party.

Yours,
Edgar

The *Milton Record* seemed to be a little slow off the mark. Its issue of 13 December, a week after Pearl Harbor does not reflect the changed circumstances. But it was soon up to speed, as issue after issue reflected the impact of war on a local community. In the first week of February it was reporting that 58 Miltonians had volunteered for the armed forces since the Japanese attack. By June more than 638 were in service and by September over 1,000. A year later it was 1,500. Victory gardens, food and gas rationing, scrap collections, war bond advertisements—and news of Miltonians promoted, shot down, taken prisoner, or killed began to feature in its columns.

Soon Mr. Hinchman's precious lawn was dug up for growing vegetables. We joined in collecting scrap metal, flattening tins, making tin-foil balls, even loading railings and anything else we could find onto our little cart and trundling it to a collection point. Collections of scrap rubber, metal, and rags and results were reported in the paper: 860 cans, readers were told, would make a ton of scrap. '226 tons of cans this week.' 'Big one day scrap collection by Milton Girl Scouts.' These scouts, too, were the 'first in the nation to contribute to a War Bond'.

Black-out curtains were fitted to the living room windows, brown-out shades added on car headlights, gas, meat, coffee and sugar rationing were introduced within weeks. Talk at the Hinchman table was of how many miles to the gallon the car would get, with pleasure trips by car forbidden. In the kitchen I helped mix yellow colouring into the white margarine. When margarine[88] first appeared in the grocery stores it was white and highly unappetizing. It looked like lard. A law the dairy farmers had pushed through

149

Congress years earlier did not allow the manufacturers to colour it yellow because they were afraid it would hurt the market for butter. It came in the shape of a brick and packed separately inside each carton was a small capsule containing yellow colouring in powder form. This had to be laboriously mixed in over the white margarine for about half an hour. Even then it looked streaky. Incidentally, we occasionally made real butter by shaking milk interminably until it solidified. I began saving for an $18.75 war bond that became on maturity $25. The cereal box tops I collected could be redeemed for pictures of liberator bombers or a mock cockpit for so many bottle tops.

All this was reflected in the advertisements. For instance: 'An automobile is unnecessary to reach the Milton Hill House for luncheon and dinner' and 'How many miles can you drive on your gasoline ration? See our carburettor man.' Also: 'This is no time for skimpy meals. Uncle Sam wants us to eat good food and plenty of it. Buy the best at Milton's oldest and largest market.'

Over the months flags began appearing in family's windows—a blue star denoted someone in the service, a silver star someone sent overseas, a gold star that someone in the family had been killed. By May 1943 Milton Academy had 545 graduates and nine former faculty members in service. Four families each had four sons in the forces—the Fullers, Garnetts, Roberts and Swifts. Two others had three.

In the first months after Pearl Harbor a few practice alerts for air raids were not taken very seriously. Angela Pelham noted, 'We had a trial black-out the other night, so the grown-ups sat in the dark except for a candle, because Maple Croft hasn't any curtains anywhere, except net ones in the lounge, and it would cost far too much to have them made, especially as we might be leaving. But the next day we asked one of the wardens how it all went off, and he said that the Hotel had refused to turn off their electric signs in case they lost business, also one of the restaurants had said the same. So you see that business comes even before patriotic cooperation (rather good wording don't you think?!)'

'Dim outs' along the East coast which persisted until April were not very successful. The first German U-boats arrived off the East coast of the United States on 13 January 1942. Coastal cities at the time provided a convenient glow against which the continuous flow of ships was silhouetted as if for target practice. The German press even ran a photo of Manhattan allegedly taken from the conning tower of U*123*. In the first two weeks the U-boats sank 100,000 tons of shipping and the rate increased in February. German U-boat commanders called it the American turkey run. U-boat ace Peter Cremer found to his amazement that on the East coast 'they seemed to be asleep, to put it mildly…it emerged that the lights and buoys were not blacked out but shining as in deepest peacetime, for the guidance of friend and foe alike.'

Off Florida (on 4 May) when evening came they surfaced and, one after another, the men came up to the bridge for a breath of fresh air and, as Cremer writes, 'rubbed their eyes in disbelief'. He went in so close that through the night glasses they could distinguish equally the big hotels and cheap dives, and read the flickering neon signs. 'Not only that: from Miami and its luxurious suburbs a mile-wide band of light was being thrown upwards to glow like an aureole against the underside of the cloud layer, visible from far below the horizon. All this after nearly five months of war! Before this sea of light, against this footlight glare of a carefree new world, were passing the silhouettes of ships recognizable in every detail and sharp as the outlines in a sale catalogue. Here they were formally presented to us on a plate: please help yourselves! All we had to do was press the button.'

Which is what he and other submariners did. In March the total sunk on the East coast of the USA and in the Gulf of Mexico and the Caribbean was almost 250,000 tons with oil tankers making up 17% of the total. A complete coastal black out—opposed by the tourist industry—was first instituted on 10 May.

Albert-Lauritz Rasmussen, three years younger than I, at public grade school in Milton remembers distinctly the changes that were introduced as the war came and America was involved. He joined with others in wrapping care packages. 'I bought cranberry sauce,' he says. He joined in the collecting of scrap metal for the war effort. 'After eating anything from a can, the can had to be washed, the label taken off, then the cans had to be stamped on and put in boxes.' At one point there was a scare that Germans had landed from a submarine. He and others from the first and second grades were warned to be on the lookout for anyone they encountered on the streets who spoke with an accent. 'I went home from school very frightened.' The salute to the flag at school was changed. Up until then pupils had put out their hand loosely towards the flag. Now they were all taught to respond by putting their hands over their hearts. The extended arm, they were told, too much resembled a Nazi salute. Suddenly he noticed that Beethoven and Bach were no longer known as German composers, they were classical composers. 'So was Wagner even though he was more a Romantic one.' When they went to the opera in Boston, the national anthem was always played before performances of such composers though this was not always done before the music of others.

Albert-Lauritz' father was as patriotic as any other American—'I remember him going out in his white air raid warden's helmet'—but, like his grandfather who had gone from Denmark to study in Germany and who lived with them in Milton, found it hard to be as wholeheartedly anti-German as many of those around would have liked them to be. When Albert-Lauritz' mother once played *Wacht am Rhein* on the piano, stones were thrown through the window. 'As a child I suffered a little,' he says.

John Hinchman graduated from MIT in the spring of 1942, with an ROTC commission, was called up in a few weeks and served for the rest of the war in a unit of maintenance engineers. He went to England in July where our parents were able to entertain him in London, including attending one of Lady Londonderry's parties. In November he went to North Africa and subsequently served in Italy, France and Germany. He performed a unique service in running flexible steam pipes from the shore at Oran to work the donkey engines of sinking freighters and so to make possible the unloading of much valuable cargo. He was given a citation and a bronze star for increasing the efficiency of bulldozers in bridge building at the Rhine. His letters home came on miniature v-letters.

Hoel was working 12 hours a day on war work with the Foxboro Company, developing radar trainers and torpedo devices, and towards the end of the war on basic trainers for dealing with Japanese kamikaze bombers. Meanwhile his brother, a Quaker, drove ambulances in North Africa but got so incensed at being shelled by the Germans that he then enlisted in the army where he found basic training less arduous.

The Hinchmans' other son-in-law, Herwin Schaefer, had been born in Germany and came to the United States when he was 20. As the war progressed he found himself teaching German to army officers who were being prepared for the eventual occupation of Germany; also to teams of mayors, police chiefs, fire chiefs, hospital administrators, museum directors, school administrators, etc.

Mrs. Hinchman's brother, Malcolm, became Military Attaché in Tangier in 1943, then was commandant of a special Allied intelligence training establishment training agents who were parachuted into France. In June 1944 he landed in Normandy and on August 25 is believed to be the first Allied officer to get to Paris, marching with the French leader General DeGaulle down the Champs Elysées. By the end of the war he had received French, American and British decorations.

Marita's husband, Carl, and all his brothers were working in the Quincy shipyard.

Many evacuees, like Ian Skinner in Dallas, Texas, whose father was in the RAF, became experts on aircraft recognition. His bedroom walls were covered with B17s, Lancasters and ME109s. His host, William McCraw, a lawyer, joined the US Army Air Corps and was posted to the Pacific.

Many members of the Milton faculty qualified as air raid wardens and on campus an exciting development added to our perception of serving the war effort. An observation post for plane spotting was set up on top of the Milton chapel tower. In the days before radar a network of amateur spotters reported to a central, coordinating point on the movement of all aircraft seen and heard. Our post, Observation Post 114A of the Boston region, received a Certificate of Authority signed by the commanding general and the regional commander of the US Air Force First Interceptor Command Aircraft Warning Service dated 15 May 1942. Airplane spotting was done regularly between six in the morning and six in the evening. Although at 10 probably under the permissible age, I and another boy in my class, Bob Morrison, whose father was a teacher were allowed to stand watch with the older boys during school vacations as we were on campus. Bob can still recall 60 years later, '"Army flash, Cunningham 2340; one-high-bi-seen-Darby four-nine-southwest-three-north" indicating one very self-important feeling kid had seen one airplane high in the sky (with two motors) somewhere south of the chapel—looked like it was going north. That kid couldn't do Latin for diddly—but he knew the silhouettes of all the American (and German) fighters, bombers, the PBY sub-spotters—the ubiquitous "yellow perils" from the Squantum Naval Training base—and even today can't hear a plane overhead without glancing up.'

One Wilkinson memory from spring 1942 was the excitement of watching the yellow T6 trainers doing 'circuits and bumps' over the adjacent fields as he cycled home from school. They were the most common planes for us to see. I think we were a pain to recent Academy graduates who would demonstrate their prowess by diving down below the gym out of our sight and then swooping up over the football field while we duly reported them for low flying. The biggest scare was a lightning strike on the chapel tower. Observers were shaken but fortunately unharmed. A bigger excitement for the school is reported in the *Milton Bulletin* of February 1943: 'Massachusetts led America in Civilian Defense, and Milton Academy, with its observatories, being a natural center for such work, took its share. The Milton Legion used the observatory for spotting, the boys and girls the tower of the chapel. The Academy is proud of the spotting record it established, and of having located and saved a "bailed out" flyer.' It told the story under the headline 'The men

Observation Post 114A in the Milton Academy chapel tower. The cupola no longer exists.

of the watch': 'On Friday, February 5, anyone in the neighborhood of Milton who had bothered to look up at the sound of an airplane would have seen just another yellow trainer going through its manoeuvres. A few seconds later the same observer would have seen the plane start to loop and a body to emerge from the plane and start its downward course. The body possessed a parachute and the parachute opened. The plane went on its way, its pilot, apparently, unaware of the loss of cargo. As the body floated down and out of a sight a report was flashed to the Boston Information Center of the First Fighter Command, indicating the position of the plane and the probable location of the fallen body. Only one report of the incident was made, but that was sufficient for the Army to send out a search party and to locate the student pilot hung up in the branches of a tree in the Blue Hill Reservation. The Army grateful for the prompt and accurate information it had received, called up the Milton Academy Chapel Tower Observation Post to thank the men who had been so actively on their job. The "men" were two Fourth Class boys who were taking their turn at watch during the mid-winter holiday weekend: Walter A. Lane, Jr., of Milton and Anthony Beecroft Moore, of Devizes, England.'

Fifteen-year-old Tony Moore and his friend, Walter, spent as many hours as they could up the tower especially enjoying the early morning shifts watching the sunrise. They took the task most seriously and felt that they were as accurate as it was possible to be. Tony recalls, 'In the few seconds the parachute was above the horizon I had seen it and we sent our "red flash", an accurate one, too, as regards direction and distance. The top brass responsible for aircraft spotting made a considerable fuss of us.'

Boys and girls at the school also contributed for a mobile canteen to be sent to England. In fact so much was subscribed locally that two canteens were purchased. The two Milton vehicles were stationed near Reading and were part of what was called Queen's Messenger convoys. A letter of thanks from Lord Woolton at the Food Ministry stated, 'In making this gift you have done much to help the people of this country in their hour of need, not only by this practical evidence of your sympathy, but in enabling us to bring hot food and drink to any place which has suffered severely from heavy air raids.'

Pearl Harbor meant a big change for Shirley Catlin in the way she and her brother were regarded in the Twin Cities. Having already moved around a great deal before she came to America this time, she was unusually adaptable for a nine-year-old and had taken to America 'like a duck to water'. But Minnesotans were strongly isolationist and the children were suspect at first. 'By Pearl Harbor the atmosphere had changed and I became the embodiment of the little girl ally. I was always being handed up on platforms like Bundles for Britain.' She even presented bouquets to Lord and Lady Halifax when they came to town.

Lord and Lady Halifax travelled widely in the United States during the war. Lord Halifax had followed Lord Lothian as Ambassador to the United States. Having been Viceroy of India and Britain's Foreign Secretary and being a Lord his voice was listened to, even though he had earlier been regarded as a champion of appeasement. He would speak in shipyards and aircraft factories and to prestigious forums in many cities. Lady Halifax was called on to launch ships and christen planes. His sense of humour is evident in his memoirs as he records a conversation heard by his private secretary after he had thought he had spoken well at a Des Moines club. One member said to another, 'It's been fine having the British Ambassador here this evening.' His friend replied, 'Yes, we haven't had a steak like that in the Club for twelve months.' He records a vote of thanks in Milwaukee: 'Up to now there have always been some of us here who would have expected, when we met the British Ambassador, that we would find him too smart for us. After meeting Lord Halifax, we shan't any more.'

Occasionally there were gaffes. For instance, after meeting the chairman of the Senate Foreign Affairs Committee he told pressmen they had been discussing the timetable of the Lend-Lease bill, which looked like British interference in the American political process. Sometimes regarded as rather aristocratic, particularly when photos were printed of him hunting, he attempted to convey a more common touch by attending a baseball game. It was not well received, however, when he commented that the game was 'a bit like cricket except we don't question the umpire's decision so much' and he was heard to ask whether the fielders were 'throwing the ball at the runners'. At the end of the game he left an unfinished hotdog on his seat. This led to a front-page photo with a comment that although King George had eaten his in 1939 this democratic food was clearly not good enough for the exalted Lord Halifax.

The Halifax's second son was killed at the battle of Alamein and eight weeks later their youngest son, also serving in North Africa, had his legs crushed by an unexploded Stuka bomb which fell on him. Roosevelt offered him his private plane to visit his son but he refused even though his son might die. He felt that others who were not ambassadors and had sons in that predicament would not get the same assistance.

Lord Halifax had initially dreaded going to the United States but came to regard his five and a half years at the Washington embassy among the happiest of his life. At the end of Halifax's service in America a senior American diplomat, Averell Harriman, commented, 'We never had an ambassador in America who enjoyed a wider acceptance.'

Evacuees often participated in unexpected areas. For instance, sisters Elizabeth and Margaret Ewert in Nashville, Tennessee found themselves christening a Vultee Vanguard for Britain. Journalists got them to make Churchillian V signs for a photograph. A 15-year-old evacuee to Canada[89], Geoffrey Hogwood, spoke to a crowd of 60,000 people at an open-air gathering outside the Parliament building in Winnipeg in 1941. The occasion was a visit from Malcolm Macdonald to appeal on behalf of the Victory Loan Campaign. One report said that 'he publicly stated his love for his country of adoption' and that 'he was determined to make Canada his future home'. It quoted his words, 'But first I want to be in the final showdown when that bad man Hitler is put down to stay.' Mary Waghorn in Toronto ran a bazaar one summer with friends and raised $1.56 for the *Evening Telegraph*'s War Victims' Fund.

Nancy Wood, host to Louise and Blanche Lawson, wrote in a letter to their parents, 'Two of our best actors, Lynn Fontanne and Alfred Lunt, have been giving special performances for the benefit of British relief and some good soul thought it would be nice for three British schoolchildren to present her with a bouquet in thanks. A friend of mine working on the committee asked if Blanche could help. I accepted and later when I told Dick he was irate. However it was too late.' The flowers were presented backstage in the actress's dressing room who presented each child with a signed book and a photograph.

Louise and Blanche and a friend, Patsy Perkins, also participated in the Memorial Day parade in 1942. At the time when rationing was getting stricter, they rode in Patsy's pony cart, carrying the notice WE NEED NO GAS, NO TYRES, JUST A LITTLE SUGAR.

The *Peru Daily Tribune*[90] in Ohio reported an unusual contribution to the war effort by English evacuees Sheila and Dina Mathews: 'The children have given their hair for use in instruments of war and for needs of science and industry. The certificate of thanks stated "By the above kind act not only has the national need been facilitated, but the funds of the USO and Red Cross have benefited as the cash market value of all hair used is being paid into those patriotic and humanitarian societies."' The paper announced, 'Hair submitted must be straight, blond, untouched by chemicals, hot irons, waving machines, etc., and at least 14-inch length.' Next to this story was the headline 'Over 8 million in US forces.' 12-year-old Sheila also made speeches. Her American mother, Jean Strohmenger, reported to her parents, 'At first I thought that I would not let Sheila go out giving all these talks, especially as we were writing up a new one for each occasion, but finally we got one speech written up and she gives that one every time. She has talked to four or five different organisations and more loom ahead for the future. I guess the practice will be good for her. I told her that she would probably have to be making speeches when she got back to England to tell the folks over there about her life in America, so by the time she is thru she should be quite a public speaker.'

In May 1942 the children from the Actors' Orphanage put on a special musical revue. Constance Collier, an English actress in New York and Gertrude Lawrence's daughter, Mrs. Cahan, directed. The *New York Herald Tribune* reported, 'Fifty English orphans from Surrey, who invaded the lower East Side yesterday to present *Gratefully Yours*, an intimate revue in eleven scenes, received the ultimate American acclaim from 500 tenement children. Their performance was greeted by a double-barrelled, royal Delancey Street salute, better known as a two-finger whistle. From the opening chorus "California here I come" to the final singing of "God save the king" and "My country 'tis of thee", the show was a success.'

Pat Ayckroyd, who was five years older than I, was like American girls and boys her age, earning money. Another evacuee, Stanley Bilkis worked as a 'car hop' in a Texas store, while Jonathan Hema sold newspapers in the Bronx and Michael Cane was a soda-jerk in Westboro, CT. Pat worked feeding animals in the children's zoo in the Bronx and played tennis and hockey in Central Park. She had first attended Scarsdale High School where she was a cheerleader and then was at Miss Hewitt's Classes, as the Hewitt School in New York was then known. Miss Hewitt was 'very English' and 'frightfully grand' and loved to have English children in her school. Pat became head girl and won a prize for 'good Americanism'. By the end of her time she had become 'very americanised' and later on return to England was 'homesick for America'. Ellie Bourdillon, in Toronto, one summer joined the Ontario Farm Service Force and worked by day or by week for farmers who needed extra help for crop harvesting, strawberry hoeing, etc. Similarly, Lord Montagu went to work for a local peach farmer, was paid $3 a week and learned how to milk a cow and hoe and prune, pick and grade peaches. At one point Mark Lucas was with his mother Dione Lucas on a dude ranch in Wyoming where she was cooking for debutantes, staff and cowboys. Although she was a Paris-trained Cordon Bleu chef and was later to have her own celebrated cooking show on CBS, she did not then have the high school domestic science requirement for a catering job in New York. Asked for their opinion, the cowboys pronounced it 'OK, but for God's sake don't give us any more of that damn *pâté maison*'.

Daniel Farson[91], who stayed in several homes in the United States when not at school in Ottawa, had his first work, a poem, published in the Front Views and Profiles column of the *Chicago Tribune*:

O, to have a little look
At England once again,
To walk once more in London's streets
Or down a village lane.
To see anew the little house
In which I used to live—
O, only just a little look,
And anything I'd give.

Farson thought it 'the most pro-British sentiment ever published by the *Chicago Tribune*'. Somerset Maugham, whom he met in Chicago, described his poem as 'very simple and very moving. I suppose one always writes best when one is impelled by a given feeling.'

In 1942 a British Children's Prayer had wide distribution. With words by Merrick Fifield McCarthy and music by Jacques Wolfe, the 'poem was used by special permission of Bundles for Britain, Inc':

Now I lay me down to sleep
Pray the Lord my soul to keep!
If this night's sleep should end in rest
That is forever keep me blest
Within Thy mercy! May I be
Child of Thy Kingdom, safe and free!
If I should wake within the night
To see the sky all red with light
And hear the rooftops of the town,
With our own walls, come tumbling down,
Though there be death within the sky,
May I not fear, O Lord, to die!
'If I should die before I wake,
I pray the Lord my soul to take!'
But should I live the long night through,
When I arise my work to do,
May I with courage seek to be
Not safe, O Lord, but free! Amen.

In Britain several hundred British parents whose children were in the US formed a club called the 'Kinsmen' to encourage Anglo-American friendship.[92] Many American foster-parents became honorary members of the club and throughout the war letters, magazines and books were exchanged. The British hosted American servicemen in their homes and took them on sightseeing excursions. In February 1942 they began a Fellowship Trust to finance education in Britain after the war for the relatives of Americans who had been foster-parents to their children. The club had a newsletter, the *Seagull Post*. Cabinet minister Anthony Eden wrote in the *Seagull Post* in 1942, 'I am confident that a victorious peace will be achieved and that a cloud of young witnesses to the warm-hearted hospitality of Americans will then return to my country and forge a link binding our two peoples yet more closely together.'

On 3 and 4 July 1943 there were major editorials in the *New York Times* in support of Britain. On 3 July at a time of military setbacks in North Africa in its editorial headed 'Faith in Britain', the paper called for a reaffirmation of 'our faith in British courage, British endurance, British honor'. 'Now, above all other times, let us give thanks for three years of steady courage and uncomplaining sacrifice on the part of the British people. Now, in a dark hour, let us both be generous enough and realistic enough to recognize that without that courage and that sacrifice our own position would be far more perilous than it is today.' The editorial ended with a salute to 'a brave people who for more than two years held the fort for us—brave people who still have endurance, faith and tremendous reserves of unused power. To the end of the road we shall go together, stanch allies in a winning cause.'

On Independence Day its editorial began, 'We must celebrate the glorious Fourth with too little gasoline and too little rubber; with priorities crowding in ahead of us when we go shopping; with our surplus cash, if any, earmarked for Government bonds or next year's taxes; with young men going off secretly on transports, when we had hoped they might be getting jobs and getting married.' It concluded, 'This is a sad Fourth of July for a nation that prefers the ways of peace to the frightful cost of war. Yet it brings us closer to the glories of the first Fourth because we, like the Fathers of the Republic, have the opportunity to give all that we are and all we have to preserve the glorious meaning of this holiday.'

One excitement for us was a three-day visit from our aunt, Kittie Carpenter, who had escaped from Rangoon when the Japanese attacked Burma, got to India and then boarded a freighter for a gruelling six-week trip across the

Pacific to the US. She recorded pages of typed impressions which must have reassured our parents that we were in good hands. She loved the garden. 'Part of it is formal and is, as you probably know, Mr. Hinchman's hobby, and then in unexpected places it merges into woods and glorious wild bits with ferns and lilies of the valley, solomon's seal, and masses of violets.' She drew the line at my picking up a 'harmless' snake in the swamp to show her. 'I had not been in the East so long without wanting to put distance between myself and it.' It is interesting to note that young Anthony Thwaite in Virginia was also encountering snakes in the wild. One of his poems has these verses about the experience:

> How to account for these snakes
> In a boy uprooted at ten
> In a war that spanned a world
> He would not see again?
>
> Eden did not have snakes:
> Only one snake, it is said.
> We know what that single snake
> Did. Or so we have read.

Kittie visited our schools. 'Michael was in an English class. They had been given a sentence which they had to complete making a small story. I was rather amused. The teacher, Mrs. Smith, was talking about adjectives and gave the word "weather" asking them to think of adjectives to go with it and going round in turn and putting things down like "cold" and "rainy" etc. When she came to Michael he said "English" and she let him get away with it!

'There are some very nice children in Michael's class. American boys are inclined to be "tough" to our eyes and the children in class have certainly more say than ever in our time, a freedom to voice their opinions and talk in class, but it probably gives the teacher a chance to really know her children in a way that the older system of awed and respectful and dumb ones didn't. America and American ways are certainly different from England and I think for those living here for any time, far the best thing is to accept them and forget the English ways and be uncritical if its manners and not principles, and it is to be hoped that allowance will be made in England for them on their return and that our system which has been rather rigid will be elastic to include all the English children from America happily, so that they won't have another spell of adjustment to make.'

In 1942 Jinny left the Hinchmans to get married to Ted Boyd who was in the Navy. We attended the wedding in Framingham. He had been with PBYs stationed in Panama and Puerto Rico. She joined him at Jacksonville Naval Air Station. 'Do you remember that I sent some silk stockings to your mummy? She had written about how all the women were wearing stockings with "ladders." We called them "runs". Ted had been sending silk stockings from Panama from time to time, so I sent a few of them to your mother.'

Before the war even began for the United States Miltonians were serving as ambulance drivers in France or were in the Canadian air force fighting in the Battle of Britain. In the war they fought in places as far apart as Dunkirk, Guadalcanal and New Guinea. Two became generals. After Pearl Harbor 939 graduates were in the armed forces out of a graduate body of 2500 and 45 were killed. The school history records that "in a war of brains, Milton also provided its share. Fliers were rescued again and again on their way to Europe because a Milton graduate had organized dog-sled rescue. Amphibious landings were made with unbelievably low casualty rates because another Miltonian invented the DUKW amphibious craft. In the construction of the atomic bomb, the administrative ability of another Miltonian helped to speed accomplishment."

As many younger schoolmasters were in the service, Walter Hinchman chafed at not being able to do more for the war effort. He did stay on an extra year and, as he says, feeling a trifle restive at so unmilitary a gesture he comforted himself by muttering, 'Set some strong man free for fighting while I take awhile his oar.' It so happened that the baseball coach, Reggie Nash, broke his legs and Herb Stokinger, the athletic director, moved in to take his place. This left the next group, the three 'league' teams, in the hands of willing but inexpert masters. Then someone remembered that in the remote past, Hinchman had coached baseball so in 1943 he was pressed into service, about 25 years after his last effort at Groton. He was proud of his fungo bat. And coached one group each day. It was comforting, he said, to find that he could still do it, though knocking flies to the outfield was exhausting 'and the whole afternoon's activity made a sedentary evening peculiarly attractive'.

Letters from home were less likely to be censored. We were not to discover until after the war exactly what work my mother and father were doing; they had signed the Official Secrets Act. I am not sure even then they told us much. One letter our father sent later in the war contained a strip of what was called chaff or 'Window'. This was a means on bombing raids over Germany of confusing enemy radar by dropping reflective strips of metal foil.

An amusing story[93] of its development by 'boffins' records that one day at the Directorate of Radar a charming, rather slight fellow walked into the office and made a startling suggestion. 'Hang on a moment,' said the officer who received him, 'I think the Group Captain would like to be in on this one.'

'Sir.' he said to Group Captain Walter Pretty, 'I've got a chap in my office who wants us to throw silver paper out of our aircraft.'

'Heavens, what will they think of next! What's his name?'

'Cockcroft,' I said, 'John Cockcroft.'

'Oh, I think we'd better listen to this one; he's the chap who split the atom.'

So Window was introduced, with which by confusing the enemy ack-ack and fighters, Allied bomber losses were cut by 30 per cent. It is also more widely known as the means by which the Germans were confused by a 'phantom fleet' on D-Day.

The extent to which evacuees followed the progress of the war depended on their age. I certainly remember Mr. Hinchman telling us of the importance of the surrender of the German 6th army under Field Marshal Friedrich Paulus in February 1943 and comparing it with Napoleon's defeat. It ended the six-month siege of Stalingrad and was one of the decisive engagements of the war.[94] I was also first introduced to the word 'liquidation'.

Ruth Hutchison was conscious in 1943 of the tide of fortune turning in the war. Every morning as she and her sisters donned their snow suits they listened to the news. They became deeply conscious of 'the Eighth Army'. She wondered about the other seven armies and said to herself one morning, as yet another advance across the desert was announced, 'I will remember the Eighth Army till I die, and that I was alive when they were doing all those deeds[95].'

In the summer of 1943 Winston Churchill came to Harvard University to receive an honorary doctorate of laws. The citation read, 'Winston Spencer Churchill, Doctor of Laws. An historian who has written a glorious page of British history; a statesman and warrior whose tenacity and courage turned back the tide of tyranny in freedom's darkest hour.'

I was there in the crowd in Harvard Yard, a small but very proud English boy among a sea of 12,000 Americans, including 6,000 uniformed Harvard students who were massed in review before Memorial Church. I think I was waving a Union Jack[96]. A special issue of *The Harvard Service News* [97] published by *The Harvard Crimson* reported, 'Holding back the crowd as the official black cars came up, the police had trouble when the familiar figure, in his colorful garb of Doctor of Civil Laws at Oxford, climbed up the South steps to Sanders Theatre and turned around to wave at the crowd.

'Secret service men were posted throughout the theatre, and two of them marched behind Churchill and President Conant amid the gowns and robes of a colourful academic procession.

'Outside in the Tercentenary quadrangle, the mob listening over loudspeakers reacted to the speech as though they were watching the ceremony go on before them. Hats went off and heads bowed as the prayer was read and the laughter and applause within Sanders was reiterated by outsiders.

'The mass of service men in ranks and the people packed on the Widener's steps, were all silent in the hot afternoon; only a few babies crying, and the hubbub around several figures who had fainted in the hot sun marred the attention to the speech.'

After the formal ceremony Churchill spoke extemporaneously to the crowd in the Yard.

Welcoming the President and the Prime Minister, Massachusetts Governor Leverett Saltonstall said that more than 300 years earlier John Harvard had brought to America from England a faith in a land that was to grow beyond his time and a firm determination that the youth of this land should have the benefits that come with learning. Today that spirit lived again in the distinguished guest from England. 'Sir, the Commonwealth of Massachusetts is proud to join Harvard in welcoming you today. Your presence here at a moment when our two countries are engaged in fighting together on a world-wide front tells us more plainly than words that victory in battle alone will not bring lasting peace; that true peace will come only with our better understanding of one another.'

In his formal address at the academic ceremony the British Prime Minister, made a strong plea for continued Anglo-American cooperation, expressing the hope that the gift of a common language might 'become the basis for common citizenship some day'.

'Whatever form the system of world security may take,' he said, 'nothing will work soundly or for long without the combined effort of the British and American people. I, therefore, preach continually the doctrine of the fraternal associations of our people, not for any purpose of gaining invidious material advantage for either of them, not for territorial aggrandisement, or the vain pomp of earthly domination, but for the sake of service to mankind and for the honour that comes to those who faithfully serve great causes.'

He said, 'If the people of the United States had remained in a mediocre station, struggling with wilderness, absorbed in their own affairs and a factor of no consequence in the world, they might have remained forgotten and undisturbed beyond their protecting oceans. But one cannot rise to be in many ways the leading community in the civilized world without being involved in its problems, without being convulsed by its agonies and inspired by its causes. If this has been proved in the past, as it has been, it will become indisputable in the future. The people of the United States cannot escape world responsibility.'

11
Transatlantic Correspondence

At present in the United States to say that a man is anti-British is only one small step lower than to accuse him of being pro-Nazi.
—American host mother Janet Matthews to English parents

As you know we have our time of trial here now. My office has been bombed, and we suffer other inconveniences which you will read about in the papers. Every day this sort of thing adds to our thankfulness that Charles is away from it—and to our indebtedness to yourselves for having him.
—English father Edgar Fay to his son's American hosts.

As the years went by families on either side of the Atlantic who were complete strangers to each other when the European war began came closer and particularly after the United States entered the war could empathize with each other's worries and concerns. Transatlantic correspondence helped build relationships. The fastest airmail letters could come in as little as thirteen days but more commonly took even three or four weeks, sea mail was much the same but could take five or six weeks. As letters were lost when ships were sunk in the Atlantic, many families took to numbering each one. Usually censored, with a label 'Opened by Examiner' and a number[98], letters from England were often written in the air raid shelter during a bombing raid and reflect rationing, job relocation, destruction of homes and the courage of ordinary people, and sometimes parents would let overseas hosts in to what they felt about the separation. One mother wrote to Canada in 1941, 'Fancy, they will have been away two years in August, seems a lifetime, how I had planned their little lives and to enjoy their company and love…little did I think someone else would be bringing them up in the best years of their life.'

Children's letters home reflected, of course, their ages at the time. And with the passage of years letter writing sometimes waned and became more of a chore. Most of the correspondence from those years, as in our case, has been long since thrown away. But some families have kept the letters and they shed light on relationships and developments and attitudes on the respective home fronts.

One evacuee, Angela Pelham, who travelled out like us on the *Duchess of York*, had her letters published in 1944[99]. She had developed the habit of writing down something each day to send her parents. Some of her first letters home reflected the excitement of discovery by a 12-year-old arriving in the US and her own observations. She described one of her visits to her local town, Warrenburg, Virginia: 'We went to the drugstore and had the most wonderful ice cream, we caused quite a stir as usual and the owner of the shop said it would give him all the pleasure in the world if he might be allowed to stand us the ice cream. That is the delightful part of Americans, they always make you feel as if you are the only person in the world that matters and quite the most important.'

She found church attendance different: 'Church is awfully nice here everyone goes that we know and it is quite a social affair, before the service begins people talk in quite loud voices and have animated conversations, we were rather surprised at first as we have always been taught to whisper if it is absolutely necessary to make a remark.'

While in town one day early on she and her younger brother were talking with the vicar, Mr. Macy, when they suddenly heard 'that old familiar wailing' and 'we were all frozen to the spot'. 'Geoffrey rushed at Mr. Macy and said: "Where can we go, quick we must take shelter." Then Mr. Macy said "Why! Its all right honey its only the 12 o'clock hooter"; but poor Geoff tugged at his arm and said: "You don't understand, that noise can only be an air raid coming; please take us somewhere quick." And it was some time before Auntie Bee could persuade him that it was only a harmless hooter telling every one that it was 12 o'clock lunchtime. It certainly gave us all a nasty turn inside, for it is exactly the same sound, Mummy, and they do it if a house is on fire and as most of the houses are made of wood Mr. Macy told us that we had better hurry up and get used to the sound, as we would probably hear it pretty often.'

Angela's 'job' was to get the 'mail' every morning: 'The letters are left in a tin box which stands on a post. Each house has one and they are all on the right hand side of the road so that the postman, or rather I should have said "Mailman", doesn't have to get out of his car, but can stretch out his arm and push the letters in. It seems funny not to have them brought to our door, but you see it saves time and the great thing in this country is to save time and labour. The newspapers arrive in the same way, they have another tin box on the other side of the drive with Washington Post written on it.'

She sent this description of an experience at dancing lessons: 'I landed up with a boy who said he was from England. He grumbled at the school, didn't like the food which seems amazing. I don't see how anyone could not like it, he said he was very homesick and hated everything American, perhaps he was just showing off, I thought what a rotten ambassador he was and felt very annoyed with him. I don't suppose he is very popular which is entirely his own fault.... At last I got the tall boy and he was just as nice as he looked and said how "cute" I looked, and when I had recovered from the shock I managed to say "Thank you" as everyone does in America. It seemed so funny at first, if you admire somebody's house or say how nice they look, they always say "Thank you", and it is quite usual to tell a person to their face that they look sweet, and they never look awkward like we do and mutter: "Nonsense, my dress is frightfully old," but smile and say "Thank you", which now I am used to it, is a much better idea isn't it? During our ballet class everyone talked and laughed while someone was doing something alone, but of course we had a little lecture about our behaviour before we went and afterwards Miss Armstrong told us she would have known that we were English because of our good manners and polite behaviour, so it is worth it.'

One family still has some 700 letters written between 1940 and 1945. The three children of Grace and John Mathews from Hampshire—Clifford aged 12, Sheila 10, and Dinah 5—were evacuated to Ohio. The son stayed with Bill and Janet Matthews (2 't's) and the daughters with Warren and Jean Strohmenger. Their correspondence[100], compiled in 1990 by a daughter, Jocelyn Statler, who was not evacuated, reveals, according to Alan Borg, Director General of the Imperial War Museum, 'a little known aspect of Anglo-American cooperation and remind us how much the civilian population of America did during the Second World War to help their British counterparts'.

As in our own case parents started off by trying to give to their opposite numbers some idea of their respective attitudes and life styles. In those years

English families knew little about the life of normal American families. Host parents would reassure English parents that the children were being looked after properly, whether it was in matters of health or education or keeping their links with home. An American magazine observed at the time, 'If the movement from Britain becomes a mass evacuation the fondest dreams of sociologists will be realised...a future generation of English will feel a lot warmer towards Americans and vice versa, than if they had never met.' John Mathews certainly believed his children had a job to do as ambassadors for Britain in the United States, a role they were later to repeat on behalf of Americans when they returned to Britain.

Early on Janet Matthews told the Mathews parents about Cliff, 'We are grateful to you for lending him to us. We in America look with awe upon the courage of the British and it is a great pleasure to do a tiny bit for our small English boy.' Cliff, after a short note, concludes, 'Well, now I had better begin my homework. It's the only thing that makes life unhappy here.'

John Mathews responded, 'When my wife and I decided to send the children to America we had no idea where they should go or to whom they should be sent. Almost the only contacts we had with Americans were with the men and women of the American Committee at Grosvenor House, London. These contacts, however, gave us the impression that if they were any criterion of the treatment our children would receive in the USA then we would be quite happy about sending them. You letter has completely confirmed that impression.'

Jean Strohmenger likewise wrote, 'We think you made a very wise move in sending the girls and the boy to America. I assure you they will be well cared for. There have been only five children sent to the Cincinnati area.'

Janet Matthews wrote Grace Mathews about Cliff, 'Our greatest problem is to keep him from getting spoiled by too much publicity and attention. A number of English children have had their heads rather badly turned by all the fuss that has been made over them. The sad part is that it makes them unpopular with their classmates as well as grownups. You have done such a splendid job with your boy's bringing up we are anxious not to have him go home to you badly spoiled. So we have turned down all offers of newspapers, magazines and radio stations for interviews, feeling that they would not be good for him.'

Grace said she 'absolutely agreed' with the policy on the press. She also wrote, 'You mentioned that you and your husband are poor substitutes for Cliff's parents—our only worry is that you seem to be making such a good job of it that he may not want to come home.'

Janet responded, 'As to your fears that the children might never want to go home, I think you can dismiss them—certainly as far as Cliff is concerned! We fully realise he is just a loan. We want him to think of us as very special friends—sort of American headquarters—but not in any way as rivals for his affection for you and his father. We talk of you every day and we try to think how you would want things done. I know how you must feel and we are trying to strike a good balance. I would cheerfully murder anyone who tried to win my own boys away from me!'

She also wrote, 'Happily for us all, Clifford really is the most tactful child I have ever seen. Never once has he criticized any of us or Americans and I know we must seem strange to him. The result is we can discuss the differences in English and American table manners, school systems, clothing, etc., in the friendliest way without anyone trying to prove that one system is superior to the other.'

John Mathews replied to a reference to the supposed arrogance of the English: 'When I first wrote to you I mentioned that I hoped he would be a good ambassador and he seems to have made a good job of it if it is he who has persuaded you we are not "an arrogant lot who despise and look down on Americans". I assure you that of the great many people of my acquaintance, the majority, on reading your remark would say "how extraordinary". They simply wouldn't understand why you might think us arrogant. Mind you, in the old days the Englishman was taught as a boy at school that one Englishman was as good as four foreigners, whereas in these enlightened days we only think one Englishman as good as three Italians or two Germans. You see what I mean; we are improving all the time. Of course, in the old days, we won more battles than we do just now.'

Subjects like confirmation and girl friends were discussed across the Atlantic. John Mathews: 'Perhaps we should be getting anxious, though, because we learn from Cliff that he has a girlfriend now. What a surprise. Old Cliff would run a mile from a girl over here, unless that is she happened to come in useful as a wicketkeeper.' Also medical matters. Jean Strohmenger wrote, 'The girls will go into the hospital to get their tonsils and adenoids out sometime this week, I think. They are looking forward to it with much enthusiasm, but I am not. Methinks, Dinah will go into one of her weeping acts, which are a little unnerving.'

Occasionally, letters would also comment on the American social scene. Janet Matthews asked, 'Do you talk much in England about stamping out all race prejudice? It is interesting here to see how much it is being discussed. The

South still believes that the Negro should be kept in his place and by that they mean in a position of inferiority, not properly educated, kept from voting and, above all, segregated. While the Northern states have always been more liberal they haven't done much about it. Now, since we have so many colored troops and allies of all races, there is a definite campaign to impress upon us the fact that our constitution says all men are created equal. It is a subject Bill and I feel very strongly about and we are delighted to notice a more liberal and broadminded trend.'

John Mathews responded, 'From what I remember of history, it is entirely our fault that we have the problem today. As an outsider, I would say that if the Negro pays taxes equivalent to the white, he should have access to the same educational facilities and the right to vote.' He was not sure, he commented, that he would 'care to work under a Negro boss'.

Sheila Mathews wrote to her parents later in the war, 'I am going to have a girl in my class out for the night. All the girls have people to their house for the night. The girl's name is Helen Martin and she really is a wonderful girl...the only trouble is that some people don't like her because she is a Jewess and that really makes me mad. Any girl that thinks about creed, color or social position when she picks her friends does not rate very high with me.'

As the years passed and small children became teenagers cultural differences, in so far as they were communicated, sometimes caused parental concern. Louise and Blanche Lawson still have the letters exchanged with their parents and with their Quaker hosts.

She builds on them for her book *A Very Different War.*

Curfew times, for instance, were disputed. 'Aunt Nancy', her American host, received a letter from the girls' mother saying that she was shocked to hear Blanche had come home from the movies at 9.30 pm. This, according to Louise, suggests 'the news of the 11.30 night out hadn't reached her yet.' Blanche wrote home, 'You just don't know your 13-year-old daughter. You will have to realise that I am older than I was when I left England. I go to bed at 9.00 pm every night so 9.30 pm is really not very late you know. After all in America we have fun especially our crowd. In America we go out with boys as Nancy probably told you. Don't get poor ideas about me please.'

Louise comments, 'The problem was now beginning to arise of getting our mother to accept and understand aspects of our American way of life and furthermore the changes in us as we grew up away from her sight and influence.'

Later in November 1943, with Blanche 14 and Louise 11, it is evident from letters that their mother is still not happy with how her daughters are being brought up. Aunt Nancy writes again, 'I have been quite troubled in realizing that you do not think I am firm enough in my discipline; and you are quite right. My experience of forcing children makes me feel it to be less satisfactory than leading them. First because it relieves them of the burden of deciding between right and wrong which I think they need to learn early and practice constantly. Secondly because it seems to me that when "discipline is maintained" there is sometimes a feeling of unease between the discipliner and the disciplinee. My hope is to help them discipline themselves, at adult suggestion if necessary, and to develop in themselves the power of acting because they feel it to be right rather than because I expect obedience.'

When homes were chosen for English evacuees care was taken wherever possible to place children with families from roughly the same income bracket and the same religious denomination. Jean Strohmenger wrote to say that she thought the Mathews would appreciate the care used in choosing homes for the children: 'They realise that the children will all be going back to their homes in England and they don't want them getting used to servants if they won't have them when they get home.'

After a year, and the sending of a photograph of a large swimming pool, it was clear that the American Matthews were considerably better off than the English Mathews. This did not cause problems but it was felt an explanation was needed. On a form that the American prospective hosts had been given to apply for an evacuee they had put down on the recommendation of a friend 'net worth $50,000'. In truth, it was several times that figure. The differential was even greater because of the impression John Mathews, who worked with the Petroleum Board, had made when he applied: 'The whole thing has its amusing side, inasmuch as when I first obtained an interview with those splendid Americans who were running the evacuation scheme at Grosvenor House, they impressed on me the intention of the Committee to place children with families in America of about our own social and financial standing, the idea being that a child should not feel out of place either one way or the other. I can only think that I must have looked as if I had been left a lot of money—I certainly couldn't have looked intelligent enough to have made a pile myself. Grace suggests that I was gazing so fervently into the eyes of the lovely American lady by whom I was interviewed that she kept putting noughts on the end of the figure which I very truthfully gave as my income. I say she stuck a nought on because she could see I was worth much more than I was getting anyway.'

Many English families felt bad that they were not permitted by financial regulations to contribute more to American hosts. Edgar Fay, the father of Charlie, wrote to the Thompsons on 14 November 1940, 'It seems very unfair that we over here should be asking you not only to make a home for our children but to undergo financial sacrifices as well. If after the war any of us over here have got any money you may be sure I will pay you back. Of course the reason for the financial ban is that there is only a limited supply of dollar exchange and we need every cent of it to purchase armaments. I am an official of the Treasury myself at the present time, and I well know the vital necessity of preventing any dollars being used for other purposes. It is quite literally true to say that the money you expend on Charles is money helping us to win the war. At the same time, from the personal angle, I can't help regretting the necessity of it.' Kathleen Fay told the Thompsons, 'We have only one regret in sending Charles to you, i.e. the financial one.'

In June 1941 the ESU newsletter *English-Speaking World* was reporting a lively discussion going on in Britain about the position of British parents who wished to bear the financial burden of their children's upkeep in America: 'While no one doubts the willingness of their American hosts to look after them, British parents feel it unfair that any such generosity should be demanded for an indefinite period.' Mrs. Beatrice Rathbone, an American woman member of Parliament, wrote to *The Times*, asking the Government to relax the rules that prevented money being sent abroad, 'However warm-hearted may be the generosity of the American foster parents—nevertheless the first enthusiastic reception might become less fervent as the war lengthens, and the expenses incurred by these child-guests increase.'

By January 1942 Edgar Fay could write to Huntington Thompson, 'I have just received official notification from the authorities that my application to remit funds for the benefit of Charles has been granted for the maximum amount, i.e. Ł36 a year. I shall tomorrow instruct my bank to remit the first quarterly instalment to you. This will be Ł9. It's a terribly small sum, but I am very glad indeed that I am at last permitted to do something in this direction. The exchange is now $4 to the Ł so it will only be about $36.'

American families sometimes sent food parcels. Kathleen Fay wrote the Thompsons on 14 January 1942, 'Your food parcel was a glorious surprise. The chocolate disappeared instantly. The tea will be broached today (thanks very much for the individual tea bags—I take tea very weak so each one is split for me and thus goes much farther). The meat of course is a windfall—we can buy these things now on a "points" rationing system only. I have to keep these mostly to sardines and other things suitable for Peter. Our (your!) sugar is being kept for visitors—we can then say, "No, really do take some. It is quite off the ration and was sent us from America." It is horrid not being able to offer people lots of edibles. The fruit—words do fail me—and it looks so pretty as well. It will be rather nice after the war when fruit is plentiful once more. Sometimes I see pictures of grapes or peaches or grapefruit and it is very difficult to put them out of my mind. I was always rather greedy. The milk is put by for emergency use. We do send grateful thanks for your thoughtful present....I am a bit busy just now. It seems wrong to keep rooms empty so I have volunteered to take in four tinies—2-5—with one paid helper. They will sleep in Charles' room, with the dining room for a day nursery and Edgar's study for the helper's bedroom. It is taking quite a lot of planning as you can imagine. Sometimes my heart fails me at the thought of the meals and the laundry but I know that if there were another blitz on London I could not be at peace with myself if I did not do this—they will be motherless or whose parents cannot leave London. Not housebroken, I regret to say—I am warned that our carpets, etc. are likely to be ruined!—it would be simpler if I did not have Margaret (14 yr evacuee) in another bedroom.'

In so far as the censors permitted it, English letters like this gave a feel of wartime Britain. On 21 August 1942 Fay wrote to the Thompsons, 'We are still talking of the Dieppe raid of two days ago. A very heartening business! I think this country can now be said to be stripped right down to essentials for the war. Luxuries, like the movies, are only tolerated as recreation essential to keep the mind fresh. Motoring is cut to the minimum, and the streets of London now bear a thin traffic of busses, taxis, and military vehicles. Chocolate and sweets are rationed—the very small ration of 2 oz per week having just been doubled. I think this has hit me more than petrol rationing, for I am a great consumer of chocolate.'

Three weeks later he wrote, 'I suppose you are now undergoing what we are here pleased to call "austerity". I gather your motoring is as severely restricted as ours. But have you got down to ankle-length socks (for men) yet? And I imagine you'll give up lots before foregoing ice cream, which has just been banned. We are now facing drastic fuel cuts too. No one seems any the worse for any of these so-called 'deprivations'; in fact, health has been better than pre-war. Many of these measures are wholly beneficial, such as compulsory wholemeal flour, thus abolishing white (and de-vitamised) bread.'

From early 1942 on American letters, too, reflected their country's participation in the war. Janet Matthews wrote in November 1943, 'One of the effects of war in this country seems to be that courtesy has been lost to a large extent. I suppose it is the result of the taut nerves. When I asked for directions in a store recently the saleswoman said, "There's the sign, can't you read?" You have a moment's irritation and then you think that perhaps she has a son or two on the high seas or in Italy. I am going to try to cultivate an extra share of tolerance and courtesy.'

Warren Strohmenger joined the navy in 1942 and by June was a lieutenant while in the following year the Matthews' two sons were in the services. By the end of the war Dr. Strohmenger was serving on the frontline as a medic on Iwo Jima. As a result of this changing situation, the Strohmengers found themselves financially stretched and they asked if the Mathews could send some money. They responded by doing the maximum the currency restrictions would allow—£6 a month.

At the end of December 1943 Janet Matthews could report 'an amazing thing' happening: 'We had a communication from Buckingham Palace, with greetings from the Queen. I have had fun lording it over Cliff, for he hasn't had any personal messages from the Royal Family.'

It was a beautifully illuminated personal message from Queen Elizabeth to guest hosts expressing gratitude for the help and kindness they had shown to the children who crossed the sea many months earlier. It read: 'Since the early days of the war you have opened your doors to strangers and offered to share your home with them. In the kindness of your heart, you have accepted them as members of your own family, and I know that to this unselfish task you and all your household have made many great sacrifices. By your generous sympathy you have earned the true and lasting gratitude of those to whom you have given this hospitality, and by your understanding you have shown how strong is the bond uniting all those who cherish the same ideals. For all this goodwill towards the children of Great Britain, I send you my warmest and most grateful thanks.'

Cliff had exciting news from Britain too. His uncle, Engineer-Commander Leonard Mathews, RNR, was awarded the DSC[101] for his part in an action in the Bay of Biscay on 28 December 1943 when the light cruisers HMS *Glasgow* and HMS *Enterprise* engaged a flotilla of eleven German destroyers, sinking three and damaging others. Cliff noted in his diary, 'Grand piece of work, wasn't it? I must write to Uncle Harry.'

His father wrote to him, 'Mummy would be writing this to you but she is frantically finishing snappy scarves for saucy sailors.'

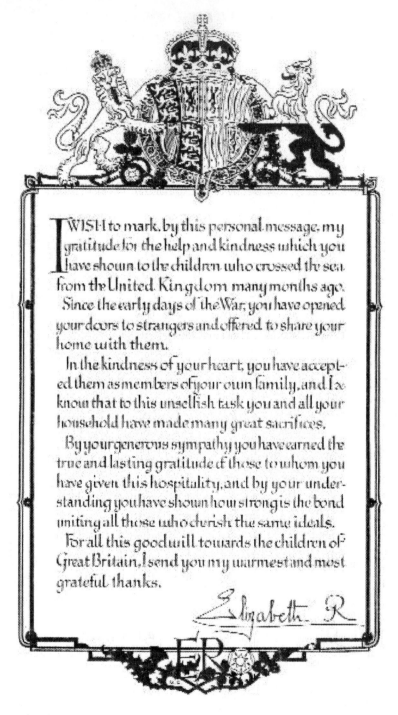

I WISH to mark, by this personal message, my gratitude for the help and kindness which you have shown to the children who crossed the sea from the United Kingdom many months ago.

Since the early days of the War, you have opened your doors to strangers and offered to share your home with them.

In the kindness of your heart, you have accepted them as members of your own family, and I know that to this unselfish task you and all your household have made many great sacrifices.

By your generous sympathy you have earned the true and lasting gratitude of those to whom you have given this hospitality, and by your understanding you have shown how strong is the bond uniting all those who cherish the same ideals.

For all this goodwill towards the children of Great Britain, I send you my warmest and most grateful thanks.

Elizabeth R

Her Majesty's message

176

The families soon became accustomed to the censor's blue pencil which hovered right through the war. Warren Strohmenger commented on the first letter that was effected, 'They cut out a paragraph in which you apparently told about a air battle.' A letter from John Mathews in August 1943, giving some war news, observes, 'There is no secret in this as the papers print it.' And a letter in November ended, 'Well, I don't want to overwork the censor, so I will close for the time being.' In June 1944 the first V-bombs fell on London. A month later Cliff wrote home, 'A letter from mummy today. It was the only one that had been opened by the censor in the last half dozen and it was heavily cut. I completely missed something that concerned Aunty Pat and an apparent robot bomb explosion. Tell me again in the next letter and it may not be censored.'

John Mathews managed in an uncensored letter to report on an aspect of the Normandy invasion. The family at this time were living in Bognor Regis near an airfield: 'We have seen some sights and the one which will always remain outstanding was that of Halifax and Lancaster bombers towing glider after glider in one long stream just over our housetop. They stretched as far as the eye could see towards both horizons, troop and freight carriers, and it was a marvellous sight.'

At one point the Mathews wrote to the Strohmengers: 'We were glad the children were able to do something for "Bundles for Britain"…certainly if anyone over here prior to the war ever felt that your feelings in America were far from friendly towards us, they must have revised their ideas in the last year. You people couldn't have done much more for us if we had been fellow Americans.'

As the years went by the prospect of a return home drew nearer and families tried to prepare for the inevitable. By late 1943 Blanche Lawson in New Jersey for instance, was beginning to feel homesick and in need of her father's support. It was becoming evident that the readjustment was going to be very difficult for all concerned. Her father wrote her a reassuring letter, 'It was brave of you to go to America and I feel so proud of you. I find myself talking of you often and thinking of you and the children a great deal. I had arrived at a stage when I dare not think of Blanche and Louise. I know this is the case. I remember so well how we felt in 1940. If we were going to be invaded at least we would have sent something of us into a free America.'

Louise Lawson, now Milbourn, writes, 'Thus we can see the heartbreak of my parents, facing the consequences of their decision to send their daughters away for the "duration", little realising what would be the outcome. For my sister and me there was also heartbreak. This time the wrench from this home was much more painful. We were older, no longer small children ever trusting in the decisions of the grown ups.'

12

Message to Garcia

It gave the boys a great summer and their families a chance to relax!
—*Annie Putnam*

When Gerald and I first arrived in Boston in 1940 we were driven in the family wooden-sided station wagon straight up to New Hampshire, to a family camp at Rockywold, on Squam Lake, since made famous as 'golden pond'. Rockywold-Deephaven, originally separate camps, had been offering 'rustic simplicity, friendly services and an unsurpassed natural setting' since 1897, and the Hinchman family went there regularly. It was our introduction to a new world, to everything from chipmunks and tennis and sailing to an incredible choice in breakfast cereals; even to going to a church service on a little island by canoe. Gerald and I won first prize at the camp's fancy dress party that summer. We were outfitted, topically and accurately, as 'bundles from Britain'.[102]

Gerald particularly remembers every Sunday attending an open-air church service beside the lake. 'It left an indelible impression on my mind, singing hymns against the lovely background of the sunset over the lake. In the beauty of that setting singing "Now the day is over" was almost a spiritual experience, if one can call it that when one was so young. I still remember it well.'

At Rockywold we were also introduced to blacks or African-Americans. For many years I assumed that they were employed simply to do lesser-paid jobs at the camp. Far from it, I discovered comparatively recently. The owner of the camp was Mary Alice Armstrong, the widow of General Samuel Chapman Armstrong, a Civil War officer who founded the Hampton Institute, the first educational institute for blacks after emancipation. These African Americans who served us so cheerfully were actually students given the opportunity of summer jobs to help finance their studies. There was a friendly relationship 'but it was not exactly equality', as a later account acknowledged.

In the years that followed I went each summer to a boy's camp at South Pond Cabins (SPC) in New Hampshire. Gerald went there for some years, also one year to camp Marienfeld. When our own daughter, Juliet, was the age I was when I was evacuated I very much wanted her to have that American experience of going to camp. My own time there had been so happy. She was able to do this in Oregon where we lived at the time. I think she enjoyed the life of camping and boating and riding as much as we did. What I did not realize during the war was that the many weeks at camp probably got us out of the hair of the Hinchmans and enabled them to relax a bit more.

South Pond Cabins was founded in 1908, eight miles from the foot of Mount Monadnock under the pines on a spring fed lake and, as its brochure stated, combining 'the traditions, experience and loyalties of more than thirty five years with a forward-looking, flexible, informal and innovative approach'. The camp grew over the years to cover 60 acres. 'All boys get some camping experience, learning what it takes to sleep comfortably in the open, to build a campfire, to cook a meal, to maintain a campsite properly, and to keep in good health in the woods and on the trail.' We did.

SPC's founders were Rollin T. Gallagher and R. Heber Howe, masters at Middlesex School. In the fall of 1907 they were atop Mount Monadnock and spied South Pond (Laurel Lake) ten miles to the south. They rented a horse and buggy and drove over to investigate. Soon each had borrowed four hundred dollars and bought about a quarter of what later became the property. Summer camps were at that time hardly known. President Eliot of Harvard University called them America's outstanding contribution of the period to the practice of education.

The camp was run for thirty years by Rollins' widow. She was from Milton and during World War II worked with Sylvia Warren to take English boys at the camp. She put a large map on the front porch of the main cabin with a star on each town where a boy lived. 'It gave the boys a great summer,' remembers her daughter Annie Putnam, 'and their families a chance to relax!' The English boys included Henry Darwin, a class mate at Milton, some whom I have mentioned already like Richard Price and John Wilkinson, also Gilbert Baker, Timothy and Ronald Barnes, Robert Day, Marius Robinson, and Robin Hitchcock, whom I was to recognize years later after I returned to England when he was playing field hockey for the Leys School when I was playing for

Mill Hill. Dominik Lobkowicz was also there. Both John Hinchman and Hoel Bowditch had been counsellors at the camp earlier and put their practical skills to work in its maintenance. There was a predominance of Milton and Harvard counsellors.

It was always an exciting time of the year going through the detailed lists of clothing and camping equipment needed, with name tags to be sewed on. We enjoyed the train trip across the southern tip of Maine and on to Fitzwilliam Depot, the nearest station.

A wonderful character whom I met when I first went there was an Englishman, Herbert Henry Haines, who had been in the British army at Gallipoli and was in charge of everything at the dock. He was a school rowing coach and all his family had rowed. He had coached at Henley, had coached several winners of the Diamond sculls and won the Doggetts Coat and Badge, a bargeman's race on the Thames

Water sports played a big role at camp. There were many canoes, a shell, rowing and sailing dinghies and one larger sailboat, the Dickie B, a gift of Dickie Barbour, who was John Wilkinson's American host. Also a scull, a kayak and an outrigger canoe from Pago Pago. There were many competitions whether in rowing or swimming or diving. Swimming races went from the raft to the area which was roped off for beginning swimmers. The raft was also used for fireworks on the fourth of July. You always had to be on the lookout, even when swimming, for large dock spiders, lest you got one in your mouth. For achieving sufficient standard in the various disciplines you could sew a red fish on your SPC jersey. One example: you had to go out in a canoe, manoeuvre it paddling on one side only, tip it over and bring canoe and paddles safely back to land. We also became knowledgeable about knots, everything from a clove hitch to a sheepshank, and definitely no 'grannies'.

When I was there the camp had three tennis courts, a large baseball field and a second field used for games like Capture the Flag and Prisoner's base, a nature cabin with its Audubon posters and butterfly collections, a well-equipped workshop, a large dining room and a meeting hall where we also had hotly contested table tennis matches. There was an infirmary which, for some reason, I associate with impetigo and eggnog!

My love of tennis was nurtured at the camp. There was a large backboard and we seemed to spend a lot of time chasing balls that had gone over it. Those were the days when, if you left your wooden racket outside the dining hall over night, it was warped and unusable the next day.

In the workshop we learned carpentry and the use and care of spoke shaves and planes and saws and the like and did leatherwork with belt and moccasin making. I admired the sailing boat models made by older more skilled boys. I managed a bird's house. The chance to study a car engine and learn how it worked seemed to fascinate young American boys. I couldn't understand why. In front of the workshop was a pump that needed priming to get water and a horseshoe pit where we spent many hours perfecting our ringers and leaners.

The first years, as younger ones, we lived in cabins. Our bed making was inspected to make sure we had used hospital corners. Behind my hut I had my first and last try at smoking a corncob pipe. Later we graduated to tents with wooden floors. The toilet arrangements were very primitive and required the spreading of plenty of lime.

Singsongs round the campfire were a big feature of the evenings; we moved indoors when it rained. One near tragedy recalled in an account by a camper does not name the culprit. It was I. It involved an Indian wrestling competition with another boy in front of the campfire. Unfortunately, I toppled my opponent into the fire. Fortunately, only his eyebrows were singed but it was an anxious moment. We sang old traditional songs like 'Oh, Suzannah', 'I've Been Working on the Railroad' and 'Dinah, Won't You Blow Your Horn' and also the ballad about the exciting encounter between Ivan Skavinsky Skavar and Abdul, the Bulbul Ameer, and old staples of American campfire singing like this one, sung quite innocently at least by the young campers:

> Drunk last night, drunk the night before
> Going to get drunk like we never got drunk before.
> When we're drunk we're as happy as can be
> We're the members of the Souse family.

Glorious, glorious, one keg of beer for the four of us
Glory be to God that there are no more of us
Cos one of us could drink it all alone.

As it was wartime, our repertoire would include service songs, like the 'Army Air Corps' (Off we go into the wild blue yonder), the Army's 'Caisson Song' (Over hill, over dale, we will hit the dusty trail, as the caissons go rolling along) and, of course, the Navy's 'Anchors Away', and the 'Marine Hymn' ('If the Army and the Navy ever gaze on heaven's scenes they will find the streets are guarded by United States Marines'). Meeting Americans over the years I have also often, to their surprise, been able to sing them their college songs which I learned round the campfire. We sang Harvard songs as most counsellors were drawn from there but also these, for example, from other colleges:

Way down in old New Jersey, in that far-off jungle land[103]
There lives a Princeton tiger, who will eat right off your hand.
But when he gets in battle with the other beasts of prey,
He frightens them almost to death in this peculiar way:
Wow, wow, wow-wow-wow, hear the Tiger roar;
Wow, Wow, wow-wow-wow, rolling up a score.
Wow, wow, wow-wow-wow, better move along
When you hear the Tiger sing his Jungle Song.

And the boastful Brown song:

Oh we've licked Harvard and we've licked Yale
There ain't no team that we can't whale
For it's Rah, Rah, Brunoniaonia, Rah, Rah Brunoniaonia
Rah, Rah, Brunonia; Brown, Brown, Brown.

And parodies:

Cheer, cheer for old Notre Dame
You take the notre, I'll take the dame
Send some sucker out for gin
Don't let a sober person in
We never stagger, we never fall

183

We sober up on wood alcohol....
While our loyal comrades go
Burping back to the bar for more

We would walk the miles on dusty roads to Mount Monadnock, carrying the horseshoe packs we had made out of blankets, blanket pins and a poncho. What a relief to stop half way at a store for 'pop'. In those days when we were on the mountain we could drink water from the springs that bubbled out. Overnight camping trips were looked forward to eagerly. They would also usually involve long hikes, and for older ones a canoe trip, carrying food and cooking utensils with us. We would build our fire and cook hash and baked beans and cocoa, and as it got darker we might tell scary ghost stories. Sometimes we would sleep by a lake where we could enjoy a morning dip and where through the woods you could hear the penetrating whistle of a train in the distance and just catch its lights. Or we would be lying back in our blankets in a field watching shooting stars, being woken up by the lick of a cow. Curiously, I can still remember a little nervousness about swimming holes because we thought President Roosevelt had caught polio in one.

Other activities might be archery and also .22 shooting contests, where we worked to get our NRA marksman or pro-marksman medals. Much was done competitively, with teams divided, for some reason, into 'hinks' and 'dinks'. This even applied to blueberry collecting when we would come back with 30, 40, or 50 pounds of berries.

The camp had its own unique game called Scouting for which our teams were called mechanics and engineers. This usually took place on Sundays after we had got to know the names of fellow campers. Down the middle of the camp, down the hill to the dock, was a path. Set back several hundred yards to left and right behind thick bushes and undergrowth were stonewalls. You started at one stonewall and had to get to the opposite stonewall and back to your own without being seen or at least identified. That scored a run. If you saw someone on the opposing side and called out his name he was dead and had to go down to the morgue, the dock. We'd have several games in an afternoon.

The war, to most of us younger ones, was far off. One boy's father, a senior officer in the Marines, made an impressive appearance in uniform. Some naval officers, like Putnam, the Gallagher son-in-law, were there at times. Supervised letters home went from each camper each week, and we had the one to England to do as well.

Heart and soul of everything was Rollin T. Gallagher, Jr, or Junie as he was known to us, who seemed to do everything with great enthusiasm. Many campers speak still of the importance he attached to the story 'Message to Garcia'. Most Americans of my age know the story well. No young and few middle aged Americans have any idea what it is about or have even heard about it. Message to Garcia is about self-sufficiency, about carrying out a task without asking how. After the declaration of the Spanish-American War, a young lieutenant in the US Bureau of Military Intelligence, Andrew Summers Rowan, was given a message to deliver to a Cuban general, Calixto Garcia, in a remote district. He landed in an open boat near Turquino Peak (24 April 1898), carried out his mission and brought back information regarding the insurgent army. Oliver Wendell Holmes wrote, 'By the Eternal! There is a man whose form should be cast in deathless bronze and the statue placed in every college of the land.' Quoting the author, Elbert Hubbard[104], he went on, 'It is not book-learning young men need, nor instruction about this and that, but a stiffening of the vertebrae which will cause them to be loyal to a trust, to act promptly, concentrate their energies, do a thing—"carry a message to Garcia."' I have certainly never forgotten the injunction.

13

On Convoy Duty

The epic fight of the liner 'Duchess of York'
—Headline, the London Evening News

That the thanks of this House be accorded to the officers and
men of the Merchant Navy for the steadfastness with which
they have maintained our stocks of food and materials; for
their service in transporting men and munitions to all the
battles over all the seas, and for the gallantry with which,
though a civilian service, they met and fought the constant
attacks of the enemy.
—Resolution of the House of Commons 30 October 1945

In 2000 a Merchant Navy Day was established in Britain. The third of
September is the date. Besides being in 1939 the first day of the war, 3
September was also the day the first merchant navy ship was sunk, the
Athenia. The next day the first Cunard ship, the *Bosnia*, was sunk. These
sinkings underline the fact that the Merchant Navy were on the front line from
day one and they continued to be so throughout the war. Sometimes their
dedication and heroism has gone inadequately recognized and so it is fitting that
in future it will be remembered each year on that day.

Richard Hough, an authority on the merchant navy's role, writes, 'The
Second World War demanded more of its sailors than any other in history in
endurance and the unremitting need to face danger, with increasingly lethal
weapons and an ever-increasing need for vigilance by night and day.' Andrew

Williams ends his book *The Battle of the Atlantic*: 'It took a very particular sort of courage; these men were at risk for weeks at a time, almost powerless to influence their own fate. Some were torpedoed twice or three times and yet chose to return to sea. They were united by a common sense of purpose, a determination to see it through no matter the risks.'

The men of the Merchant Marine may not have received the accolades of 'the few' who fought in the Battle of Britain but the Battle of the Atlantic must share honours with it as the two most decisive battles of World War II. And the debt which Britain and the world owe to the sailors should be mentioned in the same breath. At the time, for the people of Britain, writes Martin Gilbert, 'each convoy disaster at sea seemed to threaten the possibility of a German invasion of Britain itself'. For Britain only produced enough food to feed half its population and had reserves to last only a few months, oil and other raw materials were imported, and so the Atlantic was the country's lifeline. Losses were so bad at one point that Churchill ordered figures to be kept secret. He admitted that the U-boat threat was the only thing that ever really frightened him. During the war 800 million pounds of meat and fish products; a thousand million pounds of grain; 800 million pounds of fruit and vegetables; and 800 million pounds of milk and egg products were shipped across the Atlantic.

In December 1940 Churchill wrote to Roosevelt, 'The mortal danger is the steady and increasing dimunition of sea tonnage.' The decision for 1941, he said, lay on the seas: 'It is therefore in shipping and in the power to transport across the oceans, particularly the Atlantic Ocean, that in 1941 the crunch of the whole war will be found.' The Axis powers knew this too. In February 1941 Nazi Germany's foreign minister Ribbentrop told the Japanese ambassador in Berlin that the important thing now was to sink enough ships to reduce England's imports to below the absolute minimum necessary for existence.

It was not just the survival of Britain but also the possibility of the Allies going on a counterattack that depended on the men of the merchant Navy. The authors of *Convoy— Merchant Sailors at War 1939-45*, Philip Kaplan and Jack Currie, write, 'Without their sacrifice Britain could not have survived the early years of the war; Russia could not have been supplied with the weapons and raw materials which enabled her to stem and then turn the tide of German invasion; the Mediterranean world would have become the mare nostrum of which Mussolini dreamed; and, of course, the great sea-borne invasions which rolled back the Axis forces, first in North Africa, and then in Europe and the Pacific, could never have been mounted.'

Two thousand eight hundred Allied merchant ships and 148 Allied warships were sunk. And during the five years and eight months of submarine war

27,491 officers and men on German submarines—75% of the service—were killed. Out of 863 U-boats sent on operational patrols 754 were sunk or damaged beyond repair while in port.

In the summer of 1941 the bravery of the Merchant Navy was featured in some American papers the way the plight of children had been the year before. On 3 August the *New York Times* Magazine had an article headed 'Men of the Convoys—They spin yarns at the British Merchant Navy Club downtown, but they don't like to be called heroes.' The article, by Meyer Berger, reported on the Club which had been opened in March that year with British Ambassador Lord Halifax as guest of honour: 'The women get to know the faces; watch for them every time fresh convoys come to the harbor. Sometimes they tell you sadly, you miss a boyish face or two. You don't ask questions. The British have a way of conveying thought by utter silence.' A photo caption reads 'E cahn't do us in. We'll come out atop, don't think we won't.' 'Such is the spirit that stirs the seamen of Britain's Merchant Navy to heroic self-sacrifice,' Berger writes. 'Our guide thought we ought to know something about the British seamen's slant on things. He said, "I wouldn't lay it on about their being heroes. They don't go for that. They're mostly modest chaps." This was sheer understatement.' A sign on the wall stated: 'Don't help the enemy. Careless talk may give away vital secrets.' Between the dart boards another sign cautioned: 'If you've news of our munitions, keep it dark. Ships or planes or troop positions, keep it dark. Lives are lost through conversation, here's a tip for the duration, when you've private information keep it dark.'

In 1942 the BBC launched a wartime programme for the Merchant Navy Shipmates Ashore, basing its 'club' at the Hammersmith Palais. Each weekend the programme, broadcast for listeners at home and overseas featured seamen, many of whom had made their way to London after their ships had been torpedoed in the North Atlantic; reporters, who brought in interviews and shipping news from ports around Britain. The programme attracted all the big stars from the London stage, and wives and sweethearts sent messages to their men over the airwaves. The program was hosted by Doris Hare.

Some of the messages reflected the tragedy being enacted in the North Atlantic—in 1942 alone over 1,000 British merchant ships were lost to enemy action. 'Don't mention anything about his feet,' a mother wrote to Doris about her son in hospital in Nova Scotia. 'He doesn't know that I know.' The 19-year-old Londoner had had both legs amputated after enduring 13 days of icy conditions on the Atlantic in a tiny boat. On another occasion a sailor, lying in an American hospital in a coma, began to regain consciousness when he heard his little sister's voice crackling across the short waves from the Merchant Navy Club in London.

By the summer of 1942 it was a real club. The Ministry of Labour was given an astonishing $75,000 raised by the New York-based International Ladies Garment Workers Union as a tribute to the work of the Merchant Navy in keeping international trade going during hostilities. A building was found near Piccadilly where visiting seafarers could meet.

In 1949 the programme became the Merchant Navy Programme and in the eighties Seven Seas, and on its 50th anniversary was still being broadcast.

I still have a tattered autograph book with its tartan cover with 41 names of sailors I collected on our trip across in the *Duchess of York*. Besides the HMS Revenge signalman, W. Simmons, I can make out names drawn from a variety of shipboard occupations like: Thomas Charles, Gym Instructor; C. Thornton, Second Engineer; An Deas, Jr Purser; L Shannon, 5th officer; PV Pascoe, Sanitary Engineer; C Wyer, Stewardess; WJ English, Waiter; LA Griffith MB ChB, Surgeon; DW Elkington, 5th Electrician; William J Smith, Chief Engineer; F Lawson, B Room Steward; CB Chong, gunner; Albert Wood, Baggagemaster; D Fairbourne, 3rd Radio Officer. Little was I to know that within a couple of years eleven members of the crew would be dead and the *Duchess of York* would lie a wreck at the bottom of the sea. The extent of her travels give some indication of what her crew had to face again and again.

Between September 1939 and July 1943 she steamed approximately 223,000 miles, carried 73,000 military personnel, 4,000 civilians and 6,000 prisoners of war and 65,000 tons of cargo on trips to Canada, the Far East, India and the Middle East. For her last voyage in 1940, after depositing us in Halifax, she sailed to Suez via Cape Town, and in March 1941 carried reinforcements and supplies for the far eastern naval base at Singapore that had not yet been lost to the Japanese. Returning to Liverpool towards the end of July she next made two voyages to India. Late in 1942 and early 1943 she made six trips carrying 8,000 troops and supplies for the North African landings and was on several occasions the target of enemy air raids. On 14 March 1943 she was attacked by two Focke Wulf aircraft shortly after leaving Algiers and hit by a 500-pound bomb which landed on No 5 Oerlikon gun pit, penetrated three decks and, fortunately, failed to explode. Two French naval ratings were in the gun pit and the fifth engineer was in bed as the bomb passed through his room;

but apart from shock none of these men was hurt. During its passage the top part of the bomb and its nose fuse were torn off and later found in A deck alleyway. The Chief officer called for volunteers to manhandle the bomb to the side of B deck where it was pushed overboard. For this hazardous action R V Burns, later General Manager of Canadian Pacific Steamships, was awarded the George Medal and Lloyd's medal. First Officer R. McKillop was made a member of the OBE[105], two other members of the crew were given the BEM[106] and others were mentioned in dispatches.

Four months later, on 7 July 1943, the *Duchess of York* left Glasgow for the last time. She proceeded down the Clyde and joined another convoy. All went well until the evening of 11 July when two Focke-Wulf aircraft, flying at 15,000 feet, were identified. At ten minutes past nine the ship was hit by a stick of bombs. The centre of the ship quickly became a raging inferno and communication between the bridge and other parts of the ship became impossible. While the ship's guns continued to fire at the five aircraft which were now attacking other ships in the convoy, efforts were also made to control the ship, but without success. The ship had to be abandoned. Captain Busk-Wood and his chief engineer EE Vick were the last to leave the ship at approximately 22.40. As the vessel continued to float, the escort destroyer *Douglas* fired a torpedo at the burning hulk in order to reduce the risk of the convoy being found by submarines. As well as the eleven members of the crew, five members of the ship's permanent military staff and 11 RAF personnel were lost. The survivors were picked up by the escort vessels and taken to Casablanca. The official war record says the waters were searched long after darkness for any survivors.

Eleven decorations and mentions in dispatches were awarded to the officers and men of the *Duchess of York* for outstanding service in the face of enemy attack. She was the 12th and last Canadian Pacific ship to be destroyed by enemy action in World War II.

It was more than a year later when the London *Evening News*[107] told the story for the first time. The headline: 'The epic fight of the liner "Duchess of York"'

'The story of the ship's dying hours is a gripping one,' wrote the paper, 'of fire-fighters battling until finally driven over the side by the flames, of a man, horribly burned, making a bridge of his body for his mates to escape when a companion ladder was blown away, of engineers working when the whole ship was liable to explode at any moment.' It quoted the ship's log: 'Fire was opened immediately on the bombers with all available guns. Then a stick of heavy bombs hit the ship, cutting off the bridge from the rest of the ship. Ordered to abandon ship, the men stayed on for another hour to fight back. Third butcher Hughes made a bridge of his body, staying firm and unflinching till all his mates had clambered up his shoulders to safety.'

In the March 1958 issue of the *Crowsnest*, the Royal Canadian Navy's magazine the following appeared: 'In the after canopy of the Tribal Class destroyer escort *Iroquois* there is a plaque which is displayed as proudly as any battle honour. It commemorates the rescue 15 years ago of survivors from SS *Duchess of York* sunk while on troop transport duty on 11 July 1943.'

On the eve of D-Day General Eisenhower said, 'Every man in this Allied Command is quick to express his admiration for the loyalty, courage and fortitude of the officers and men of the Merchant Navy. We count upon their efficiency and their utter devotion to duty as we do our own; they have never failed us yet and in all the struggles yet to come we know that they will never be deterred by any danger, hardship or privations. When final victory is ours there is no organisation that will share its credit more deservedly than the Merchant Marine.'

14
Rectory School

If Only

If only there had been no war,
No battle, strife or tears, or gore.
No sinkings, killings, deprivations,
No quarrellings between the nations.

But we must all return to facts,
To a world with secret pacts,
A world that's full of strife and hate.
Where no man knows his death or fate.

And we must all remain today
Partakers in this terrible fray,
Till pass the weeks of fear and doubt,
And comes the day when we will rout
All strife and terror from the world,
And battle flags will all be furled

Michael Henderson
Rectory News, spring 1945

As the years passed, as host families aged and children grew, while the war effort and shortages made more demands on them, some American families began to feel the pinch. Marion Dunham, a Boston member of the English-Speaking Union, pointed out, 'Many American sponsors are finding it financially very hard to carry on for four years when they imagined it would be for one.' In the middle of the war there were changes going on at the Hinchman household, too, which necessitated for us to move schools. A letter[108] from Walter Hinchman to our parents outlines the issue and is to my mind an indication of his great care and sensitivity:

Your letter of August first took over a month to get here. Our latest from John (No. Africa or Sicily), we're not sure which) took only ten days, but I suppose they expedite servicemen's 'V' mail. John, by the way, seems pretty cheerful. He says they have been repairing everything from tanks to cigarette lighters, and he adds that in spare moments he made an ice-cream freezer out of odds and ends he picked up. Where do you suppose they get the cream? I wonder if our spendthrift government, while we pay taxes, sends cream, by some sublimated refrigerating process, to North Africa. I'm glad to have the boys have the cream, but it does seem out of proportion! Probably John is using goat's milk.

You do not feel a whit more remiss than I in not writing oftener. I fancy we both lean back on our wives, who keep the story of your boys up to date. But I think I have some news which Julia has not yet written, as she has been very busy the past few days—in fact, past few months!

We have decided to send your boys to the Rectory School, Pomfret, Connecticut. Julia's parents in Victoria, BC, are very low, a neighbour friend who does errands for them is seriously ill, and she must go to them. Her father is 89, practically blind, and able to do little for himself; her mother, 80, though active mentally, is in bed most of the time with serious heart trouble and blood pressure. Obviously, Julia must go; and it is not as if she could run across the street—she must go 3000 miles and stay possibly for months. When she does go, she will have to leave no 'staff' here but a decrepit if willing, crone of seventy—a French Canadian who could not look after the boys, who could not even telephone adequately in an emergency. We have canvassed all the schools and agencies for a replica of Jean or Jinny, but there just aren't any. It is very different, I fear, from the time two years ago when Mrs. Hinchman visited her parents. We then had two competent maids and Jinny. Now, when she goes, if the boys were here, I should not be able to leave the place during the evening or weekends; and, at that, it would be pretty dreary for the boys, with only the crone aforesaid and me for companions! The only solution, since the boys cannot go back to England and since we did not wish to experiment with placing them in another household, was to send them to a boarding school. Incidentally, they are delighted with the prospect, so we hope all will go well.

We have looked into the school problem rather carefully, and we think the Rectory School is a good choice. It takes boys up to fifteen. Michael will have approximately the same course of study, with Latin, that he would have had in our sixth class ('First form' to you) and Gerald, I think, may have rather better (that is, more exacting, more masculine) instruction than he would have had in our Lower school.

It is a small school, and Michael may have a happier time, socially, in such a group than if he had been the smallest boy in our Milton Upper School of 260. So, apart from Mrs. Hinchman's emergency, it may not be a bad move. We are very fond of the boys, and I think they feel our house is their home, but it did not seem possible to give them a good home, even an adequate one, this winter if Mrs. Hinchman has to be away a good deal; so we feel you will understand and approve of our decision. In any case we shall have them during vacations.

If you have a map of New England, even though Pomfret may not be on it, you can locate it approximately as 50 miles northeast of Hartford, Connecticut. It is lovely country, about as hilly as Western Shropshire. The watershed ('height of land' in our lingo) between the Connecticut River valley and the Atlantic starts in New Hampshire (mountains there) and runs southeastward through Michael's South Pond region (about 1200 feet) across Massachusetts and Eastern Connecticut (about 600-800 ft. at Pomfret). Far better than suburban Milton! Pomfret is a trifle less than two hours from Boston by rail, so we should be able to visit the boys easily.

I quite understand your position in regard to the boys' returning to England, and I agree with your arguments against it under present

194

conditions. I hope that you, too, understand that we feel it more than an obligation—in fact, a pleasure and a privilege—to look after them. But you must see, as we do, that under present conditions here, we do not feel that we can do as good a job as we could earlier. That is, we shall have to put them in boarding schools and camps more than we did in view of Mrs. Hinchman's obligations to her parents and the impossibility of getting adequate help; and that means less personal touch and home life. Incidentally, too, we have had four grandchildren born since Michael and Gerald came to us and that means all sorts of time- and energy-consuming occupations for my wife. No good telling a grandma to ignore her grandchildren!

But these are minor reasons. The main reason in my mind for you to consider the return of the boys as soon as it is *safe* and *feasible* is that Gerald does not really remember his parents at all. Even England is a good deal of a blank. He has 'got up' a kind of second-hand picture of his country. How long that can be allowed to go on without irreparable damage I don't know. As regards Michael, he has an astonishingly clear memory of you both (considering that he was only eight when he came), and he keeps up his knowledge of and feeling for England by reading, radio, etc. His loss will be of quite different nature—some difficulty (how much, it is hard to say) in adjusting himself to the social and scholastic ways of your country. I say all this not because we want to get rid of the boys—far from it!—but because I think it is a real consideration for the good of the boys.

In a former letter you were good enough to suggest that I speak quite frankly if the cost of keeping your boys was a serious burden. At the time I answered 'no', and I can hardly say yet that it is 'serious'; but with increasing taxes and reduced income, the margin is decidedly smaller than it was. The boarding school venture will cost us about $800 a year more, I figure, even allowing for the saving on Jinny and food. If you could see your way to defraying part of that, it would help; but please understand that I don't wish you to do so unless you conveniently can. The figures for the two boys, as near as I can estimate them, were $2060 in 1941-2 and $2095 in 1942-3. I have no figures for 1940-1, but I should think they were about the same, perhaps a trifle less. The estimate for 1943-4 comes to about $2905—or $810 more than last year (figured Sept. to Sept.). I am giving you all this merely because you asked me to be frank about it; but I hope you understand that we recognize clearly our obligation and do not wish to present a 'demand'!

This letter has already run to such length that I won't attempt to say much about the boys, except that they are well and developing normally. Michael is beginning to thin out and to shoot up, without much gain in weight, but he continues strong and active. Gerald is still a chubby boy, but as he is growing, he is laying on weight and has almost caught up to Michael. He is a little more mature, I think, a little less of a baby, but he is about four years behind Michael in his social adjustments—whether with friends, in games, or in his sense of responsibility, or in interests. But Michael, I think, is ahead of his age in his consideration of others and his desire to share with others. Scholastically, Gerald certainly improved last year and I hope will 'find himself' this year. Michael, if his new teachers can develop habits of thoroughness in him, will be an exceptional scholar. I have talked with his new headmaster about this, and, as the school is small, I think that aspect may be better looked after than in Milton Academy Upper School. A careless boy, if he is bright, can slip along unnoticed in a large group. But don't worry about Michael. He is learning a lot outside of school—in his reading, his stamp collecting, his listening to the radio. It is these things, I think, which widen the gap between him and Gerald to more than their calendar years. Also Michael is absolutely honest and straightforward and cooperative in every way—a 'good citizen'.

Please give my regards to Mrs. Henderson and tell her that Mrs. Hinchman will write her as soon as she can get the boys outfitted for their new school.

With best wishes,

Very sincerely yours,

Walter S. Hinchman

PS Don't feel any rush about the foregoing suggestions. The coming winter is provided for, both as to care of the boys and as to funds.

The Rectory Headmaster, John Bigelow, or Mr. John as we came to know him, had shared in the decision by the association of Junior Boarding School heads to offer scholarships to English youngsters. Being a small school it was possible for the staff to give a great deal of individual care. During the war the school thoughtfully even hung a Union Jack in the assembly hall so we were not embarrassed at the daily Pledge of Allegiance time. We could turn and face our flag when the American boys faced the Stars and Stripes. Reminiscing about Rectory, Gerald says, 'I remember with gratitude as a nine-year-old the care and the family atmosphere. There was also the expectation that I sensed from Mr. John that each one of us should contribute our best and his real concern if we fell short.'

There were a number of English boys at Rectory when we came. One, Jeremy Thorpe, later to lead Britain's Liberal Party, had just returned to England and the school paper, *Rectory News,* that November carried a letter from him:

I am writing to you now, wearing a stiff collar, striped trousers, tail coat, and vest and bow tie (a perfect butler) It is very nice here, but, as all old Rectory boys write, that they miss the sleep that they used to get there. We get up at 7.00 for 7.30 class, next breakfast, and 9.20 chapel, then two more periods, and recess ('chambers' here), either one to two more periods, and then pupil room, where you do your Latin, or what have you, with your housemaster, or tutor. Lunch, games (a peculiar game called 'field game', which is one half soccer and one quarter rugger, and the rest is entirely mongrel) and if it isn't a half-holiday, two more periods; then a delicious tea, which, except for the bread, you buy yourself. You don't have to hide Coca-Cola or chocolates, as (1) you can't get anything like Coca-Cola (unfortunately) and (2) you have such a small sweet ration over here that you hardly taste them. You have your own room, but I don't think one could find anything anywhere to compare with Rectory in absolutely anything whatsoever. I broadcasted from BBC to America about two weeks ago on my experiences at midnight to WBZ, so it got to you around 7.00 in the evening. Well, if I can herd in enough shekels, as McCorkle used to say, I'll definitely be popping over to see you after this beastly war is over. Think of me when you eat your oranges for breakfast, as they're ungettable in (as Jacob used to think) that queer, savage land! Well, this brings all my best. Will be sending you some photographs soon.

Jeremy Thorpe wrote in his autobiography *In My Own Time* in 1999 that he was extremely happy at Rectory. He points out that we all had some responsibility for the domestic side of the school—'my privilege was to look after the pigs'. He describes a visit from his American aunt Kay who came to visit him during his first winter there just after a heavy snowstorm: 'By way of a compliment, I invited her to come with me on my toboggan, taking the food down the hill to the pigs. Rather nobly she accepted and, wrapped up in her mink coat, sat behind me whilst I clutched between my knees a pail of swill which I had collected from the kitchens. The worst occurred. We hit a rock hidden by snow and Kay, myself, the garbage and mink coat were thrown off the sledge and landed in a heap! Needless to say she was not best pleased.' He had apparently already developed a sense of social justice He objected to a Pomfret resident's garbage as having 'too rich garbage' for WW 11 austerity. He admonished him or her for 'nor going without like everybody else'. His headmaster always remembered him well as 'a charming fellow, very bright and very articulate'.

My own 'war job' was looking after chickens. And my first published article was on how to do this. This literary contribution was followed by articles on citizenship and on sports, serious and satirical, and even my first and last poems. It is only on later reflection that I realize how many of the interests I developed at Rectory accompanied me through the rest of my life. I was obviously very involved in plays then, and have been over the years; I was in the school ice hockey team (We twice beat Pomfret Lower School), captain of the soccer team and tennis champion. And nearly fifty years later was able to play all three sports in Oregon. We were proud to wear orange and black, the Princeton colours, at football. At compulsory rest time I used to sit out in the corridor and read from books to the other boys in their rooms; perhaps a preparation for reading radio commentaries and doing voiceovers! And, thanks to the influence of the weekly Promptness Honor Roll, I have never felt comfortable coming late to anything!

I joined a Society for the Promotion of the Study of Latin which had a regular newspaper with Latin words invented for current objects like planes. The headmaster was pleased that I got honourable mention in a high school competition sponsored by a national church paper with an essay about prejudice.

Thinking of those two years at Rectory my childhood memory recalls all sorts of images: the Saturday picnics where we cooked hot dogs and devoured doughnuts; the ravine where we constructed our makeshift huts; an expedition to the place where General Putnam killed the last wolf in Connecticut; our hockey master, Charles Cook, falling through the ice on the pond; our weekly candy bar ration from Miss Gertrude Jones; weekly movies, often Abbot and Costello, or patriotic or war themes like *Gunga Din, Corvette K225* and *Paris Calling* and George Formby movies, as well as *A Yank at Oxford, The Invisible Man, Bambi, Lassie Come Home* and *National Velvet*, starring fellow evacuee Elizabeth Taylor[109]—on the strength of which connection I have a portrait signed 'love Elizabeth Taylor'.

Gerald and I both served as acolytes in the chapel (now a classroom). One boy used to fascinate us by taking out his glass eye in the pew and playing with it! I also vividly recall music teacher Annie Ashe playing on the organ 'Now the day is over, night is drawing nigh' as the last rays of the sun poured in the window behind her head. Gerald writes that the experience of serving in the chapel was 'a special one that has lived with me over the years, one stepping stone in a faith journey'. Annie, to our delight, was a lover of Gilbert and Sullivan and would have groups of us to her home to listen to the Savoy operas.

I seem to have developed a strong conscience somewhere along the line and will never forget one evening at chapel. Before the service a crowd of us were in Mr. John's rooms and were offered chocolates. I took one that was much larger than any of the others. That particular chocolate, I discovered a few minutes later, was intended for Mrs. John, as the headmaster's wife was known. Mr. John asked who had taken it. No one owned up. During the chapel service afterwards I felt terrible. I had to rush up to him afterwards and tell him that I had taken it! Occasionally, disagreements were settled in the boxing ring, which I did not like. I seem to think one I had was something about England.

Those years were, of course, very much affected by the fact that from December 1941 onwards the United States was in the war. By the time we were at the school the *Rectory News* was reflecting the difficulties of rationing, staff shortage and above all the fact that some 200 alumni were in the services. The headmaster noted in February 1944 that with more and more joining up, that there were too many alumni to put a star for each on the service flag. The paper's columns indicated that they were spread round the world 'somewhere in England' or 'somewhere in the Pacific' and that some of them were being killed or wounded, and some being decorated. Gerald writes, 'When we were there the European theatre of war was coming to an end but I remember the pain of the reverses in the Pacific where American soldiers were giving their lives.' Indeed, the war was brought home to us when the father of one of our school friends, Ward B. Wack, who had the room across from mine, was killed.

Articles by students sometimes reflected the war. One wrote, in an article about the Battle of Britain, 'Food was scarce. Butter, for instance, was a mere memory. Everybody, even His Majesty, had to eat margarine.' The Hinchmans, it was recorded in the school paper, had presented the school library with a subscription to *Britain.*

As the war progressed, and as I got a little older, I began to take a more intelligent interest in world affairs. At Rectory we were encouraged to read *Time* and to enter its annual current affairs quiz. Mrs. John used to get near perfect scores in the *Time* quiz (104 when the average for college students was 58). I was aware of the Allied landings in North Africa and remember Mr. John calling us in to hear a broadcast by President Roosevelt when the Allies entered Rome. By the time of the Normandy invasions I followed the breakout from the beachhead and the encirclement of the German troops in Cherbourg. I was aware of the Four Freedoms enunciated by the President in 1941—freedom of speech, freedom of worship, freedom from want and freedom from fear—and Norman Rockwell's illustration of them in 1943, and was pleased to add to my stamp collections the new issue of flags of oppressed nations.

At the school I was entrusted with responsibility for hoisting and lowering the flag, learning to fold it correctly and never to let it touch the ground. We spent time marching and drilling and practicing the manual of arms with model wooden guns and had a colour guard. We also got fitter with an obstacle course on Cow Hill and marching up to Caterpillar Hill where there was an Army Air Force spotting post. We trained in skills like Morse and semaphore, and on graduation day the boys wowed the parents by conveying messages correctly from one end of the football field using their flags. Gerald remembers feeling important sitting in the back of a truck being driven to the fields to dig vegetables as part of the war effort.

Mr. John wrote in the *Rectory News* of the sad news of deaths reported, 'The price of winning the war is tremendous. May we find means to make the peace which will follow it universal and lasting. That is the least we shall owe to our dead.' Perhaps the commitment of our lives, both Gerald and mine, to peacemaking, and my books in this field, are an unconscious echo of that challenge.

Occasionally evacuees were fortunate, as we were, to have their fathers come over to the United States. Our father came on a mission to Washington, DC.[110] Of course, being wartime there could be no advance warning of a visit. I was woken up shortly after going to bed one night during the holidays. The Hinchmans were excited. It was our father on the line. I apparently commented, as I put down the receiver, 'Gee, he talks just like in the movies.' He came for two days to Milton. We enjoyed being given the chance to polish his buttons, with a metal plate under the buttons to protect the cloth and duraglit for polishing, to go out with him on a shopping expedition, though slightly embarrassed when he was buying underwear for our mother, and having tea at Schrafts. Peggy recalls, 'I remember your father going to a department store to buy some face cloths to take home. He found it a bewildering experience as he kept asking for flannels.' It gave him a chance to see where we were growing up. We obviously had adopted our local attitudes for when our father, trying to unbend, said, 'I suppose you find things swell here,' I replied, 'Daddy, we don't say swell in Boston.'[111] The Hinchmans invited Jinny to come for lunch with our father.

We do not know what took him to the United States at that point but I did discover later he was involved in two of the projects that helped make the Normandy invasion a success—PLUTO, an acronym for the pipeline under the ocean that supplied gas to the invading army, and MULBERRY, the code name for the huge artificial harbours made of concrete whose components were floated over to France, a harbour that was essential for the landing of supplies for the invasion army. So secret was the concept of a pipeline to Normandy that one of Britain's leading architects, Basil Spence (later Sir) was commissioned to design and build a phoney oil dock at Dover. The fiction was so thorough that it was visited by King George V1, and General Eisenhower spoke to the 'construction workers', while Dover's mayor paid tribute to this new facility 'the precise nature of which must remain secret until the war is over, but which will bring the borough material benefits of consequence'. The phoney dock was built with the help of film and theatre stagehands and consisted of scaffolding, fibreboard and old sewage pipes.

We were proud that our father came to Rectory in uniform. He arrived at the school just as I was in a rehearsal of a play about Nathan Hale and walked in as I, as Tom Adams, was saying, 'I will not sing "God save the king".' I wonder what subversive indoctrination he thought we were getting! We enjoyed going out to lunch with him at the Pomfret Inn and having a 'Pomfret special', a concoction of cake and ice cream and chocolate sauce. We proudly wore his regimental badge that he gave us.

Jinny still has a letter she received from our mother in March 1944, thanking for the stockings she had sent. 'I had almost forgotten what silk stockings look like,' wrote our mother. She refers to Col. Henderson's four days with the boys at Milton and adds, 'It would be unwise to bring them back now that things are warming up a bit here.'

With our father in Milton

My last Christmas in America I was invited to go with my English Rectory friend, Charlie Fay, to his adopted family, the Huntington Thompsons, in South Tamworth, New Hampshire. Mr. Thompson was a master at Rectory. Pleasant Patch, their home was up a steep hill. Other members of the family lived down the road from where they had a dramatic view of the mountains. Even to this day I can remember the names—Chocorua, White Face, Paugus, and in behind, Mount Washington. Two young English girls, who were adopted by other members of the family, joined us—Eleanor and Meggie Milne. A variety of impressions remain with me. Church attended by people in ski pants. It didn't seem right! Exploring the mountainside and valley and frozen-over streams on snowshoes with Charlie who loved to blaize trails and had formed a Little Larcomb Mountain Club in which he enlisted me. At night we would play board games. One was called, I think, Target for Tonight. You would throw dice to go on bomber raids over Germany. It was where I first learned names like Dortmund, Essen and Hamm. On Christmas Eve I was asked to bring from the upper house precious, breakable Christmas decorations. Riding low on my sled down the steep hill, I imagined I was one of the Norwegian children I had just read about in a book *Snow Treasure* who used sleds to spirit gold away from the Germans!

That was my fifth and last evacuation Christmas.

15
Return Journeys

We are sailing without a convoy. The first crossing without one. We are going to go fast. If any child falls overboard, we will not stop.
—*Captain of the* Mauretania

As early as 1942 a trickle of boys and girls had begun to return home. Some because they had reached the age of military service, some because parents were worrying about the adverse effects that prolonged separation could have on relationships or felt their child was not in a suitable home, some fearing that their children might have become too American. Jeremy Thorpe said his father thought it was high time he came home 'otherwise I would become a complete American and lose contact with my country. A number of parents who had sent their children across the Atlantic took the same view.'

One parent making enquiries in April that year was told in a letter[112] that the prospects of a return passage were not good. 'In the last eleven months out of three to four hundred children for whom passage applications were made, only just one hundred were able to leave. The reason for this is that available sailings have recently diminished, due no doubt to a military need for the ships, while the number of applicants has increased.' The letter added, 'There is no possibility of travel by air.' Daniel Farson sailed on a banana boat, *Jamaica Producer*, in a convoy from Halifax on 19 April 1942. On the first day they were attacked by a U-boat which was sunk by an accompanying destroyer.

Another early returnee, Angela Pelham, had a similar experience. She wrote, 'Life is full of surprises, did we think we might be sailing on the *Queen*

Mary? Well, we aren't, No! Sir! When we were at last allowed to see round the corner of the canvas that was rigged up to keep everything secret, there was a little boat alongside the dock and Aunt Amanda said, "I suppose that is the tug that is going to take us out to our ship." We were soon put wise and found that it was the ship we were crossing the Atlantic in.' With them were other children and mothers returning to England and also soldiers' wives who have come from the West Indies to join husbands who were already at home. The boat was 10,000 tons and was built to make trips up the Amazon. 'There are lots of boys and men who are called the "Survivors", poor things they have been torpedoed and some of them are too bad even to come on deck, but have to have an attendant with them below. One boy who walks around with Molly and plays with us was on the *City of Benares*, and in an open boat for days, and had to watch the children who fell asleep, get washed overboard, he says he will never forget that part of it.

'There was the most terrific crash the other night, it turned rough again when I was going to bed, and suddenly there was what I thought an explosion under my bunk which nearly threw me out, but it was only a wave hitting the ship. One of the sailors on the boat deck told us that a torpedo struck the ship on her outward journey, but it happened to be a dud, and he showed us the dent it had made, and it was just under Aunt Amanda's porthole.'

Also returning in 1942 was 16-year-old Granville Bantock from the Actor's Orphanage. His mother wanted him home despite the risks and his passage was booked on a Norwegian ship, MV *Thorstrand*. It had been a German-owned ship that was in a Norwegian port when the Germans invaded the country, and had been commandeered and sailed to England by a Norwegian crew. By 1942 it had made some twenty Atlantic crossings. The vessel's smallness alarmed him: 'I would have thought twice before crossing from Portsmouth to the Isle of Wight on this boat.' The *Empress of Australia*, on which he had come to Canada, was 23,000 tons and even she rolled around a lot. 'What then would the ocean do to this tiny tot?' He was soon to find out as the ship encountered storms. Like others who have endured seasickness he would say, 'The next 36 hours was hell—where, oh where, was that torpedo?' At one point they joined a convoy but as the convoy was averaging seven knots and the *Thorstrand*[113] could do 18 knots they soon departed from it.

In November that year Gillian Stronach (8) and her brother, David, (11) and their mother sailed from Baltimore to Lisbon on the Portuguese ship *Serpa Pinto*. This was a neutral ship doing a regular run with all its lights on, always fully booked for many passages ahead and sailing full. 'Our parents had been convinced even after Dunkirk that we hadn't a hope,' says Gillian. 'Now we felt we were not going to be overrun. We all voted.' They had been the two years first in Toronto and then in Buffalo, New York. From Lisbon they flew to Bristol, being attacked and damaged by a German fighter over the Bay of Biscay. 'An experience a child does not forget,' she says. A few months later the same plane, named Ibis, was shot down and actor Leslie Howard was killed.

The Royal Navy agreed to take school children home but cautioned that the sea-lanes were still not safe even for convoys. In fact, in March 1943, in what turned out to be the climax of the Battle of the Atlantic, U-boats sank 39 ships in four successive convoys. One of Lord Montagu's friends had died on the way home but he pressed for an early return. 'At fifteen I was old enough now to make up my own mind and the truth was that I was embarrassed about what others and I could only regard as "funking the war".' A berth was found for him on HMS *Dasher* which was due to escort a convoy from New York to the Clyde. As able-bodied young men he and the other returning evacuees were required to keep watch. Apart from one submarine sighting and a barrage of depth charges in mid-Atlantic, it was a quiet trip.

Jeremy Thorpe was one of ten children taken aboard HMS *Phoebe* sailing from Norfolk, Virginia, to an unnamed British port, which turned out to be Liverpool. They too had the exciting but demanding task of doing four-hour stints on the bridge on watch duty. Another 25 children travelled in the same convoy on the battleship *Queen Elizabeth*.

John Wilkinson, then 14, sailed in March from New York on the 16,000 ton submarine depot ship HMS *Wolfe* along with six other boys: 'Our own convoy was extremely fortunate as an Atlantic storm, which lasted for most of the two weeks of the voyage, prevented the U-boats from successful attacks.' Tony Moore, also from Milton, and his sister, Bridget, joined 40 boys, one other girl and a few naval wives on HMS *Khedive*, an escort carrier on its way to the European theatre. Henry Jacobs and his mother went back that same year on a Portuguese freighter, probably the *Serpa Pinto*, which was stopped by a German submarine. 'It seems from talk on board after we were underway again that our skipper had been asked if he had Jewish evacuees on board and had bravely denied it,' says Henry, who was himself Jewish. 'What a man!' They docked in Lisbon and spent some days in Estoril before being flown by flying boat to Ireland and being reunited in Liverpool with his father. 'For us kids it was lovely to have a father again—but for mum and dad after three years apart after only ten years of happy marriage 1930-40 what wonders and what joy—and I guess the difficulties of settling down to a partnership again.'

Geoff Towers returned on a Norwegian freighter, *Tunsha*, in July 1943 in the midst of a huge convoy, nearly a hundred ships. 'This was a fantastic adventure for me. The crew treated me with great respect and saluted me reverently.' They were so hospitable that on his 10th birthday they gave him rum and a large cigar, the results predictably making him exceedingly ill. Most of the time he spent roaming the decks submarine spotting 'with several unconfirmed sightings'. The British gunners made him their mascot and he was excited to spend time on the gun platform while they tested the Bofors and Oerlikon guns. The arrival at Liverpool was heralded by the coming aboard of the pilot who was delighted to receive a banana and an orange. 'We did not realize rationing,' says Geoff. 'We were soon to find out!'

In October 1944 'in view of the improved war situation' Noel K. Hunnybun of the London branch of the US Committee for the Care of European Children contacted British parents of evacuees: 'I am now writing round to all parents who have children in America to ask if they would like to sign these release forms, so that when the time comes for return there need be no unnecessary delays. The signing of the forms merely means that the children's names are entered in New York on the Consul General's list in readiness for return after the hostilities are over.' In March 1945 she responded to a letter from John Mathews:

I am afraid we cannot make any arrangements for girls to come back on naval boats. I quite agree that this has been done on one or two occasions but how we do not know. We have a definite ruling to the effect that this method of return is only available for boys who have not yet reached their seventeenth birthday. If Clifford returned to England before 31 July of this year it might be that we could get him a 'Special Sailing' by naval boat, which would cost you just a few pounds, as the navy only charge messing fees, but we should have to be very quick in making our arrangements. If you would like Clifford to return by this route, will you let me have a letter signed by you and your wife to say you are anxious for him to return by 'Special Sailing' and that you are prepared to defray expenses up to the sum of L10. Now with regard to the return passages for the two girls. At present the rates vary between L28 and L35 per person and we see no hope of any reduction. We have made efforts in this direction but have not been successful. I am sorry but there it is. The demand for passages is very great and the matter rests with the respective shipping companies. The parents of children who went out under the care of this Committee only paid about L25 for each child, but at that time the shipping companies gave special terms for evacuees.

Faith and Toby Coghill went home in 1944 on the escort carrier HMS *Arbiter*. On another escort carrier was Martyn Pease. Being several years older than I am, and indeed enjoying a high school graduation ceremony[114] just before leaving, he was glad to get back while the war was still on. 'I always felt guilty being in America,' he says, 'and was pleased to get home in time for the "Baby Blitz" of early 1944 and the subsequent V-weapons.' He and half a dozen other English boys were on HMS *Searcher*. They sailed from New York but found their first destination port was the Newport Naval base in Virginia from whence they returned a week later to New York and then joined a huge convoy of some 60 or more merchantmen. The ship in the next lane to his was the *Dominion Monarch* which in spite of the February cold had every inch of deck space covered by soldiers. The convoy's speed was dictated by the slowness of HMS *Ramillies*, an elderly battleship provided in case the new German dreadnought, *Tirpitz*, made a sortie from its Norwegian lair. Destroyers and corvettes patrolled the convoy's flanks and the captain told them there were two heavy cruisers and further destroyers thirty miles ahead. The rough weather was welcomed as it lessened the chance of torpedo attacks. 'We were on board for three full weeks for which each boy was given a mess bill of L2.0.6. And that was the total cost of the Atlantic crossing.'

Shirley Catlin returned at age 13. From 1942 onwards her parents were taking steps to get her and her brother back. They deliberately wanted them to experience the war. The *Daily Mail* at the end of October 'revealed' the peril Shirley and others faced, when the weather almost succeeded where the Germans had failed: 'Most of the children were travelling unaccompanied to Lisbon on the *Serpa Pinto*. Halfway across the Atlantic the cyclone struck. The captain said afterwards it was the worst storm he had known in 26 years. All the lifeboats were swung out from the davits ready for launching—but the voyage had ended before the master of the ship told anyone of his fears that none of the boats would have survived in the raging sea.' On its many trips the *Serpa Pinto*, picked up survivors of torpedo attacks stranded in the Azores.

Shirley faced another peril on that ship. In later years, in talking about predators on children, she recalled her experience: 'As a young girl of thirteen, I was confronted by a group of sailors intent on raping my best friend and me on the ship on which we returned to England from three year's evacuation in the United States. We escaped into the gentleman's lavatory and from there into one of the lifeboats on deck.'

Juliet Rodd, who had been with her mother and sisters in Long Island, was the same age on the same ship. She, too, remembers the storm and the care of the valiant Baptist missionaries returning to Africa without which many of these unaccompanied children would never have survived: 'For three days the hurricane raged, tossing our ship like a toy on waves as high as houses. Our propeller was out of the water for most of the time and we made little headway. The captain decided on a new strategy and turned the ship 45 degrees to head in a different direction, so that the propeller would remain in the water. He did the manoeuvre in the middle of lunch without warning. Chaos! Waiters, children, soup, chairs and table settings tumbled in confused heaps in the wildly pitching dining room. Bread rolls ran like marbles among the debris. My mother thought the cargo had shifted and that we were finished but the ploy worked. Gradually the waves decreased and our ship rolled and wallowed into smoother seas. We heard later that a fire had knocked out our radio.'

She recalls the Hollywood star Lynn Fontanne and her husband smoking, bored to tears, while the large sofa on which they were sitting rolled from one end of the lounge to the other. When the grand piano started it was time to abandon the lounge! There were eighty unaccompanied British children on board and Juliet, now a grandmother, realises what a daunting prospect the employment and entertainment of all these children must have presented. 'I hugely enjoyed everything, the company, the games, the acting and dressing up evenings and even the rudiments of embroidery that someone taught us.' The ship stopped twice, at Madeira and the Azores: 'There was magic in these islands appearing first as tiny bumps on the horizon and the little boats that came out to meet us as we arrived, selling embroidery and local crafts. For years I treasured a handkerchief, my first attempt at bargaining.'

Also on a Portuguese ship were Fabian and Dora Pease who had been in Chester, Nova Scotia. Fabian, 7, writes, 'That trip I remember well, spending the first few days miserably seasick and the rest of the two week trip utterly bored. I made a vow (which I have kept) that never again would I cross the Atlantic by boat.' Those on the Portuguese boats had in some cases to wait a long while for a plane or a flying boat to take them home from Portugal. For one thing flying boats could only take off in calm weather and they had to fly at night to avoid German interception. Juliet Rodd remembers their clothes being stuffed with newspapers for insulation as there was no heating in the plane.

The poet Anthony Thwaite went back in June 1944 on another escort carrier, HMS *Ruler*. He was in mid-Atlantic on D-Day. 'It was a bit wild; there were a dozen or so other unaccompanied British boys with me, and we behaved in characteristic young teenage fashion, even though we were supposed to obey "naval discipline". I remember being summoned before the commanding officer, with some other boys, to be reprimanded for breaking an ink bottle and splattering it about in a cabin.'

The Hutchison sisters and their mother were was also at sea on D-Day in an old New Zealand ship, *Rangatiki*. They were assigned bunks in an enormous communal cabin below the waterline, along with eighty-three other children. The surrounding ships of the convoy were a comforting sight and gave a sense of security which, however, the nightly announcement over the loudspeakers undermined: 'You are advised to sleep in your clothes as we are passing through dangerous waters,' followed by the unforgettable tune of Liliburlero introducing the nightly BBC news. The Hutchisons never did sleep in their clothes because, as Ruth says, 'Even a twelve-year-old could reason that, dressed or undressed, there would be no escape were a torpedo to strike.' None of them would like to repeat such a voyage. 'Dysentery was endemic on the ship and we all got it,' says Anne. 'In a slow convoy the crossing took two weeks going as far north as Iceland. I don't remember eating a single meal in the dining room and my life-long dislike of milk chocolate sprang from being given it daily by poor mother no doubt to try and keep us alive.' The voyage was enough to put Ruth off sea travel for life. The night before their arrival in Liverpool Anne went on deck and looked astern: 'The convoy stretched back in two lines right to the horizon where the sun was setting as an immense orange ball with a fiery carpet stretching up the centre.'

Vivien and David Brawn returned on the sister ship, *Rangitata*, in November 1944. She regrets that when visiting the Empire State Building before leaving she had turned down the chance to record her 'strong American accent'. One exciting event for her was when escort ships depthcharged a submarine and another when her ship was rammed by another ship whose rudder was defective and was steering with its engines. It hit her vessel near the stern, a temporary patch was placed over the hole and they were on their way: 'When it backed away there was an incredibly narrow triangular hole in our side ending just above the waterline.' The ramming happened during mealtime: 'There was an incredible sight in the dining room. The ship had heeled so violently that all the food had spilled on the floor. The passengers had panicked and I could see skid marks in the fallen food where they had scrambled to get out on deck. Some people had lost their shoes in the struggle.'

Sir Martin Gilbert who was evacuated to Canada gives an interesting sidelight from his perspective as Churchill's biographer. Shortly before the Normandy invasion in 1944, the Prime Minister, noticing that the *Mauretania* was to return from New York with only 3,000 troops, said, 'Why not bring the children back from Canada.' Messages were sent out and Martin, then seven, found himself on this big liner. He says, 'I found in Churchill's papers a little note where he put against the *Mauretania* file "make sure there are enough lifeboats on board for the extra children". Now, that's interesting to me. This man, who then was having to defeat Hitler in Normandy, counter the bombs, deal with the whole problem of defeating Japan, still remembered there were extra kids and to make sure there are enough lifeboats in case the ship goes down.'

On the *Mauretania* was Susan Lawson who was then nine and had been given 48 hours notice to pack up. She remembers an officious customs man who searched her luggage before she went on board and turned the whole lot out onto the ground losing some marbles from a set of Chinese checkers. 'He was American-Irish and anti-British!' The First Class lounge was full of hammocks for troops. 250 mothers and children were put in there. The bottom bunks had canvas put round them so that if it was rough the children would not fall out. Before sailing they were all called up on deck and the captain spoke to them: 'We are sailing without a convoy. The first crossing without one. We are going to go fast. If any child falls overboard we will not stop.' She recalls the friendliness of the crew who when they arrived gave every child a lunch box on a string containing an apple, an orange, sandwiches, a small bottle of coca-cola and a Hershey bar. Also on the *Mauretania* was Janet Young.

Sheila Christine, now 16, returned on the *Athlone Castle* which had become a troop ship and been remodelled to accommodate as many people as possible. The bunks in her dormitory were in four tiers across the whole breadth of the ship, beneath the bridge. Her fellow passengers were other returning "war guests" and brides of British servicemen who were on their way to rejoin their husbands. She remembers a very fat bride looking in despair at the small space allocated to her and saying that it would not do and she would speak to an officer. 'Good luck,' thought Sheila, but the bride was soon installed in a cabin of her own. 'I had learned lessons about squeaky wheels and the ways of the world.' Submarines still lurked 'but we sailed alone this time and no alarms came to spoil the pleasure of the voyage'.

Wendy Clarke travelled home in September 1944 and recalls the experience graphically:

Total devastation of farewells in New York. Sailing next day in a tiny Mediterranean cruise vessel under the Cross of Lorraine, manned by Free French crew. Later discovered to be part of the largest convoy of the war, comprised of 2,000 ships. Travelled for 17 days at top speed of eight knots. Not a single book on board but every day something spectacular. A tornado, water spouts and massive waves towering above the ship. Deck forbidden to the 20 passengers, but nobody really caring so two days sheer bliss lashed to a stanchion, staring through walls of green and purple water. A tiny brown sparrow fellow traveller. A school of whales, so thick the sea was red with blood as the ship cut through them. A calm and beautiful moonlit night when the ship was outlined with phosphorescence. Thoughts of U-boats inevitable but quiet conviction we'd be safe. Our nearest neighbour was sunk. Nearing Ireland enemy planes bombing ships at the edge of the convoy. Our sole armament an AA gun, firing as I stood at the base of the turret. Both Paris and Brussels were liberated during the voyage. Captain celebrated to insensibility and first mate followed suit. US navy radar experts locked them in their cabins and took over the ship for a few hours. Arrived safely in Cardiff all the same.

Neil Maidment returned on 14 August 1945 as American soldiers were beginning to come back to America. He sailed out of New York harbour past a sign on Staten Island WELCOME HOME BOYS and thought, 'Strange, I'm going home too.' The ship carried thousands of men and women in uniform with him and his sister being practically the only children on board. Soldiers took turns looking after them. On 15 August the Emperor of Japan announced the surrender of his forces. 'The ship went mad with happiness, everyone was so excited and delighted. There were parties going on everywhere. I shall never forget the atmosphere of sheer exhilaration and good nature of that day and night, it will remain with me forever.' On 18 August he celebrated his birthday. 'I was loaded down with Hershey chocolate bars, packs of gum and enough lifesavers to preserve the whole ship's complement.' The next day they paraded up the channel with ships of every shape and size escorting them and increasing in number as they reached the shores of England. 'There must have been hundreds of them, filled with cheering people. There was one large ferry, I remember, leaning over almost to the rails in the water because of the weight of passengers crowding her port side. There were boats with brass bands playing and people singing. It was all because that frightful war was over at last. Britain's finest passenger ship, the *Queen Elizabeth,* the largest and fastest ship in the world was coming home in public for the first time. Everyone was bursting with pride, happiness and tears. Looking back now, I realize it was the greatest moment of national glory in my life. But then, I thought how appropriate it was that half the population of England should be turning out to welcome me and Jackie back home.'[115]

From the beginning of 1944 the number of women and children returning home had gone up each month. For instance, 598 in March and 727 in April. There was a reduction in September that year as news of the V-bombs landing in Britain discouraged some from returning. By the end of the year nearly half of the evacuees in the US had returned home.

For all its inevitability, our own return to England in 1945 after five years in the US was very sudden. We had a few days notice, to pack up things at school, take the train to Boston, and collect belongings in Milton and then set off again by train with Mrs. Hinchman to New York. The school had rushed through an eighth grade graduation certificate and gave me some awards. Gerald was presented with an album of Tschaikowski's First Piano Concerto played by Vladimir Horowitz, signed by his friends. The suddenness of the departure was underlined in the next the issue of the school paper, *Rectory News*. In a review of a theatrical production it says, 'The show went off with a bang, even though Michael Henderson, who was chiefly responsible for the production of the play, left for England three days before' and his original script was changed because 'we decided it didn't have enough slapstick'. The author of the review was another evacuee, Donald Westbury. In the baseball news it says that 'the loss of our catcher was a heavy blow'. The headmaster wrote in the paper, 'Michael's and his brother's return home had long been expected, but when the spring term rolled around and they still had no word from the shipping authorities, we all thought they would be with us for the entire school year. The departure of no other two boys could have left a larger nor more obvious gap in our school life.'

The deputy head was a little upset. Huntingdon Thompson thought our departure 'unfortunate'. He wrote to Charlie Fay's parents, 'They ought to have finished their year here. One can understand Colonel Henderson's and Mrs. Henderson's longing to have the boys back again as we can understand your longing for Charles, but if one has stood it for four years it would be supposed that a month more could be stood. Somehow it also seems to indicate a slight contempt for this school. Probably, Colonel Henderson didn't see this possible interpretation.'

The abruptness of departure is underlined for me in the fact that I can recite the first half of the presidents of the United States. I can't get beyond 22, President Grover Cleveland, because that was where I had got to in memorizing when I was whisked out of school. I do not remember the parting from the Hinchmans. I suppose our focus was on the excitement of going home.

We had been told to report at New York's Barbizon Plaza hotel with our luggage labelled 'Peru'. I don't know whom we were trying to fool! This was 24 hours after VE-day. Jennifer Clarke, who left earlier, still has her luggage label from that trip home. Her supposed destination 'Sydney'. All I recall of the hotel, which was the shore base for Royal Naval personnel, was that breakfast was passed in through a slot at the bottom of the door. Keith Douglas-Mann who had got there a day earlier remembers being taken to Times Square to see the VE-day celebrations, and seeing sailors scaling lampposts. To discover that we were travelling on a Royal Navy ship, HMS *Patroller*, was exciting. Not quite HMS *Revenge* perhaps but the chance to see Royal Navy uniforms close up instead of just studying them in the *Illustrated London News*.

HMS *Patroller*

Anthony Bailey, who sailed on an escort carrier, HMS *Ranee*, earlier, in October 1944 says that a petty officer told him that the crew called the ship a Woolworth carrier, or banana boat and advised the evacuees not to dawdle if they heard the sharply clanging bell announcing action or an emergency. 'These are real coffin ships,' he said cheerfully. 'They go down like a stone.' He and eleven other evacuees travelled as unofficial Boy Seamen.

Our 11,400-ton CVE, or aircraft escort carrier, was built in the Todd Pacific shipyards in Tacoma, Washington and launched on 6 May 1943 as the *Keweenaw*. She was assigned to the United Kingdom in June and transferred to the Royal Navy under lend-lease in October. The 'Ruler' class escort carrier was armed with 2 5" guns, 16 40mm Bofors guns and 35 20mm Oerlikon cannons. It was initially employed as a Ferry carrier for aircraft for the Eastern fleet between the US and Cochin. In March 1944 it was lent to the US Army for transport of their aircraft to Pearl Harbor and then fulfilled a ferry role between the UK and USA. She was lent to the US Navy for further ferry duty in the Pacific from January to May 1945. To our great interest when we joined her she had a Japanese zero plane in the hangar. As with some of the other escort carriers conveying evacuees the planes were not operational but being ferried to the British Isles. Fighters filled the hanger deck and the flight deck was covered with more lashed down aircraft with folded wings.

Escort carriers were built because of the submarine threat in the Atlantic and to protect the long supply lines in the Pacific. They could be quickly produced from merchant hulls. At one time during the war they were being launched at the rate of one a week. As the war progressed their role became more an offensive one. From mid-1944 to the end of the war they furnished fighter protection and direct air support to the invasion forces, spotted for gunfire, and sent strikes against enemy air bases. In our case she was carrying a squadron of planes on the deck and in the hangar bound for Northern Ireland.

Jennifer Clarke, who was also on an escort carrier, HMS *Speaker*, which was ferrying planes, still has her mess bill for 12 days costing L2 and a list of 29 instructions for the civilian passengers. They are very comprehensive ranging from where children could and could not go on the ship to details about meals and what to do if the alarm sounds. It was made clear that only the Commander (The Hon R.A. Southwell) had the authority to deal with matters affecting passengers but 'should the problem be one of such delicacy that lady passengers feel diffident about approaching the Commander direct, they should see Mrs. Jones (The Commander's Representative for lady passengers)....' Instruction 28 stated, 'It is hoped that it will be realised that an HM ship at war is not able to give the service of an hotel, and that the normal inconveniences experienced by Officers at sea in war time will be accepted by all passengers.'

On 10 May we sailed out in the cold, calm, misty weather past the Statue of Liberty and joined the other 27 ships in our convoy (FX-3712), cargo ships, tankers and four escorts from the US Navy. Towed behind each ship was a fog buoy designed to produce a wake for the next one to steer by. Four other ships were to rendezvous with us later. In the official report our ship was listed as 'miscellaneous', probably because our planes were not operational. Our convoy took ten days to reach Europe, travelling at 14.5 knots, zigzagging and coping with terrible weather.

We were about 20 to 25 young British housed in the pilot's ready room, sleeping on specially erected wooden bunks. We were put in charge of a petty officer. We took our meals in the officer's mess, with breakfast at 6 am as we ate before they did. 'Wakey, wakey, rise and shine' came blaring out of the loudspeaker followed by some other line which I am sure was more restrained than usual due to the presence of children. The mess tables had edges that could be put up and were also fastened to the floor in a storm which we, indeed had, for nearly a week. I have never been so sick and for so long. Keith Douglas-Mann had his liver and white springer spaniel 'Socks' with him. He had a terrible job getting the dog up ladders to the flight deck in the pouring rain with the ship pitching and tossing and was always afraid he would be lost overboard. Everyone including the captain paid the dog special attention.

After the stormy period had subsided it was bliss to sit in sunshine on the flight deck with calm seas and the sight of all the ships in line port and starboard. We were impressed the way the officers walked across the deck and always seemed to know how to turn in step. We had the chance to sit at the controls of the guns and manipulate them. We were given the duty of cleaning grease off the cartridges. Up there on the deck one day we saw a German submarine. We had always thought that it had surrendered to us. Keith writes, 'Tremendous excitement when convoy stopped to accept surrender of U-boats. Also further excitement when off Ireland, convoy stopped again and we were told a U-boat was depth-charged for not surrendering.' However, the report of the convoy commodore does not confirm our childhood memories of a submarine surrendering only the fact that we passed a submarine under escort.

In fact, one submarine did actually surrender in the North Atlantic a few days later on 19 May, a fact which was never disclosed because of its cargo.

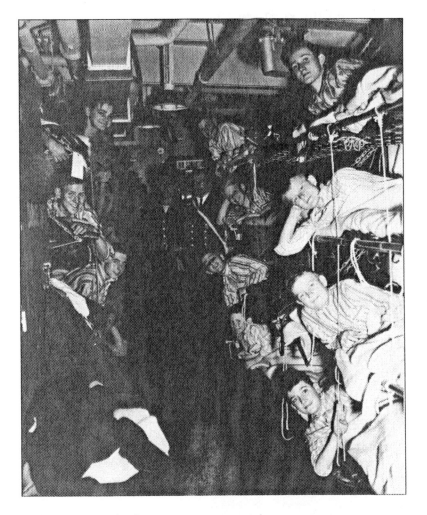

Evacuees returning home on an escort carrier

It was carrying 1,200 pounds of uranium oxide, ingredients for an atomic bomb, bound for Japan. Two Japanese officers on board were allowed to commit suicide. The oxide is believed to have been taken to Oak Ridge, Tennessee, to bolster supplies for the Manhattan Project, the US atomic bomb program.

When we neared England the convoy split up, some ships heading to London and French ports, some to Merseyside, and with us going to Glasgow. The official report says that station keeping was at the beginning poor, partly due to unfavourable weather. Another criticism: 'The smoking of ships in this convoy was generally excessive and perhaps was, in the opinion of the Convoy Commodore, due to a general letdown by the ships concerned.'

Before we landed the petty officer opened up a store under the ready room and we could buy things for our parents, things they wouldn't have seen much of for years, like tins of grapefruit juice and assorted bars of chocolate. I had a little grey purse which I carried round my neck, also the metal disk on a chain with my national health identification which I wore on the way out and still have. The Hinchmans had thoughtfully provided us with some money.

Entering the Clyde Keith hatched a plan with the crew to smuggle Socks ashore to avoid quarantine. His father had different ideas as a cutter met the ship to take the dog off. 'My mother and my younger brother Stewart came back on the *Queen Mary* on the occasion when it very nearly turned turtle because of the weight of the people returning from the states in a violent storm.'

From Glasgow we took the train to London to be reunited with our parents.

16
At Home Again

In the early days we undoubtedly annoyed people in Britain by praising American virtues too extravagantly. Now we take a more balanced view of the good and bad in both countries. One American virtue we can never overrate is their unhesitating generosity.
—*Jocelyn Statler*

In Dayton I had been compelled on several occasions to stand up for England but now I found myself forced into the role of spokesman for the United States.
—*Anthony Bailey*

The fear of not recognizing their parents was uppermost in the minds of many children as they returned after their years away. Anthony Bailey remembers, 'Finally, I put out my hand to shake that of the woman, with premature streaks of grey hair, who met me at Glasgow, who I thought might be my aunt, but who, as she put her arms round me, I realized was my mother.' Alastair Macbeth, who had been one of the Oxford party, saw a crowd of people at the end of the platform and a man he did not recognize stepped out, held out his hand rather formally and asked, 'Excuse me, are you Alastair Macbeth?' It was his father. Jean, returning to Middlesborough from Canada, didn't recognize her father and when he came forward and put his arm round her she reacted violently: 'I thought he was a stranger about to abduct me.' Brian Proctor, five years in Canada, says, 'My parents seemed like strangers when they met me at the station. It must have been terrible for them to have given up so much for so long and to be faced with a teenager with little appropriate comprehension.' Penny Moon, who returned from Montreal, did not recognize her mother. She believes that a lifelong anxiety about not recognizing someone she ought to know dates from that experience. 'The upside of that,' she says, 'has been that I smile at everyone just in case.' Asked if she was pleased to be home she replied in a broad Canadian accent, 'I sure am.'

Parents had the same fears of not recognizing their children. When Vera Brittain went to meet her 15-year-old son at Paddington, after three years separation, she could not tell which boy he was. 'It would take time to get to know him again.' Her daughter, asked later by her mother if she remembered her return home, told her, 'You weren't real to me at all. You seemed more like a person in a book.' Ellie Bourdillon came back in 1946 on the *Queen Mary*. Her parents were at the dockside in Southampton. 'Happily we did recognize each other though my North American accent must have been a shock. The years of separation were overlaid by joyful reunion though never quite forgotten. Being a parent has made me realize what a gap my absence was in all our lives. But the benefit to me was unquestionably valuable and greatly valued.' She also met her future husband in the US.

Anthony Thwaite arrived back in Sheffield: 'There were my parents on the platform—looking strangely old, even a bit grey-haired. The whole episode— my going to America, the time there, the coming back—is clear in my mind; but I can't quite make sense of it. Maybe the main thing is that it made me independent, and restless, and eager for change—but at the same time I know I value roots.' Lord Montagu's mother met his train and, she wrote in her diary, 'found him very quickly'. 'He's taller than me and talks with a soft, low Canadian accent. Just too odd.' She claimed that almost his first words, confronted with the car that was to take them home from the local station, was, 'Say, where did you get that gas?' It had not occurred to Daniel Farson that his arrival in London, still at war, would be so disillusioning. He scarcely recognized his mother, they were strangers. 'I looked out of the taxi with dismay, expecting the bomb damage but not the air of desolation—the streets almost empty, the shops boarded up or shut, the public houses closed. And it was raining. My God, I thought, England is destroyed. I forgot one thing: it was an English Sunday.'

John Mathews wrote to his son's host family in the United States, 'I suddenly saw a head sticking way up above everyone else and after looking at him two or three times I decided that the worried-looking fellow must be

Cliff. I waved and suddenly he discovered me and waved back and we forced our way towards one another and once again I was holding the hand of my favourite son. What a moment that was. All Cliff could say was "Gosh". It was a terrific moment because all around us were people meeting their sons and daughters and husbands for the first time in years, and some of them were openly weeping. This made things all the more difficult, my own eyes became pretty watery, but everybody else in the family put up a good front so I had to pretend I had a bit of grit in my eye.' His two daughters were to return a little later. When they departed from America, their hosts wrote to the Mathews, 'This is a very sad evening. We are going to hate having the girls leave tomorrow. We know that we are terribly lucky—having the three nicest children in all England for so long—but I wish they were not so attractive and had a few irritating traits so that we could be a little pleased to see them go. What a thrill for you to have them all again.'

Blanche Bradley returned with her two sons, John and David to their home in Horsforth, Yorkshire. John writes, 'The kitchen door of The Gables was unlocked so mother walked straight in and there, as usual, was her mother standing by the kitchen sink. She glanced up as she heard the door open and nearly died of shock. In the interests of security our departure from Canada had been kept so secret.' The Bradleys had been on the *Rangitata* returning just after the Normandy invasion. One night Blanche was playing Bridge with a group that included an Indian princess. During the game the princess was called to the Radio room. On her return she confided that her embassy had told her that a mysterious flying bomb had fallen on London.

Indeed, those who returned while the war was still on had to contend with the 'doodle bugs'. Penny Moon can still recall her 'terrifying fear'. She was also baffled by her friends who had stayed in England and seemed unafraid. Some evacuees did not have familiar homes to come back to. Brian Hall-Tomkin returned early with his mother and sister on the *Serpa Pinto*. His father, in the medical corps, had been evacuated from Dunkirk, later saw service in Holland and Germany and in the last days of the war was caring for the survivors of Belsen. Their home in Exeter had been destroyed by firebombs while they were in Toronto.

For most children it was a reverse culture shock, getting used once again to familiar ways. To Angela Pelham the first surprise was at the policemen's helmets: 'Wasn't it a silly thing to be surprised at? They looked so funny and strange to me after the flat hats in America.' Jan Struther and her children, Janet and Robert, returned the same month we did in a banana boat, the

Bayano. Looking out of the taxi window at the thin and war-weary Londoners near Victoria Station, Jan, according to her daughter, Ysenda Maxtone Graham, 'tested her conscience'. She was deeply moved as she knew she would be to see the people who must have lived through the bombing, and to see the city of her childhood so changed, with unexpected empty plots and vistas where buildings had been. But she did not feel the violent assault of guilt which other Londoners claimed to have felt on returning from wartime exile. 'She reflected that in her own way she, too, was war-weary after five nomadic years as Allied propaganda.'[116]

Author Lynne Reid Banks had been ten in 1940 when she and her cousin Chris were sent to Saskatoon in Canada. She remembers her return after five years: 'At last the war in Europe ended and we sailed home. It was early summer of 1945. London was in ruins. My father's hair had turned white. My aunts looked much more than five years older. We came back into a poverty-stricken, ration-blighted, war-torn country, licking its still-open wounds. Our loved ones welcomed us with utmost warmth and helped us, as far as they could, to fit back into our places. They never let us feel like deserters. But that's what I knew I was.'[117]

Gerald and I had been fortunate to see our father during the war, but we had not seen our mother for five years and did, indeed, walk right past her on the station platform. One of the first tasks on getting home was to try to get off the accumulated grime from two weeks on the aircraft carrier. The next, which took longer, was to re-establish the sense of family.

Some evacuees report that the biggest difficulty of the whole evacuation experience was this adjustment after coming home. *Back Home*, a gripping novel by Michelle Magorian, is built round the story of 12-year-old Rusty returning to England after five years in the United States. She seems to encompass in her attitudes every criticism a returning child might possibly have had towards her newfound country and to suffer at school and at home every possible variation of uninformed attitudes to 'yanks'. No doubt some children will have identified with Rusty's story but it was not our story or that of most of our friends. We did not in our reactions progress to 'dramatic and devastating rebellion' as she did. But then peaceful reintegration, like planes that do not crash, is not the stuff of engrossing fiction. 'I cannot remember conscious turmoil,' says Anthony Bailey.

Our reunion and subsequent life together had its stresses and rows. It was naturally hard for us to live into the lives of parents who, after years of bombardment and nightly fire watching, would jump at any loud noise. A British

Information Service pamphlet at the time warned that returnees would find that after the years of war 'many people are easily tired and sometimes, therefore, abrupt in their manner' because of the cumulative pressure on nerves and physical and mental endurance. Our army officer father expected a quicker obedience perhaps than we gave him. Mother and father's admonitions were constantly met with the refrain, '*We* don't do it that way in America.' '*We* don't do this, *we* don't do that.' So much so, that America in our family soon became known as '*We*-land.' In much the same way that in some families a common refrain in those first post-war years was 'Before you went to America....'

An article in early 1945 in the *Evening Standard* may have alerted parents to some of the possible difficulties. New York correspondent F.G.A Cook interviewed boys and girls from the Actors' Orphanage who would be returning home shortly: 'They are bringing some shocks with them for parents who probably do not realise what four years and America have done for them. Little girls who were eleven when they said "goodbye" with sticky fingers and their hair in pigtails are completely self-assured young misses today, with fashionable "hairdos" and well-cut clothes. Little boys who were nine or so when they left home, manfully sniffing back the tears, are muscular young footballers now, some of them cheerfully hoping war will not be over before they get their chance in the RAF or Navy.' He added, 'I would not be a truthful reporter if I did not straight away warn their parents that not all of them are in the least enthusiastic about the idea of going home.'

Many evacuees had the reaction, as we did, that everything was somehow shrunken, distances were shorter, roads were narrower, cars and homes smaller. Anthony Bailey 'found it hard not to bump into things'. London, and other cities, were also understandably very shabby. We soon got used to the London Underground which still had gauze across the windows, the water tanks ready for the fire service, the rubble of demolished buildings all round where we first lived in Abbey Road, St. John's Wood—a street which twenty years later would have more famous occupants. There were new slogans to take in, for instance, like London Transport's Billy Brown of London Town: Face the driver, raise your hand, you'll find that he will understand. The first winters were particularly cold and London fog was real and in those days justified, as it no longer does, a raincoat being so named. At the newsreel cinema Studio 2 I saw shots of Arsenal against Moscow Dynamo with players looming up out of the fog. In fact, Granville Bantock, from the Actors' Orphanage school, thought 'the filthy fogs were the worst part of being back in England'.

Muriel Harrington (Russ), who had the advantage of having her parents with her in Canada because her father went there as an Inspector of Munitions, still had to cope with a different England: 'We returned to freezing houses and food rationing. After the warmth of the Canadian homes and the plentiful food, life in England was very austere.'

There was, indeed, strict food and clothes rationing to contend with. In 1945 there was 'utility clothing', bread was 4" p a loaf, Pom was a useful substitute for mashed potatoes and we had only powdered egg, and by law you were not allowed to pay more than 5 shillings for a meal in a restaurant. The British restaurants with cheaper meals were still around (with a spoon for stirring your tea chained to the counter). We were glad to get back to English sweets, like Cadbury's chocolate, humbugs, Old Fashioned Butter Drops and Bertie Bassett's Liquorice Allsorts—even if they were rationed to a few ounces a week; and also to other essentially British items which we had missed like Tate and Lyle Golden Syrup, and Ryvita, and custard, and crisp cold toast in a rack as opposed to soggy hot toast in a napkin. We soon got hooked on the radio programmes we had missed, ITMA, Much Binding in the Marsh, Dick Barton, special agent, and used to the theme of Music While You Work.

We arrived back in England in time to celebrate VJ night on the cobblestones streets of Cirencester and on Victory day, June 1946, to join the hundreds of thousands who lined the Mall as thousands of Allied troops in their battle khaki, led by the Guards and the US Marines, marched past the reviewing stand.

All of us returnees had to contend with an educational syllabus that was different. Coping with English money sums was particularly challenging. One Milton mother, writing back to the Academy in 1946 about how her daughter had fared, commented: 'The return to arithmetic—an essential School Certificate subject—with pounds, shillings and pence, has been a real torment and has sorely tried her otherwise enthusiastic patriotism!'

Henry Jacobs and I found ourselves later at school together. He had come back earlier and felt that by the time he was 13 and sent away to school a good deal of the brashness he had developed in the States had worn off, although he was always trying to catch up his education. 'But instead of blaming the standard of education in the States at that time,' he says, 'perhaps I was naturally not very good at the learning process.'

Jane Redway (Fry), who spent the war in Ontario, says her only regret after having 'a truly wonderful war' was her educational gaps. 'After 4 " years, I returned to England never having learnt any English history or literature.'

However, she insists, 'I had learnt a lot about life!' Or as Douglas Wilde, 4 ″ years in Manitoba, puts it, 'Evacuation to Canada gave me a foundation for my future life and my comparative success in life but my knowledge of General Wolfe, Montcalm and the Heights of Abraham were not much use in trying to get a place in a grammar school back in England in 1945.'

A group of boys and girls who had spent three or four years in America was brought together at the Toc H Centre in Dean's Yard, London to answer questions about their life and schooling there. 'These children,' according to one report, 'now almost grown up, impressed their hearers with their fair criticism, frankness and good humour.' 'None of us is afraid to work, thanks to America,' said Ann Fry, of Welwyn Garden City. They were all keen about co-education. Peter West, who attended West Town School, Pennsylvania, said, 'You grow up with girls and learn to be free and at ease with them.' They all liked and missed the informality of American homes, where one can 'drop in at any time and not upset anybody'.

The points they liked about American schools: Fewer rules and fewer temptations to break them; no canes or prefects, the only punishment being detention; fewer history dates to get by heart; self-government by the students. Anne James (McCready), returning from Farmington, Connecticut, found single sex schools less fun than co-education and had to get used to wearing a uniform and a school hat. The teasing about her accent was 'a big hurdle'.

Tony Moore, who came back earlier from Milton than I did, says that his English school took the line that at aged 15 ″ he had got back just in time to be rescued from an inferior education in the States; just as some Americans had tended to imply when he arrived there 3 ″ years earlier that he was fortunate to be saved, not so much from the Germans as from the British educational system. He and his sister were 'a little edgy' about their return, surprised at the readiness of people to assume that they had returned from America as it were in the nick of time before accents, dress and habits were completely moulded in the American way of doing things. 'Bridget and I became fiercely defensive of our American experience.' He looks back on his time in America as a boy of 12-15 with great pleasure, a lot of fun and some tears. 'One gained self-confidence and sometimes lost it. We missed our home and family. But we never doubted it was only a matter of time before we returned. The possibility of any outcome to the war other than an Allied victory was quite beyond contemplation.'

He wrote, in 1988, 'In some ways the experience of the evacuation did not end with our return to this country. I came back influenced by the kindness and richness of the experience and I have remained conscious of it through the years. Some understanding of international prejudices has been a lasting benefit of the experience!' He would be surprised if the vast majority of children who went across the Atlantic were not equally happy. 'Children are almost infinitely adaptable and resilient. They only get hang-ups when adults get too tense about things.'

Martyn Pease, who was at Milton Academy's rival Browne and Nichols, feels on balance that overseas evacuation was probably a mistake but he has no doubts about American hospitality: 'The enormous generosity of the American hosts, and of the schools, only nominal fees or none at all, is never forgotten by us recipients.' His cousin, Richenda, returned with what she called 'a new outlook, much more international, pro-American'. In fact, she found herself 'very quick to leap in to defend the Americans'.

Alys Rickett retains very happy memories of her childhood in the United States. She lived in Providence, Rhode Island and only returned to Britain in 1947. Her brother Brian now lives in the US and she regularly travels there to see families and friends and to arrange lectures on American museums, music, gardens and other arts for the English-Speaking Union in London. Always noted on the programme is that the lecture is 'in memory of Mr. and Mrs. Harvey A. Baker who took a little English girl into their home during the Second World War'.

Meg Weston Smith (Milne), who went on to teach in the US and in Britain where she was Head of Mathematics at South Hampstead High School, confirms what I have often felt, that it was not that one system was necessarily that much better or worse than another but that we learned things at different stages. Which means, at least for me, that there are great gaps in my education and that my own educational challenge on returning home was centred on trying to pass the Common Entrance exam that would get me into my father's old school. I took it shortly after getting back and I think I was below 20% in practically every subject. But a term and a half of intensive cramming at The Hall School, Hampstead, was enough to bring me more than up to speed so that when I took the test again only one mark, history, was less than 90%. This was done by again and again going through previous common entrance exams. As a later classics master would say repeatedly about the learning process 'Repetitio, repititionis'. I was fortunate that I never again got asked to stand up and decline nouns after I did so once and although it was clear that I knew my declensions I had learned them in a different order in America and therefore would confuse the other boys. At The Hall I remember having to give a talk to the whole school about my experiences on HMS *Patroller*[118].

To Meg, her five years with Miriam and Theodore Dunham 'stand out clearly, and were a tremendously happy period, formative and colourful, that have stood me in good stead'. As Ruth Hutchison (Mackenzie), who was evacuated to Ottawa, says, 'These second families we were all given was the great plus from it all.' Barbara Shawcroft still regards her wartime Canadian hostess as 'mother'. 'These were my formative years,' she says. 'I believe the experience was freeing and gave me a special kind of independence.'

Jennifer Richards (Clarke) found coming back to England a shock. 'Although I had never had doubts about the outcome of the war or my eventual return to England, I don't think that I realised or understood what England had gone through in the years I had been away. My first sight of Liverpool and the bombed buildings was a shock, as was everyone looking tired and shabby. After four years of luxury, I couldn't believe how cold English houses were, and the great lack of foods like margarine, sugar and meat. We had to queue for bananas, oranges and grapefruit which were practically unheard of. I returned before D Day so have memories of all the thousands of American troops and the huge formations of bombers on their way to Europe. I also have memories of the sound of the big guns booming away on D Day and afterwards. I did recognise my parents on the station platform in London but am not sure how they recognised me from the 10-year-old leaving to the 14-year old with a strong American accent.' Those years away affected Jennifer greatly and were an important part of her life and 'perhaps made me into the person I am today'. Like some others she has a slight feeling of shame about being out of Britain and escaping the worst years of the war. Apart from bouts of unhappiness and homesickness and feeling rather on her own, she considers the four years she spent in America a very exciting time of her life and a wonderful opportunity. Sixty years later she is still in touch with friends she made at school and she has been back often. 'A lot of Americans were incredibly kind and generous to us English children and I very much appreciate and am grateful to them and to Milton Academy for giving me those years of good education.'

For parents, too, there was gratitude for the generosity of American[119] and Canadian families. Canadian novelist Guy Vanderhaeghe writes of the ordinary folk who were moved to make sacrifices on behalf of people they often didn't know: 'These sacrifices were not, of course, ones commonly considered heroic. They were small, pinching, disrupting sacrifices that upset households and which were made day after day, week after week, month after month, year after year, for the sake of strangers' children.'

Daphne Dunkin (James), one of the Oxford party invited by Yale, feels that this sacrificial commitment of American families has not always been fully appreciated. She and her sister Anne lived with John and Perry Lee in Connecticut. A couple in their mid 30s, the Lees were very busy, he working with the Pratt and Whitney research division and she involved in the League of Women Voters. Besides looking after their own four children and the two evacuees, they took on fundraising and care for more Oxford families. 'They gave of themselves 100%,' writes Daphne, 'and continued to do so until they died. I am still in constant contact with the Lees whom I consider an extended limb of my family.'

In 1946 when the London branch of the US Committee was about to close it received hundreds of letters from parents expressing appreciation for what the committee and American foster parents had done for their children. Though in some cases this was tinged with regret for missed opportunities to be with their children in formative years. Vera Brittain expressed this in several books. She writes, 'The carnation pressed in my diary from the parting bouquet which John and Shirley gave me remains a poignant relic, for the lost years of their childhood are lost to me still. The small gallant figures which disappeared behind the flapping tarpaulin of the grey-painted *Duchess of Atholl* have never grown up in my mind, for the children who returned and eventually took their places were not the same; the break in continuity made them rather appear as an elder brother and sister of the vanished pair.' Nobody was to blame for this, she says, it lay in the logic of a world situation with by-products which neither their magnanimous hosts in America nor her own family could prevent.

Janet Baker, who had done a freshman year at Mount Holyoke before returning to take up a place at Oxford, spoke to me enthusiastically of the generosity and kindness of her host family: 'I shall be everlastingly grateful for the family. They were not a rich family. They made sacrifices. They gave without counting the cost.' Her own family set aside all the money they would have spent on their children if they had stayed in England and after the war asked the American family to come and spend it. Which they did. It helped, for instance, the oldest son who won a scholarship to Cambridge.[120] 'Father thought it would be totally improper to be making money off the scheme,' she said.

The years overseas made a 'huge difference' in her life, in the first place in how she thought about America. In later years, whenever the Americans did things with which she disagreed, she remembered their generosity and that 'they would have kept us forever'. The fact that she had stayed with an intellectual family who had engaged in passionate discussions about the soul, about political issues, about pacifism—they were pacifists—about the meaning of life and what you were going to contribute, may have been a bit daunting at the age of 13 when she arrived but had a profound effect on her and helped strengthen her arguments. Baroness Young, as Janet became, found her American years most useful when she was Minister of State at the Foreign and Commonwealth Office. The fact that she had attended Mount Holyoke stood her in as good stead with American diplomats as the fact that she had been at Oxford with Margaret Thatcher. At her 50th class reunion Mount Holyoke gave her an honorary degree. Having adopted an American accent during the war she soon lapsed back into it whenever she returned there.

The war years spent in the United States opened new horizons in this way to the children. Shirley Catlin, now Baroness Williams, enjoyed what she calls 'freedoms I had never enjoyed in England' and felt her years there gave her a sense of the promise of 'a new world where everything is possible'. She was even at her young age there conscious of the way different people whether plumbers or doctors or secretaries were not judged by their social backgrounds. 'There was a sense of the high possibility of a society ready to pull together.' She was horrified on her return to Britain, coming back to 'pigeon-cooped slots', at the extent to which Britain was "mired in class'. She says, 'It is one of the things which drove me into politics.' Likewise, Eric Hammond, who was later to become General Secretary of the electricians union, EETPU, was delighted to find that 'you didn't have to accept British assumptions or its supposedly insurmountable class barriers'.

Anthony Bailey found England 'poorer for these demarcations'. He writes, in *England, First and Last*, 'Certainly those four American years left me feeling slightly unsure of myself in Britain when dealing with both workers and toffs. It also made them unsure of me. They weren't able to place me. I wasn't to be precisely defined, as foreigner or native, and, within the classes as upper, middle, or lower. Mostly I'm grateful for this escape from what seems to me a generally pernicious habit of categorization—a need to compartmentalize people, to decide *a priori* what can or can't be said to them or expected of them; a means of arranging society according to one's assumption about it, a way of giving oneself less bother. But it results in the lessening of mobility, flexibility and interaction—or it did so then, even more than it does today, after nearly forty years of the Welfare State.'

Bailey also speaks of the 'impetus' derived from those childhood years which offset the disruption and separation. And Alistair Horne believes that in a funny sort of way evacuation helped him and all the 'bundles' who went to America to also appreciate their own country the more. 'Thank you, my other country,' he writes.

John Bland, who was a ten-year-old CORB evacuee along with his sister to Canada, looking back on his four years in Regina, says that their experiences greatly changed their lives: 'I am retired now but I have had a successful career ending up as managing director of several companies. I would never have had the push to do this unless I had been made to stand on my own feet away from parents for so long at so early an age.' Similarly, Doug Wilde who spent five years in Manitoba along with his younger brother Peter, says, "Our Canada adventure made us self-reliant and more confident, an experience we would not have missed." And Geoff Towers, who was in Nova Scotia, feels he too learned a certain self-reliance, to accept whatever came his way if he couldn't influence it, to be self-contained but appreciative of friends, to be tolerant of others and always to try to be happy.

Fifty years after the evacuation of her brother and sisters to the United States Jocelyn Statler, who compiled the book of the exchanges of correspondence between her parents and the American hosts which I quoted from earlier, writes: 'My father hoped the evacuation scheme would help to promote better transatlantic relations. Within our family it certainly has[121] and perhaps we have managed to help spread this a little more widely. In the early days we undoubtedly annoyed people in Britain by praising American virtues too extravagantly. Now we take a more balanced view of the good and bad in both countries. One American virtue we can never overrate is their unhesitating generosity.'

Both in Britain and in the United States at various periods, particularly at the 50th anniversary, there have been reunions of evacuees, whether it was the children of British employees of the Hoover Company or the occasion of the launching of Jocelyn Statler's book at the Imperial War Museum or 200 CORB evacuees meeting at York University. A Hoover mother, Charlotte Carter, then 94, whose daughter Ellen was evacuated, said, 'It was very hard to let them go. But we felt one had no choice.' Hoover evacuee Peter Soundy said, 'It was too exciting for us to be sad about leaving our parents.' At a reunion of the Oxford party fifty years after they had left the only common factor in their conversations, according to Meg Weston Smith, was that all felt they couldn't slip back into the ways that had been. 'It was a gap that was never patched up,' she says. This point is echoed by Mark Lucas who has gone back to the States regularly. He says he resonates with Americans perhaps more easily than most English and has sometimes felt more mid-Atlantic. He adds,

'Maybe people don't realize now how devastating the war and evacuation was for families.'

Neil Maidment, who lives in Hong Kong and was part of the Oxford party, has always felt that gap. The greyness of life in post-war England, the poverty, the shortage of food and its poor quality, the snobbery of the English boys at school over his American accent and clothing—all combined, he says, 'to lodge in my psyche a sense of discomfort about England which I have never managed to overcome in the nearly sixty years since'. In contrast he has always been an Americanophile and a strong defender of the US in countless discussions and arguments during his working life: 'I'm not blind to their faults but neither am I quick to condemn their every foible. For sheer spontaneous generosity of mind and kindness of spirit, the Americans can't be beaten. I'll never forget what we owe them.'

The Oxford reunion was 'a seminal moment' for Isabel Lawson (Raphael), the daughter of a law professor at Oxford. She and her older sister Susan had been evacuated with their mother. Susan hated her time in America but to Isabel it was 'paradise' and the Americans 'could not have been kinder'. However, the return to life in England had been dreadful. At school, teasing became victimization, and they were made to feel bad that they hadn't shared in the wartime suffering of those who had stayed behind. There wasn't much time or energy for anything but survival, all aggravated by cold housing and low pay. 'It was a long time before we felt established again and I never got to know my father,' she says. 'At the reunion a great burden was taken off my back when I saw what other people had been through. The stiff upper lip had stopped us from talking about it. We weren't alone.'

Dorothea Hudson, a CORB evacuee, would have liked to have stayed on in Canada on the Saskatchewan farm where she spent five years. She describes the welcome hugs that greeted her on her return to Hull but writes, 'I was made a great fuss of—it was not reciprocated. My heart was three thousand miles away on Grange Farm.'

In 2001 as Dorothea Desforges she published a book *The In-between Years* in which she gives an evocative account of her years on the Canadian prairies: 'Even though the life was harsh and my relatives battled endlessly with hail, drought, crop failure, extreme weather and poverty, the over-riding emotion was happiness, not the beatings and sorrow that is well documented in many other evacuee stories.' She was more remote from the war than many. It is hardly mentioned in her book: 'It didn't impinge on our lives, mainly because no one had a telephone, papers were unavailable and the radio was only used for an hour once a week, so news was sparse. At such a young age the conflict was never discussed. When the sons came home on leave, I didn't know what a uniform was, so just accepted they'd just come home for a few days.' During her time in Saskatchewan, she says, she had never encountered envy or hate, had never craved possessions or become dissatisfied with her lot. The space, beauty and solitude of the Canadian wheat lands affected her attitudes for the rest of her life: 'No toys, no comics, no playmates, no running water, no electricity, no toilets, no holidays, no money. Experts today would be unanimous in labelling me "underprivileged". Underprivileged. Me? Oh, no. They've got it all wrong, because I consider myself to have been a very privileged child indeed.'

On the 60th anniversary of the start of World War II and of the mass evacuation of children to the countryside to get away from German bombing, there was a procession to Westminster Abbey by evacuees. Most were those who had been evacuated within Britain; but some had been sent overseas. By then in their sixties they bore little resemblance to those anxious little boys and girls who, parted from their teary-eyed parents, boarded trains and buses and boats to they knew not where. The one thing they had in common is that they were all wearing luggage labels, as they did sixty years earlier. This time it was their ticket of admission to the service in the Abbey. The *Evening Standard* wrote, 'Three and a half million former wartime evacuees are finally to receive official recognition, 60 years after the world's biggest movement of children.'

The impetus for this anniversary event came from the founding in 1998 of the Evacuees Reunion Association (ERA) at an occasion at the Imperial War Museum. After forming the ERA James Roffey received thousands of letters and phone calls, some of them cheerful, some of them with memories of great unhappiness. The need for such an association became apparent, he says, at the time of the 50th anniversary of the end of the Second World War when a few evacuees participated in the big parade in London, wearing luggage labels in their lapels. They were cheered by the thousands of spectators lining the Mall, many of whom shouted, 'I was an evacuee'.

Roffey said on the eve of the occasion that it would 'finally ensure that the part we evacuees played during the Second World War is properly recognized and never forgotten. We didn't fight any battles. Some people don't think we took part in the war. But we did, and although we don't have any medals, we do have luggage labels. We shall wear them with pride.'[122]

Thanks to a grant from the Heritage Lottery Fund to the Evacuees Reunion Association, a Research Centre for Evacuees and War Child Studies was set up in 2004 at the University of Reading.

17

A Bond Was Forged

What happened to the children—Sabrina, James and Romulus? They grew up. That is a process one cannot avoid. It is a thing that happens. And then? Well, that is all there is to tell. The world comes in and demands its share and unless we are clever—or lucky, perhaps—we forget a very great deal. But two things, I am certain, these children will always keep—their memory of those rich and varied years and their love for the country that welcomed them so largely. —From a 1966 foreword to I Go By Sea, I Go By Land *by P.L.Travers, of Mary Poppins fame, a novel written in 1941 about North American evacuation.*

Over the years much has been made of the special relationship between Britain and the United States. Some of this can be attributed to the extraordinary closeness that developed between Roosevelt and Churchill and which had begun even before Churchill became Prime Minister in May 1940. 'However turbulent,' writes[123] Jon Meacham, 'however tinged with sentimentality, however much resented by others in the world, in fact the deep connection between the two nations has been a force for democracy and liberty through what Churchill might have called the "storm and strife" of battles against tyrants and terrorists. When an American president and a British prime minister walk through the woods of Camp David or confer on a transatlantic telephone, they are working in the style and in the shadow of Roosevelt and Churchill.'

The Germans were well aware of the significance of the rapport between the two men. In March 1941 the German Foreign Minister Ribbentrop told Japanese Ambassador Matsuoka that there was no doubt that 'the British would long since have abandoned the war if Roosevelt had not always given Churchill new hope'. After the war when an appeal was launched in Britain for a Roosevelt Memorial in Grosvenor Square, the needed money was forthcoming in six days through 150,000 individual contributions.

This special relationship was also helped by the calibre of men who represented Britain in Washington DC during the war including Lord Lothian and Lord Halifax. Another was Field Marshal John Dill, whom Roosevelt described as the 'most important figure in the Anglo-American accord'[124]. The enduring testimony to the place he came to occupy in American regard was shown later in the erection of an equestrian statue to him in the American National Cemetery at Arlington.

The presence of several thousand British children in the country had a part, too, in bringing home to the American public the reality of the war in Europe and subsequently in continuing to foster the special relationship. You will not hear from most of them any glib anti-Americanism. They may at times have disagreements with aspects of US foreign policy but their prevailing sentiment, as it has been for sixty years, is one of appreciation of American generosity. Many of the families continue close ties into the third and fourth generation on both sides of the Atlantic. Richard Himsworth writes, 'We remain part of the extended family of our hosts and our children and their children and grandchildren continue the relationship with frequent visits on either side of the Atlantic and grand reunions for weddings.' He regards his four years in Cambridge (USA) as 'very formative and important to me and wholly beneficial". Ann Spokes Symonds, from the Oxford party, regularly returns for reunions at the Master's School on the Hudson River which she attended 1942-44. Her brother, also an evacuee, is an American citizen living in Minneapolis and is father and grandfather of Americans.

Richard Price found his four years with his mother and sister in Milton 'a hugely memorable time' and the lessons he learned had varied applications. He and his mother encouraged his Unitarian minister father to start a children's church as his Milton host, Dr Vivian Pomeroy, had done. In his work as a TV producer and distributor dealing a lot with Americans he drew on his experiences to understand the American point of view, having his own American company for over 20 years. Coincidentally one of the TV stations he continues to work with is Boston's WGBH. More than 130 hours of

Masterpiece Theatre have, over the years, come to the US via this station and Richard. As a result Alistair Cooke (Letter From America) who introduced the programmes on air became a friend and later in 1990 when Richard was chairman of BAFTA (The British Academy of Film and Television Arts) he presented Alistair with a special BAFTA award for his services to broadcasting.

When in New York Richard would regularly take the shuttle to Boston to see the station as well as many friends like ex-Miltonian Dan Pierce and Gertrude Donald who had befriended the Prices in Milton, continuing to do so until she died in 1996, aged 105. He spoke at the 80th birthday celebration for his sixth grade teacher, Frank Millet, and has continued regular contact with Milton Academy. On his year's 50th anniversary he showed his Emmy award winning film of Rodgers and Hammerstein's *Oklahoma!* at the school, its American premiere, and is now developing links between Milton Academy and his own Leeds Grammar School. He regularly returns to the Boston area, often with his daughter, Annabel, who has particular friends in Wellesley.

Louise Milbourn (Lawson) is sure that her experience of evacuation had more positive outcomes than negative. She writes, 'My character was strengthened by the whole episode. By nature a cheerful and optimistic person, having to cope with adversity early in life meant I learned to cope with difficulties all through life when they occurred.'

Summing up the experience, Merle Witkin wrote,[125] 'The evacuation of British children to the United States had a powerful impact on the lives of those children who went. It strengthened personal Anglo-American ties among those families affected. It may well have added to more widespread Anglo-American affection and understanding. And though the threatened invasion of Britain never materialized, no one will ever know how many of the children who escaped overseas would otherwise have been killed in bombing raids, or whether the number thus saved outweigh the 77 children lost at sea.'

Personal Anglo-Canadian ties among families affected have of course also been strengthened. It is noticeable that even among many whose experiences were less than satisfactory the gratitude to their host country and families is pronounced. Joyce Swinbank, whose family, her mother, her two brothers and herself, encountered difficulties in sustaining themselves, says, 'We were fortunate we were able to stay together and have nothing but praise and admiration for the Canadians who welcomed us with kindness wherever we went.' While John Bradley, whose family was split up in three different places in Ontario, can still say, 'We survived thanks only to the astonishing generosity of the Canadians who took us in and looked after us without any hope of repayment.' Sometimes that generosity was not enough to overcome the upheaval. J.M. Brice (Gasper) says, 'The Canadians were very kind to take us in but the strain on my parents was great. My mother had a breakdown.'

Penny Jaques (Moon) was separated from her mother at the age of 3 and lived in Montreal. The trauma of return to a family she did not remember left her with difficult emotional problems. 'I overcame these in my early adult life,' she says, 'and, perhaps not surprisingly, trained first as a social worker and then as a psychotherapist.' She specialised in working with people who have been traumatically separated, usually through adoption. She adds, 'I still have the book I was given when I left to return to the UK. It is called *Paddle to the Sea*[126]. It is a magical story of a small carved Indian canoe which travels from Lake Superior, through Lake Michigan, Lake Huron, Lake Erie, Lake Ontario and then along the great St Lawrence River and past Newfoundland and out across the ocean. This journey took four years which was the time I spent in Canada.'

Some like Ron Hart, who was evacuated to Creston, British Columbia, were one of a number—in Canada and the United States—who had such a good time that they returned reluctantly to Britain after the war. It never occurred to Grace Baldock, enjoying 'five lovely years' near Niagara Falls, that she would have to come back to Britain 'so I was very upset when I had to'. Some wished they had not done so.

John Crawshaw, who was evacuated to Winnipeg under the CORB scheme, sixty years later thinks of Canada as his second home. His experience is still sharp in his memory and treasured. His foster parents, Gertrude and Einar Anderson, treated him as their son. 'At the time I did not really appreciate what Canada gave to me and it is only in these latter years that I realized what a debt I owed to all those kind people who made me so welcome. They accepted me so readily and made me feel so much at home that half of me did not want to return to England in 1945. The Canadian children accepted me with less comment than did the English grammar school boys on my return home. I will think of myself as a Winnipeger to my dying day and will still be able to sing the chants we used to support the St John's Tigers at rugby matches.' He adds, 'I think Canada changed me and made me more outgoing than I would otherwise have been.'

Lord Montagu says that there is no doubt that his years in Toronto taught him much: 'On the more academic level we learned Canadian and American history, the decimal system and coinage, science, public speaking and acting.

They also taught us ice hockey, Canadian football, skiing and canoeing.' He was 'torn by guilt' over not being in England for her 'finest hour' but has no doubt that 'my time in Canada greatly enhanced my life and I do not regret the experience in any way'[127]. 'North America gave me self-confidence and opened my eyes to a different sort of life,' he wrote in his 2000 autobiography *Wheels Within Wheels.*

Most evacuees seem, like my brother and I, to have retained these close links with host families. Visits both ways, over the more than sixty years is quite common. Many, when they were older, returned to live permanently in Canada and the United States. In fact, from the Actors' Orphanage, less than half of the original group returned home and remained.

Many American and Canadian families retain stories about their wartime visitors that get handed down. Heather Ashton (Champion) records one that was retold to the grandchildren of her American family. She had lived for six years in a house near Brandywine Creek in Westchester County, Pennsylvania, the site of a famous battle won by the 'rebels' in the American revolution, a battle which the American rebels won. A relic of the fight, an old cannon, was preserved in the garden of the house:

'What was this cannon for?' I asked in my youthful ignorance.

'To drive the British away,' was the answer.

'Well, it wasn't very successful, was it?' said I, as I straddled the cannon with my American siblings.

Some grown-up evacuees would identify with Margaret Hanton who says, 'I've always felt like a mid-Atlantic person, not quite either, or perhaps both.'

Sixty years on, of course, the world has shifted. At the time everything was so real, so immediate, so tangible, so exciting to us youngsters, and now in many cases time has obliterated the traces of what was. Just the memories remain. The main actors in my story moved on to other fields and in many cases have left the scene.

The *Duchess of York* was, as described earlier, sunk, as was the *Duchess of Atholl* and four other ships from our outgoing convoy—*Oronsay* and *Georgic* and the destroyers *Vortigern* and *Hurricane*, which was a few weeks later to rescue survivors from the *City of Benares*. '*Hurricane* was a very happy ship,' says Dr Peter Collinson, who was the ship's medical officer from its launching in Barrow until it was sunk by the Luftwaffe in Liverpool docks. Referring to the loss of lives on the *City of Benares*, he writes, 'I am afraid the sinking was used a little for propaganda at the time although the captain of the U-boat had no prior knowledge the Benares was carrying such a precious cargo.' Collinson has been to several reunions of survivors of the *City of Benares*—one including two members of the U-boat that sank her. The U-boat's wireless operator told him of the deep sadness of the captain and crew when on their return to base they were told of the immense loss of life, and especially of so many young children: 'He shed real tears when the survivors stood on the dais and we had 2 minutes silence. He was very moved and explained to me that he had children of his own and was deeply sorry.' After one of the reunions, forty years after the sinking, a daughter of an engineer in the *City of Benares* married a mechanic from the U-boat that had sunk her father. And 63 years on, Collinson writes, 'I still get a Christmas card from the two "girls" (now in their mid-seventies) who clung to the keel of the upturned life boat for 14 hours.'

One of them, Beth Williams (Cummings), discovered at the end of 2003[128] that a crewman from the submarine which sank the *City of Benares*, Rolf Hilse, had married an English girl and for many years had lived just 35 miles away. He had heard about her through a newspaper article and got in touch. Beth says, 'I can't feel bitter and I can't blame him, because what happened took place in wartime. It was a nasty war.' Rolf, who was 19 at the time, says, 'I was very pleased to hear Beth say she feels no bitterness. It was a war and we both know it could have happened the other way round.'

On 17 September 2000 a tree was planted at Britain's National Memorial Arboretum in memory of evacuees, escorts and crew of the *City of Benares*. A sea of saplings at the Memorial is a visual reminder to visitors of the number of ships sunk.

HMS Patroller was returned to the US Navy and in December 1946 was sold to the Waterman Steamship Corporation as *Almkerk*. It was renamed in 1968 *Pacific Alliance* and in 1974 was broken up in Taiwan.

On 1 July 1999 there was a grand launching of the Pier 21 Society in Halifax. This Canadian National Immigration Heritage Centre is at the immigration shed through which several thousand guest children, like my brother and I, passed in 1940 and from which 494,000 Europe-bound Canadian troops departed in World War II. For 43 years it was the gateway to Canada. At the Maritime Museum of the Atlantic, along with a scale model of SS *Nova Scotia*, is a brass plaque with the words 'Our unbounded gratitude'. One who came through Pier 21 as 'a frightened 10-year-old' on the *Nova Scotia* in the fall of 1940 escaping with his family from the Nazi occupations of Austria and

Czechoslovakia was Canadian writer Peter Newman. He helped raise the money for the Centre and spoke at its launching. He described how for almost 18 months they had been on the run, finally retreating to France until they were machine-gunned by the *Luftwaffe*. "This was pretty scary for me…my father had obtained a Canadian visa by promising to buy a farm….Jews were not allowed into Canada,' he said. They were met by the Jewish Immigrant Aid Society. 'I was handed a fig Newton[129], he recalls. 'Nothing has tasted better since."

Toby Coghill, who with his sister, Faith, accompanied us on the *Duchess of York*, went on to become the much respected headmaster of Aberlour House, the feeder school for Gordonstoun. He also became chairman of the board of governors of Aiglon School in Switzerland. An evaluation of his work there in *Aiglon Life* in May 1999 stated that through his four-year period of schooling in the United States and Canada, he was 'well placed to be an informed advocate of international schooling with all its attributes: open-mindedness, flexibility, cultural curiosity and concern with global issues— refreshing antidotes to parochialism.' His obituary in *The Times* stated, 'His own childhood evacuation to America and subsequent schooling at Gordonstoun gave him an indefatigable confidence, and Cambridge Blues for rowing and ice hockey proved his sporting prowess.' Toby gave his son the middle name Farley after his American family. In 1991 Faith had a 50th reunion in Oxford of seventeen children who had been in Boston. She says, 'We never said thank you enough. We took it for granted.' Toby, she says, had a particularly happy time. The Farleys had had three daughters 'so they reared Tony as the son they hadn't had'.

Tim Sturgis, a Milton boy who was at the reunion, says, 'Those of us who came were only children, and we took it all very much as it came, amazingly unquestioning. The overwhelming feeling of us all was the unbelievable, open ended, and endless generosity of our American hosts, so often given without our knowing, in the hope that we would never know. They were memorable years, and a bond had been forged, which has lasted these fifty years.'

I had the temerity also to draw on my experience of American sports by applying to join Wembley Lions ice hockey team. But I was told that wasn't possible as I was going to boarding school. My skating ability only came in useful at public skating sessions at Wembley. They always ended with the national anthem when I could come to a smart stop while some embarrassed novices would eventually either fall over or crash into the side. I was soon learning rugby and field hockey and reacquainting myself with cricket. I have a very clear memory of opposing wicket keepers in school matches making rude remarks at my batting style which, though sometimes more effective than it deserved to be, betrayed some influence of five years of baseball. In my first game of rugby, where I was put as a three quarter, I couldn't figure out where I was meant to be half the time as I was more used to the more structured American football game.

Of the Hinchman family we knew so well only daughter Peggy, or Daisy, is still alive and son-in-law, Herwin Schaefer. Another son-in-law, Hoel Bowditch, who made the model of HMS *Rodney* for us, died as this book was going to press. He became an inventor with a number of patents to his name and chief engineer at the Foxboro Company. In 1989 he was even cast as Edison in a TV feature made by ABC. Filmed at Menlo Park, it was called 'Out of their minds' and was aimed at inspiring young people to creativity. We last saw him and his wife, Mary, at their granddaughter's wedding in Hood River, Oregon. The Bowditches celebrated their golden wedding in 1999 by renting three cottages at Rockywold camp for a week with nearly all their family joining them. In 2002 I had an email from Hood River announcing the arrival of a Hinchman great, great grandson!

A book of Julia Hinchman's poetry was published, but only after her death when the poems were discovered. The book, *Reflections of a Person*, contains this tribute to Winston Churchill written in June 1943 at the time I heard him speak at Harvard:

> On tides of happier portent
> Than ever touched our shore,
> Man of immortal courage
> You come to us once more!
>
> Heedless of doubt or anger,
> Forgetful of applause,
> You labour, proud and humble—
> Mindful but of the Cause.
>
> You come in trusted friendship,
> Part of ours by blood and breath,
> You stand a world's deliverer
> From evils worse than death.

God keep you, Winston Churchill,
This day and every day!
God keep you Winston Churchill,
And guide you on your way!

I visited Jinny and Ted Boyd in the 1990s. She says, 'I shall always be grateful that God guided me to the Hinchman family and "my boys".'

Milton is much as it was. My much-frequented public library does not look to me any different. The chocolate factory whose delicious smells was appreciated by generations of children has been converted into affordable housing with city and community cooperation. In fact, I have on my shelf an aerosol can of chocolate spray produced for the groundbreaking ceremony in 1985. If I ever get nostalgic I can reproduce that sweet smell of chocolate in the air.

Milton Academy has impressive new buildings. I climbed the chapel bell tower early in the nineties and there lying on the roof was the cupola which used to protect us from the elements as we spotted for planes. When I returned a few years later it had been disposed of. Hinchman House, as it is now called, belongs to the Academy and has been divided into various apartments occupied by faculty. Mary Bowditch went back to visit a few years ago and told the occupant whose sections of the home contained Mr. Hinchman's study about the hideaway behind the panelling. They opened it and discovered whisky bottles! When her niece visited later the occupant was an English teacher who used it to store a set of Dickens.

The grounds, sadly, seem today to be no one's responsibility. Perhaps my brother and I are, apart from Peggy, the only persons alive who could take you to where the goldfish pool was and to Mr. Hinchman's proud rose garden or locate the apple orchard whose trees we used to love climbing on. Of course, what we remember as little trees and shrubs have grown tall.

John Wilkinson came back to Milton on his honeymoon in 1956. In an account in the Milton Graduates' Newsletter in 1998 on the school's 200th anniversary, he wrote, 'The outstanding feature of my stay (and that of my mother and sister who lived in Brookline) was the immense kindness and generosity of our American hosts, something which left on me a deep and lasting impression. The wealth and size of America was breathtaking. The open and easy way of life was a revelation. Suddenly, the constraints of the conventional schoolboy's upbringing in England had vanished. This was quite a change—wonderful but unnerving. Looking back on those days, it seems that changes in our way of life now accelerate every decade, but my generation was conditioned by the unforgettable events of World War II, and I pray that the deep friendship and alliance between America and Great Britain so vital then, will grow ever stronger in the future. I wish Milton Academy every possible success in the future and would declare that a very special possession I have is a gold wristwatch. This was a gift from my foster father, also a Milton graduate, inscribed "Dare to be true—March 1943".'

Tony Moore writes, 'The part played by Milton Academy and many other schools in the USA and Canada has probably never been fully recognized. Milton had some dozens of English children in their midst[130]. I believe our host families paid for expenses such as meals and equipment, while the school provided us with a free education over three years. Never controversial. It was straightforward warm hospitality in a common cause.'

Although I never got into the Milton Academy upper school, having gone for two years to boarding school at Rectory, I am regarded as being of the class of '49 and so I have occasionally attended reunions at the school with those in their late sixties and now seventies with whom I was in 4th, 5th and 6th grade.

As one gesture of thanks after the war the heads of the forty-five schools that had been hosts of overseas students were invited as guests to the 1947 Oxford Summer School.

South Pond Cabins is no more. I sought it out in the New Hampshire woods in the 1990s and must sadly report that some archaeologist in the future may stumble on the overgrown ruins and ponder what went on there. I can just make out where the tennis courts, the nature hut, the cabins and tents, and the dock were. The camp closed in 1979. It was the last time they sang the old camp song:

> Cheer on cheer for South Pond Cabins
> Loud your voices sing.
> Cheer on cheer for South Pond cabins
> Here the echoes ring.
> We shall love and we shall cheer her
> Here's to SPC
> For we'll fight, fight, fight
> For we'll win tonight
> For dear old SPC

'It was a wonderful way of life for all of us, particularly Annie,' husband Hugh Putnam told me. 'We hated to close it, but in those days, small private camps were folding up all over.'

Sylvia Warren wrote after the war to a British official, 'Our hope is that, though the whole evacuation scheme was on too small a scale to be really effective, what scope it had will to some extent create bonds between your country and mine.' She herself received a letter from the British Embassy in Washington, DC dated 27 May 1947. Signed by H.R.F.Brett of the Honours and Awards Section, it stated: 'It is with much pleasure that I inform you that The King has been pleased to award you His Majesty's Medal for Service in the Cause of Freedom, in recognition of the valuable services you rendered to the common cause. Lord Inverchapel, the Ambassador, has asked me to convey to you his personal congratulations on this well merited award. Owing to the shortage of metal in the United Kingdom, some time will elapse before the insignia of the decoration can be sent, but arrangements are being made for a ribbon to be presented to you in the near future by the British Consul General at Boston.'

The fortunes, non-financial, of the Lobkowicz family, whose children, Martin, Dominik and Oliver, had stayed with her, have seen dramatic change. We had no idea at the time of the distinguished pedigree of our friends. The family is known not only as Princes of the Holy Roman Empire but also as patrons of Beethoven, Mozart, Goethe, Haydn and Dvorak. Indeed, Beethoven's 3rd and 5th symphonies were dedicated to Martin's ancestor, Franz Josef Maximilian Lobkowicz, and first performed at the Lobkowicz Palace in Vienna.

Maximilian, the father of the three Lobkowicz boys, returned after the war to Czechoslovakia but had to flee two months after the Communist take-over in February, 1948. With the ending of the Cold War, however, the Lobkowicz family, one of the oldest noble families in Bohemia, had nine castles returned to them, although most were in a state of disrepair. With the onset of the 'velvet revolution' in 1990 Martin and his son, William, returned to Czechoslovakia and the family has since been actively pursuing projects surrounding art and cultural life in what is now the Czech Republic. They have begun the long process of trying to restore the collection of art, books, and other objects to its former grandeur for the benefit of the public. They set up the Roudnice Lobkowicz Foundation to help raise the funds for this monumental task.

Charlie Fay, who became a barrister in London (and returned to the more formal Charles), kept close links with the Huntington Thompsons and returned from time to time to Rectory School and to his favourite haunts in New Hampshire. The Executive Director of the local 'Lakes Region Conservation Trust', Thomas S. Curren, wrote these reflections in his newsletter in 2000:

> Late in the spring, I was invited by a landowner to climb one of the lesser known summits in the region. The morning was cool and showery and the air still free of blackflies. We set out along an old woods road to gain the top of a ridgeline which separates several watercourses.
>
> Our talk was of forest trees and wildlife signs, of cellar-holes and old-timers' tales in the misty spring morning. After reaching one summit we found our way to an adjoining ledge, where the faint footpath that we had been following was joined by a more defined trail leading back down into the valley. The second route was marked by a unique set of blazes, a series of tin-can lids painted orange and nailed into trees along the trailside. Some sprouted rust through fading paint, others sported fresh coats of blaze orange. I made a mental note that if we were ever to protect this land, we ought to find a more suitable way to mark the trail.
>
> My guide had shared a wealth of knowledge on the history of her valley, so I inquired about the source of the trail markers. Her response was something like this: 'Before the United States entered the Second World war, my mother and father took in a group of English children whose parents sought sanctuary for them from the dangers of the Blitz. There was one boy who loved the view from those ledges; he used to climb them nearly every day and spent long hours looking out over the valley....He's the one who put those markers here, and every so often in the ensuing fifty years or so he would come back to us for a visit and quietly slip away to freshen or replace the old ones. He passed away just a few years ago.'
>
> I thought of that homesick English boy climbing up through the forest, hugging his knees on the ledges, and taking what comfort he could in the view of Mount Chocorua. It dawned on me during that same time the American ambassador to England was former New Hampshire Governor John Winant. Night after night, as the air-raid sirens wailed, John Winant walked the streets of London in a business suit, giving what comfort he could to the British people in the months before Pearl Harbor.

I made a mental note that if the Trust was ever to protect this land and if anyone was ever so dumb as to suggest that those tin can lids should be removed, my response would be: 'Over my dead body, pal.' There are a few things we won't forget about here in New Hampshire. Even those of us who were born in Massachusetts.

I was grateful that at the 75th anniversary of Rectory School I was able to express publicly to our headmaster John Bigelow, shortly before he died, our gratitude for the school and its decision to take all the young English in at greatly reduced fees.

Friends who were evacuated to Canada have much the same appreciation of their hosts. After describing her experiences, Ruth Hutchison writes, 'I cannot end without setting down, however inadequately, the debt we owe to those generous Canadian families. They opened their hearts and homes to complete strangers, for an unknown period of time, and shared their means and their lives with us. We are forever grateful. Now we each have two families and the Canadian friendships have survived and grown over the years.'

She also reflects on the emotional effect of evacuation: 'Many years later, when I was in my twenties, I realised that there was a part of my heart closed up. The whole evacuee experience came into my mind and I knew that was where it all began. By coincidence, I received a letter from my mother. She, too, had been reliving this period. She wrote at sorrow of her inability to help me over the first difficult months. "I was unhappy, too," she wrote, "but it was war and I felt I should maintain a stiff upper lip! If I had just been honest I might have helped you to say what you really felt. I am so sorry." That opened the door to freedom from the past for me, and I know that I need never shut my heart again, no matter the rocks that any of us must climb. No blame; no bitterness. For this I must also thank my evacuee experience.'

In the US Committee's final report it said that here had been, of course, some rough moments after the return home. Children had difficulty with parents who were hurt at their un-British frankness and horrified by their American speech. Some of the more mischievous youngsters could not resist using all the slang at their command in order to tease. Sixteen and seventeen year olds had trouble with mothers and fathers who kept telling them 'to wash that paint off your face' and to 'be in by nine o'clock'. Parents had difficulty having to face children with healthy appetites and (what seemed to them) luxurious tastes, with the realities of British austerity. One mother received a shock when her twelve year old son, trying to be thoughtful on his first night home, told her he didn't want much for breakfast, 'just a banana and a glass of milk'. Bananas, she had to remind him, had not been seen in England for six years, while fresh milk was available only for infants and tots.

The Committee, which had brought 861 boys and girls between the ages of 5 and 16 to the United States, concluded, 'Aside from material comforts, educational opportunities, and excellent medical and dental care, most of the children who came to America reaped a rich harvest in new and deep friendships. While their knowledge of the world was being broadened by first-hand acquaintance with the customs and manners of another land, they experienced an exchange of warmth and affection which attested to the essential humanity of people in far away places. They had an applied lesson in international understanding, which, because it came to them in the formative, growing up period of their lives had a chance to sink deep. The British were not the only ones to reap benefits, for American sponsors, Committee representatives and social workers who knew the children well also gained new friends and a quickened appreciation of another culture, plus a deepened perception of the basic needs of all children.'

Soon after the war Milton Academy invited English parents to comment on the evacuation and schooling from their point of view. The *Milton Bulletin* of February 1946 carried some of their responses. A father of a boy who was 2 " years in the Milton Academy Junior School wrote, 'He has gained greatly in breadth of experience and of interest in the large world, and one of his early remarks was that USA was the most civilized nation in the world, although he said in an after-thought it was a pity the women were so bossy. I was surprised that he had not picked up any new mannerisms or intonation of speech and hadn't even fallen victim to the OK! His independence and self-confidence as well as curiosity in intellectual matters have increased.' Another father wrote of his son, 'He admires the product of our public school life but doesn't at all like the hard work necessary and argues that in USA you are as well educated and intelligent as men here and somehow have found a method of scholarship without hard work.' A father of three boys in the Junior School wrote, 'The joint influence of school and foster-home seems to have had two effects on the boys. First, they have a definite sense of world-citizenship which is lacking in the brother and sister who have lived in England throughout. The Western hemisphere is as real to them as the Eastern.' Of the two older boys he added, 'They have acquired something of the "unshyness"—confidence in themselves and in the people they contact—which we regard as the characteristic and charm of American children.' A 1948 Milton Academy report stated: 'The Academy's life was enriched by these visitors. Not only did they give it an opportunity to serve, they taught Milton much. To this day the faculties of the three schools use the experience they have had of teaching overseas students as a criterion for judgment. Milton is proud of the accomplishments of the students it sent back across the Atlantic, the records they subsequently made, and above all the friendships so begun.'

In 1990, Eric Hammond, 50 years after he was taken by Bowaters to Canada, wrote to the West Newfoundland paper, the *Western Star*, 'War brings tragedy and loss to many people and there are few redeeming features. But here and there the decency and kindness shine through the shadows of conflict. The warm welcome we were given not only by our "new" families but also by the whole West Newfoundland community, must surely count on the side of man's humanity to man amongst all the inhumanity. I have never forgotten the people of Corner Brook, Nicholsville and Deer Lake. Across those fifty years, I remember that frightened boy of ten who lost his fears amongst you. On his behalf, I salute and thank you.'

Jessica Mann, the crime novelist, whose parents were Jewish refugees from Germany and who has written about overseas evacuation[131], never had any doubt about the rightness of her going to America. If England had been invaded, the family were not expecting to survive. She writes, 'British society had been accustomed for centuries to Empire-builders sending their children away from hot climates to foster homes or boarding schools. Our contemporary horror at the idea of parting children from their parents is a post-war development, and although it is often tempting to use that early 'trauma' as the excuse for all my deficiencies, I have the impression that the majority of the evacuees survived intact and even enriched.'

Walter Hinchman in an autobiography published in 1952, *The Only Paradise*, writes about 1940: 'In August we took on "for the duration" two little English boys and soon added, to help us with them, a charming friend of Dody's, Virginia Rorstrom, now Mrs. Boyd. These boys, Michael and Gerald Henderson—no relation of my wife though the same surname—turned out to be delightful members of our family. Different as one could imagine two brothers Michael forthright and Saxon, Gerald imaginative and Celtic they came in nearly five years to seem "our" boys. Only eight and six when they arrived, they were here during a highly formative period of their lives, and we still feel somewhat responsible, as in the case of our own children, for whatever is good or bad in them.'

Gerald writes, 'To this day I marvel at the generosity and open-heartedness of the Hinchman family who looked after us both for nearly five years in Milton, as if we were their sons. I was shy, but I was quite a handful, I am sure. Their patience, generosity, discipline and affection, even their over-protectiveness to ensure that we were in some degree still English boys when we were returned to our parents, showed a depth of care and love for which I will ever be grateful. Through it we came to love America.'

On our return to England in 1945 our parents, who had been totally immersed in the war effort, may have been a little irritated by our belief that America won the war; our uncle, an artillery officer in North Africa who had been shelled by his American allies, may have been a little jaundiced in his view of the Yanks; but the predominant thought of our family and of the nation was one of gratitude to America and the Americans and what they had done to help preserve liberty in the world. It has affected for good our attitude to the United States ever since.

Notes

[1] *America Lost and Found* and *A Bundle from Britain*

[2] Now Lord Rennell of Rodd

[3] *Postscripts*

[4] According to Foreign Office records (DO131/27 and DO131/7) the total of British children evacuated to the United States and Canada from June to December 1940 (inclusive) is 9,578, with most of them sailing in June, July, August and September.

Out of that total the US figure is 2,928 of which 838 went through the American Committee and 2,090 went privately, among them 476 children who travelled with groups like Hoover and the Actors Orphanage in August and September. 2,271 children were between 5-15 years and 657 between 0-4.

The Canadian figure is 6,650 children of which 1,532 went through CORB and 5,118 went privately. These private figures include children who were accompanied by their mothers as well as a few school and company groups.

In addition, 253 children under the age of 16 were sent to Canada in 1939, 260 were sent in 1941 and 120 in 1942. In 1941 102 evacuee children came to the US but there seem to be no records of children evacuated to North America privately before June 1940.

[5] The Children's Overseas Reception Board

[6] *Five Days in London*

[7] *The Holy Fox*

[8] When the Evacuees Reunion Association (ERA) was formed in February 1996 it chose a luggage label as its logo.

[9] See bibliography

[10] The King and Queen travelled to North America by sea. Thanks to fears of a German surprise attack, precautionary measures were taken to prevent their ship being intercepted and their being kidnapped by the German pocket battleship *Deutschland.*

[11] 30 October, 1939

[12] Earlier William Randolph Hearst had signed up Hitler to write for his newly fashioned op-ed page but he was unable to meet his deadlines and fell out of favour.

[13] In June King George VI had shooting ranges laid down in the gardens of Buckingham Palace and at Windsor at which he and other members of his family and his equerries practiced regularly with rifles, pistols and tommy guns.

[14] Tim Clayton and Phil Craig

[15] British Expeditionary Force

[16] In 1941

[17] *Memoirs of a Fighting Life*

[18] Generous offers also came from Latin America, from Argentina, Brazil, Colombia, Chile, Cuba and Uruguay, but were refused as it was felt that children should only go to English-speaking countries.

[19] *The Absurd and the Brave*

[20] Whereas in 1939 only 253 children under the age of 16 were sent to Canada, all of them privately, nearly 5500 would travel in 1940, of which 1532 were under the auspices of CORB.

[21] A Home Intelligence Report of 16 July 1940 stated that the postponement of plans for evacuating children to the Dominions was leading to 'sharp recrimination against the rich, whose children were enabled to sail'.

[22] Senior cabinet minister

[23] 20 December 1940, by Wilson Harris

[24] An approach by the US Government on safe passage was turned down: 'Germany must decidedly reject every request referring to this matter...It is entirely contrary to our interests if the power of resistance of the British people is strengthened by the evacuation of children and refugees.'

[25] Merle Witkin, Yale University prize essay, 9 April 1979

[26] Sir Martin Gilbert, himself evacuated, says, 'I'm grateful because I was let in, but I wasn't let in as a Jewish child. I was let in as a British child.'

[27] A well-known British shoe shop

[28] In its final report (August 20, 1944) the committee stated: 'Our records show that since 1940 we have participated in the care of some 1200 cases. Without a long list of figures, difficult to compile and boring to read, it would be impossible to gauge the exact extent of our involvement in each case. Our telephone bill gives some idea of the outgoing calls involved. Sometimes it was only one telephone call; sometimes it included every arrangement from England to the United States and back to England, and a blow-by-blow account of the intervening four years.'

[29] Between 1893 and 1908 Philadelphia sent three teams to England. Derek Birley in *A Social History of English Cricket* (Aurum Press 1999) writes that it was 'as gentlemanly a cricketing community as you could hope to find'.

[30] Now the Home for Little Wanderers

[31] *Churchill* (Macmillan 2001)

[32] I was afraid of going near Underground stations because of IRA bombs. The IRA had set off bombs at Tottenham Court and Leicester Square Underground stations and at Victoria and King's Cross.

[33] Ripley Court School was itself evacuated in November to Betton Strange near Shrewsbury. The school magazine reports: 'Ripley was not exactly a healthy area that autumn, and when suitable premises presented themselves it seemed wise to move while, so to speak, the going was good.'

[34] *Thank You Twice*

[35] Telegram No. 1116 29 June

[36] Later Baroness Young

[37] Local Defence Volunteers, Britain's amateur defence force

[38] 26 June 1940

[39] On 29 September *Mrs. Miniver* was number 1 on the national bestseller list in the US. *Mein Kampf* was 17th. Churchill said Struther's book would do more for the British cause than a flotilla of battleships.

[40] He was made ambassador to London for the Czech government in exile headed by Eduard Benes and remained in that post until 1945

[41] *Clementine Churchill*, Cassell 1979

[42] Lord Beaverbrook wrote Samuel Hoare in Madrid: 'It is felt that as our Minister of Morale, in effect, he should display more personal faith in our ability to beat off attack and stand together as a united race.'

[43] He and his sister sailed on the liner *Washington* six weeks before the war. On the same ship were Patricia and Pamela Mountbatten who were sent to New York to live with the Vanderbilts. Responding to criticism Earl Mountbatten said, 'With their Jewish blood, they would have been the first for the gas ovens if the Germans had invaded.'

[44] 'A splendid letter from your boy,' Prime Minister Churchill wrote to the father. 'We must all try to live up to this standard.' Churchill sent the son an autographed copy of *My Early Life* and received a thank you: 'I am glad that I am not to be ushered into safety.'

[45] Beatrice Ward

[46] In an introduction May Lamberton Becker writes, 'The most touching and beautiful gesture in national history was the sending overseas, for the duration of the war, of great numbers of British children to welcoming homes in the United States and Canada.'

[47] Ten-year-old Eddie Bell thought the balloons "looked just like pigs having a good time after the most tremendous dinner a pig had ever eaten".

[48] A pseudonym

[49] There is some question on the colour as another evacuee in the same convoy, Martyn Pease, remembers the ships being painted yellow, an experiment in camouflage that was later abandoned as ineffective. 'It was thought that a submarine officer staring through a periscope would "see" phantom yellow splodges and so miss the ship. What went wrong was that U-boats attacked convoys on the surface.' I certainly remember one liner in our convoy being very light coloured.

[50] Prime Minister Churchill wrote to the Home Secretary: 'I cannot imagine why Mr. Shakespeare should leave his duties in London to see off a hundred children.'

[51] *Let Candles Be Brought In*

[52] I suggested as the title of an earlier book of my radio talks ' I was brought to America by a drunken duchess and other perspectives of a resident alien.' It was not accepted by the publisher.

[53] There were Canada-bound CORB children on the *Oronsay* and *Antonia* as well as on the *Duchess of York*

[54] John Crawshaw, who was an eleven-year-old in our convoy on the *Oronsay*, recalls a blackboard set up on deck showing the Battle of Britain scores. The *Oronsay* had participated in the evacuation from Dunkirk.

[55] She wrote fifty years later, 'I suppose this summed up the state of mind of the younger travellers—it was an adventure, fun at that stage because we were a party and leaving home hadn't made itself felt. And we had no idea how long the separation would last. One thought in round terms of a year or so. In my case it was almost six years.'

[56] Professor R. B. Mowat 14 October

[57] Some evacuees, seeing a destroyer on the horizon apparently dropping depth charges, got all excited thinking they might be sinking a submarine, and a young evacuee asked an officer about it. He was told that perhaps the destroyer had run out of fish, because that was the way to catch them.

[58] During the war Halifax was to become a key North Atlantic port. More than seventeen thousand ships sailed in convoys assembled or regrouped in Halifax. There they collected the escorts of Canadian corvettes and destroyers. By the end of the war, Canada which at the start had only six warships ended up by providing more than 400 ships, almost half the North Atlantic escort force. More than seven thousand war-damaged ships were repaired in the Halifax yards. Broadcaster Robert MacNeil, who served there in the Canadian Navy, writes, 'Trains from across Canada ground in to the ocean terminals with troops, wheat, munitions, ambulances for the London Blitz, and Bundles for Britain of clothing and food to be loaded into transport ships'.

[59] This may possibly be another case of getting it wrong. Because that song became a hit the following year!

[60] Member of parliament in 1954, baronet in 1963 and life peer in 1983 (Lord Eden of Winton)

[61] Later the whole party transferred to Breakeyville, Quebec where they were lent a house by paper magnate Colin Breakey. John Eden then attended St Paul's School in Concord, New Hampshire.

[62] One paper pointed out that Boston lawyer Farley as well as being chairman of the Community Fund and of the Red Cross War Relief Fund was "a substitute end in Harvard's 1898 and 1899 winning football teams and was Harvard football coach."

[63] written at sea on 27 September 1940

[64] *New York Times* 3 September 1940

[65] The ship was sunk by Germany's most successful U-boat *U48* under Kptlt Heinrich Bleichrodt which sank 53 merchant ships during the war, 300,000 tons in total.

[66] He won the Nobel Peace Prize in 1945 for helping to create the United Nations.

[67] *Hurricane* rescued in her time more than one thousand one hundred survivors, earning her the nicknames Atlantic Lifeboat and HMS Rescue.

[68] Actress Carmen Silvera was listed to sail on the *City of Benares* but at the last minute, she told me, was transferred with a dozen other youngsters to the *Duchess of Atholl*.

[69] Richard Jolliffe and his two brothers had been preparing to travel on the *City of Benares*. When his mother heard the news of the *Volendam* she cancelled their passage. By a curious twist he later married Mary Justham who had been saved from that ship.

[70] *How We Lived Then* by Norman Longmate (Pimlico 2002) By September, according to Longmate, worldwide 2,700 'official' evacuees and 11,000 private ones had left Britain 'when the scheme came to a tragic end'.

[71] 11 July 1940

[72] The Actors' Orphanage school in England

[73] It was reported that an aunt and uncle said to one evacuee who came over to stay with them, 'Your father and mother must be awfully glad you got safely across the ocean', to which she replied, 'I'm not certain. I think father rather hoped the ship would be sunk. He said he'd rather see me torpedoed than acquire an American accent.'

[74] By Gaby Rogers and Harry Phillips

[75] *The Last of the Radicals—Josiah Wedgwood MP* by C.V. Wedgwood

[76] He entitled a chapter about evacuation in his autobiography *Never a Normal Man*, 'Minor Ambassador'.

[77] 1 October 1940

[78] Caroline and Eddie Bell who spent time in Ontario and Connecticut also met a new phenomenon—mosquitoes: 'We think it very strange that the mosquitoes in Canada and America bite English people so much more than Americans. It almost seems as though they were a branch of the Nazi Air Force.'

[79] On the day of the fall of Paris in 1940 the Commencement address was given by Robert E. Sherwood of the class of 1914: 'You can not Dare to be True in a world ruled by Hitler. You can not dare to be free. You can only dare to die.'

[80] *Milton Academy 1798-1948* by Richard Walden Hale

[81] Historian Michael Beschloss writes: 'In 1939 and 1940 against the advice of hard-boiled advisers who warned that most Americans were isolationist, the President risked his career by campaigning for military preparedness and aid to Britain. Had

Roosevelt been more meek or short-sighted, Hitler might have won World War II (*The Conquerors*, 2002).'

[82]Ten-year-old John Spooner, who was on the *Oronsay*, wrote home listing all the ships in our convoy but adding in capitals DO NOT TELL ANYONE THESE NAMES.

[83] Air Raid Precautions

[84] *The Only Paradise* (1952)

[85] A new catchphrase had just entered America's vocabulary: 'It's a bird, it's a plane, it's…superman.

[86] Host to huge jazz festivals

[87] Isaiah Berlin was at the time working with the British Information Services in New York. When he arrived in the office on December 7 British officials were in a state of celebration: the goal for which they had been working for more than a year, America's entry into the war, was now assured. Only Daphne Straight—half American by marriage—was in tears.

[88] Flag Margarine ad: There's a rumor that Hitler has a number of 'doubles' all exactly like him—and equally nasty! But it's a fact that FLAG margarine is exactly like butter—equally NICE and equally NOURISHING

[89] Apart from those who went privately, CORB transported 1532 evacuees to Canada where the Governor General was appointed as 'sole guardian' for the children.

[90] 6 May 1943

[91] TV personality

[92] Founded 19 March 1941

[93] *Pioneers of Radar* by Colin Latham and Anne Stobbs

[94] The Germans lost more than 250,000 men, killed or captured.

[95] Ruth, whose husband ARK Mackenzie became British Ambassador to Tunisia, writes, 'Little did I realize that, 30 years later, I would find myself living, with my husband, in an Arab palace in Tunis, which had been General Alexander's headquarters at the end of the North African campaign, and that our reception hall had been the final mess room for the officers of the Eighth
Army before the push into Italy.'

[96] Another evacuee, six-year-old Richard Himsworth, was also in the crowd that day: 'My recollection of Churchill is of a fat man in an academic gown leaning out of a window and beaming for no obvious reason that I could understand.'

[97] 6 September 1943

[98] Richard Himsworth, who was evacuated to Cambridge, Mass., remembers holes cut by the censor. That I do not is probably accounted for by the fact that our mother was a censor and therefore presumably knew what could and what could not be written.

[99] *The Young Ambassadors*

[100] *Special Relations* Imperial War Museum

[101] Distinguished Service Cross

[102] I had always assumed that I was going to call any book on evacuation *Bundles from Britain*. Alistair Horne beat me to it with his *A Bundle from Britain*.)

[103] This song which can be found in *Carmina Princetonia*, the old Princeton song book, is apparently not known to later generations of Princetonians.

[104] *A Message to Garcia* (March 1899)

[105] Order of the British Empire

[106] British Empire Medal

[107] 30 November 1944

[108] 15 September 1943

[109] Seven-year-old Elizabeth Taylor saw her first movie on the liner *Manhattan* in April 1939. It was The Little Princess starring Shirley Temple. She whispered afterwards, 'I want to be an actress.'

[110] The British presence in the American capital had grown significantly during the war from a couple of hundred Britons living in the embassy at the start to some nine thousand working in various military and civil commissions by 1945. President Roosevelt used to remind Lord Halifax that there were more English in Washington, DC in 1942 than there had been when they burned The White House in 1814.

[111] Ann MacBeth's father was able to fetch her in Hartford when she returned home. Her 6th grade teacher invited him to speak to the class but she dissuaded him because she was embarrassed by this English accent of this man who kept saying, 'Jolly good'.

[112] British Consulate General 6 April 1942

[113] A year later the *Thorstrand* was torpedoed with a loss of four lives.

[114] With draft age being 18, courses were speeded up and summer classes permitted graduation the following January rather than June

[115] In 1972 he was to see the *Queen Elizab*eth sink before his eyes after disastrous fires in Hong Kong.

[116] *The Real Mrs. Miniver* by Ysenda Maxtone Graham

[117] *Celebrity Childhood Memories* by Henry Buckton

[118] A report of this talk in the *Hall Magazine* in early 1945 describes it as 'a thrilling account' but I note that it contains many inaccuracies, either through my story telling or the listener's notes.

[119] Massachusetts had taken just under 600 evacuees; 284 officially under the US Committee, of which 204 were thanks to the *Boston Transcript*; in addition 305 came privately. The US as a whole had taken 1000 children through the auspices of the US Committee with probably several thousand coming privately.

[120] Similarly, at the end of the war a surplus of L5000 given to support Roedean girls at the Canadian Edgehill School was used for a scholarship to commemorate the connection.

[121] Three out of the four children married Americans.

[122] ERA has members now all over the world and puts out a monthly newsletter. It has helped many people to contact their wartime friends and to exchange memories with others who, from personal experience, have an understanding of the long-term

effects of the evacuation. It also meets an ever-growing demand from schools, colleges, universities and other organisations for information about the evacuation.

[123] *Franklin and Winston* (Random House 2003)

[124] Also much helped by the US ambassador to Britain, John G. Winant

[125] Yale University prize-winning essay 1979

[126] Written and illustrated by Holling Clancy

[127] He is Chairman of the Ridley College Old Boys' Association, UK Branch

[128] *Liverpool Echo* 2 Feb 2004

[129] a cookie or biscuit

[130] The Milton Academy class lists show 33 boys and 25 girls from Britain during those war years.

[131] *Out of Harm's Way*

Bibliography

Bailey, Anthony *England, First and Last* London: Faber and Faber 1985

Bailey, Anthony *America, Lost and Found* New York: Random House 1980

Bantock, Granville, *Lucky Orphan* 1993 (unpublished)

Barker, Ralph *City of Benares* London: Methuen 1987

Bilson, Geoffrey *The Guest Children* Saskatoon: Fifth House 1988

Brittain, Vera *England's Hour* London: Macmillan 1940

Brittain, Vera *Testament of Experience* London: Fontana 1957

Clayton, Tim and Craig, Phil *Finest Hour*, London: Hodder & Stoughton 1999

Collins, Harry *An Evacuee's Story* Bognor Regis: Woodfield Publishing 2001

Crosby, Travis L. *The Impact of Civilian Evacuation in the Second World War* London: Croom Helm 1986

Dalgleish, Alice *Three From Greenways* New York: Scribner's 1940

Desforges, Dorothea *The In-between Years*, Yorkshire: Buttercup Press 2001

Fethney, Michael *The Absurd and the Brave* Sussex: The Book Guild 1990

Hollingsworth , Hilda *They Tied a Label on my Coat* London: Virago 1991

Horne, Alistair *A Bundle from Britain*, New York: St. Martin's Press 1994

Husted, Helen *Timothy Taylor* New York: Coward McCann 1941

Huxley, Elspeth *Atlantic Ordeal* Chatto and Windus 1941

Inglis, Ruth *The Children's War* London: Collins 1989

Jackson, Carlton *Who Will Take Our Children?* London: Methuen, 1985

Johnson, B. S. *The Evacuees* Edited London: Gollancz, 1968

Johnson, Derek E *Exodus of Children*, Clacton-on-Sea: Pennyfarthing Publications 1985

Lorimer, Jean *Pilgrim Children* London: Muller 1942

Magorian, Michelle *Back Home* Penguin: Puffin Books 1987

Mann, Jessica *Out of Harm's Way* London: Hodder 2005

Massey, Victoria *One Child's War* London: BBC 1978

Michell, David *A Boy's War* Singapore: OMF 1988

Milbourn, Louise *A Very Different War* Oxford: Isis 2003

Montagu of Beaulieu, Lord *Wheels Within Wheels* London: Weidenfeld and Nicolson 2000

Parsons, Martin *I'll Take That One* Peterborough: Beckett Karlson 1998

Parsons, Martin and Starns, Penny *The Evacuation* Peterborough: DSM 1999

Parsons, Martin *Waiting to Go Home* Peterborough: DSM 1999

Pelham, Angela *The Young Ambassadors* London: Andrew Dakers Ltd 1944

Schweitzer, Pam ed. *Goodnight Children Everywhere* Exchange Theatre Trust 1990

Shakespeare, Geoffrey *Let Candles Be Brought In* London: Macdonald 1949

Shead, I. A. *They Sailed By Night* London: Faber & Faber

Statler, Jocelyn comp. *Special Relations* London: Imperial War Museum 1990

Symonds, Ann Spokes ed. *Havens Across the Sea* Oxford: Mulberry Books 1990

Travers, P. L. *I Go By Sea, I Go By Land* London: Harper & Brothers 1941

Warren, Margaret *Sylvia Warren* Ashfield Publishing Services 2003

Van de Wiel *Faces of Fate* Amherst NS: Acadian Printing 2002

Wicks, Ben *No Time to Wave Goodbye,* London: Bloomsbury 1988

Index of Proper Names

English-Speaking Union (ESU), 36,37
English-Speaking World, 173
Enterprise, HMS, 175
Evacuation Sub Committee, 23
Evacuees Reunion Association (ERA), 232
Evans, Harold, 29
Evening American, 96
Ewert, Elizabeth and Margaret, 157
Fairbanks Jr, Douglas, 105,111
Farley, Mrs, 93-4,98
Farson, Daniel, 87,120,159,204,220
Faulkner, Frederic, 125
Fay, Charlie, 55,59,73,203,242
Fay, Edgar, 73,147-9,166,173-4
Fay, Kathleen, 173-4
Fethney, Michael, 39
Field, Cyrus, 134
Field, Marshall, 42,107
Fields, Gracie, 116
Fight for Freedom Committee, 65
Fiji, Government of, 40
Finest Hour, 32
Flynn, Errol, 87
Fontaine, Joan, 111
Fontanne, Lynn, 157,209
Ford Company, 68
Foreign Office, 32-6,38,41,45
Forester, C S, 113
Forester, George, 113
Fowey, 46,48
Frankfurter, Felix, 110
Freeman, Hardy and Willis, 44
Friend, The, 146
Fry, Ann, 225
Fulton, Dr John, 66
Gallagher, Jr, Rollin T, 180,185
Gallup Poll, 28,40,108
Garcia, General Calixto, 179,185
Gates family, 109
Gentlemen of Philadelphia, 49
George VI, King,, 17,27-8,32,36,72,103,139,147,201
Georgic, 81,237

Printed in the United Kingdom
by Lightning Source UK Ltd.
103819UKS00002B/85-93